MW01247066

Shifting the Mindset

Socially Just Leadership Education

A Volume in
Contemporary Perspectives on Leadership Learning

Series Editor:
Kathy L. Guthrie, *Florida State University*

Contemporary Perspectives on Leadership Learning

Kathy L. Guthrie, Series Editor

Shifting the Mindset

Socially Just Leadership Education

Edited By

Kathy L. Guthrie
Florida State University

and

Vivechkanand S. Chunoo
University of Illinois at Urbana-Champaign

Information Age Publishing, Inc.
Charlotte, North Carolina • www.infoagepub.com

Library of Congress Cataloging-in-Publication Data

CIP data for this book can be found on the Library of Congress website:
http://www.loc.gov/index.html

Paperback: 978-1-64802-558-7
Hardcover: 978-1-64802-559-4
eBook: 978-1-64802-560-0

Cover photo by Artie E. White.

Printed in the United States of America.

DEDICATION

"Ours is not the struggle of one day, one week, or one year. Ours is not the struggle of one judicial appointment or presidential term. Ours is the struggle of a lifetime, or maybe even many lifetimes, and each one of us in every generation must do our part."

—The late Rep. John Lewis (1940-2020) in
Across That Bridge: A Vision for Change and the Future of America

To all those who stand in the struggle, fight with compassion, and lead with brave vulnerability.

CONTENTS

PART II:
SOCIALLY JUST LEADERSHIP EDUCATION CONTEXTS

ACKNOWLEDGMENTS

Kathy L. Guthrie and Vivechkanand S. Chunoo

No book is constructed in isolation, especially when it is focused on collective voices coming together to move forward and take action. It takes countless conversations, listening, thinking, reflection, and learning to build upon each other's ideas and concepts into something worthy of others reading and, hopefully, learning. When we think about all of the individuals who have taken us up on engaging in the tough conversations about leadership and social justice, those who have taught us, and not only modeled what socially just leadership education is, we probably could write a book on just those lessons. However, there are some people who directly influenced this book which we cannot miss the opportunity to mention. Derrick Pacheco, you answered our call for support in a time of extreme complexity. Thank you for your thoughtfulness, dedication, passion, and support in helping advance this book to the finish line. Brittany Devies, you are always willing to jump in and talk through the best ways to get engaged in the conversation. Your support in conference proposals to highlight author voices is appreciated. Artie E. White, thank you for sharing your brilliant photo for the cover. This captured what we wanted to share.

Kathy wants to thank the professionals in the Leadership Learning Research Center at Florida State University. I am continually in awe of being able to work collectively with such an intelligent, passionate, fun group of people. Mostly, I am thankful for Team Guthrie, I am nothing without you. Brian, you have always been the love of my life, my biggest fan, and the greatest partner I could ask for. Kinley, you have sharpened

Shifting the Mindset: Socially Just Leadership Education
pp. xi–xii
Copyright © 2021 by Information Age Publishing

my focus, given me purpose, and motivate me every day to be the best version of myself.

V is grateful for his team in the ALEC program at the University of Illinois at Urbana-Champaign for their grace, feedback, and patience. I would also like to thank Marilé Quintana for her keen intellect and abundant creativity. Also, to my mom and dad—Patsy and Yogin—all of my success comes from your stories, your work ethic, and your love.

FOREWORD

Jamie Washington

As I write this foreword the year is 2020. Most of us in higher education will mark this as one of the most challenging times of our professional lives. While we have heard, "the one thing that is constant is change," the changes we have experienced this year have required a *shifting of mindsets*. When I was first invited to write the foreword for this book, I was excited because social justice and leadership are deep passions of mine. I did not realize the importance of this book would be so evident in my life and all our lives given our current context.

When we first became aware of the COVID-19 health pandemic, most of us were caught off guard. We had to immediately shift our mindsets from in-person learning and working to remote life. Leaders on college campuses and other industries rushed to make sure they could continue to function in our new reality. I was well aware institutional responses would have a differential impact on members of minoritized populations. However, I also knew these impacts would not be at the forefront of our efforts in managing this crisis. As we moved through responses, there were folks at many tables who had to keep saying, "Don't forget about ...," or "What about ...," or "That's not going to work for...." While leaders were not setting out to harm or leave out its most vulnerable communities, their approaches did not place them front of mind.

When the COVID-19 health pandemic collided with the historical pandemic of systemic racism, through the murders of George Floyd, Breonna Taylor, and Ahmaud Arbery, we had yet another opportunity to see how social justice and leadership requires a shifting of mindsets.

Shifting the Mindset: Socially Just Leadership Education
pp. xiii–xv
Copyright © 2021 by Information Age Publishing

I have spent the last several months working with campus leaders on the importance of this shift. I believe one of the most significant challenges for us today is attempting to do the work of social justice, diversity, equity, and inclusion with outdated mindsets. I tend to illustrate this problem with the analogy of technologies. Many of you may remember the Palm Pilot, the beeper, the console television, and the VCR. These were cutting edge technologies in their day. However, attempting to use these devices today would leave us literally in the dark. In order to be successful today we need to upgrade our technologies or shift our mindsets.

Here are some examples of older social justice mindsets:

- "I don't see color; people are just people";
- "'LGB' inclusions";
- "differently able or handicapable";
- "treating all people equally (the same)";
- "America is the land of opportunity; all you have to do is work hard"; and
- "as a minoritzed person, I 'get' all oppression and injustice."

I am sure you can come up with others. However, my intention with these examples is to begin wrapping our minds around why this book is so important. In the first section, the authors invite us to shift our mindsets from a "one-size-fits-all" approach to leadership education. They invite us to consider how social identities matter. They challenge us to consider how identities do not matter just for those who are leading these populations, but it also matters to those who are leaders within these populations. While there has been increased scholarship on the experiences of some members of the populations described in Part I, the intersection of leadership and leadership education has not often been explored. As a leadership educator, building my capacity to support and challenge my students and colleagues to shift their mindsets is what these chapters prepare me to do.

Part II of the book invites us to consider leadership education context. Whether we are talking about the social change model or Covey's seven habits, these models and frameworks leave us with opportunities to go even further. From ethics to activism, partnerships, virtual engagement, and navigating White fragility, each discussion of these contextual dynamics guides us into new challenges and opportunities. As a 60-year-old, Black, gay, cisgender, Christian, able-bodied, man with a several degrees, and years of experience, my take on and approach to addressing these dynamics may look different from someone who does not share my combination of identities. Not only do I need to be aware of the identities and the lenses I am bringing to these situations, I also need be conscious about whom I am working with and how they might experience me. Here is a story to illustrate my point:

I was asked to do a professional development workshop for senior leaders at a nonprofit organization led by a White, cisgender male in his mid- to late-50s. He asked for a session on becoming effective White allies and microaggressions. He then proceeded to tell me his people did not need to hear anything about privilege; they were well beyond that. When I pushed back and explained it was difficult to talk about being allies and microaggressions through the lens of race without addressing White privilege, he snapped back at me with, "How dare you tell me what my people need? I've worked with them for over 25 years and you've only know them for an hour." Enter, White fragility. Yes, this was a moment where I was glad that I had shifted my mindset from *being right* to *being effective*. I knew at that moment the leadership challenge was informed by identities and context. I knew if I was not able to manage my own triggers and ego that my response might have ended this relationship forever.

I think about shifting mindsets, the same way I think about upgrading technology. I realize upgrading, like shifting mindsets, creates a degree of discomfort. We often feel like we do not have time to learn the new ways or we just got comfortable with the old way. We often struggle with the questions of mistakes, and resets, and time, and energy it will take to make those adjustments. For these and other reasons, many people decide to hold out until they absolutely have no choice. This book is like a notice you get on your computer when there is an update available for your system. Sometimes that notification can sit for days, weeks, even a month before we decide to click on it. *Shifting the Mindset* is that notification. I hope you decide to take the upgrade. I believe it will improve your leadership and social justice operating systems greatly.

AUTHOR NOTE

Rev. Dr. Jamie Washington (he/him/his) is the president and founder of the Washington Consulting Group (WCG). WCG was named by the *Economist* as one of the top 10 global diversity consultants in the world. Dr. Washington has served as an educator, administrator, and consultant for more than 37 years. He serves as an invited instructor in the Harvard Graduate School of Education and Lancaster Theological Seminary. He is the president and cofounder of the Social Justice Training Institute and a past president of the American College Personnel Association.

CHAPTER 1

NOW MORE THAN EVER

The Imperative for Socially Just Leadership Education

Vivechkanand S. Chunoo and Kathy L. Guthrie

An unprecedented pandemic. An historic election. A renewed mandate for racial justice. A deeply divided nation. An increasingly unstable global stage. With only a week left in 2020 (at the time of this writing), many of us have passed the point of exhaustion multiple crises ago. While pundits and economists struggle to accurately account for the political and capital costs of enduring these trying times, the psychological and emotional prices paid by each of us is felt daily and profoundly. Insidiously embedded in this calculus, however, is the pressure to keep moving forward, lest the forces of oppression push us back. Although some seek to make us *great again*, others are working to make society *better than it has ever been*. This is the backdrop against which we are shifting the mindset of leadership education toward justice, equity, diversity, and inclusion.

Despite these dark times, we persist with hearts and minds filled with optimism. Since our first attempt at changing leadership education's narrative around social justice and equity, we have encountered innumerable stories of hope: educators, scholars, researchers, community members, activists, and students at every level who have found themselves in our

Shifting the Mindset: Socially Just Leadership Education
pp. 1–8
Copyright © 2021 by Information Age Publishing

writing and in the recommendations of our previous contributors. These courageous stories span conversations in classrooms to presentations at conferences; dialogue in workshops and disagreements in online staff meetings. We could not be more humbled by how our efforts, and the intentions of our colleagues, have been taken seriously, considered deeply, and leveraged meaningfully by those who champion fairness and resist inequity.

We, too, have been listening. Although the feedback others have graciously provided has been overwhelmingly positive, we know we missed the mark in some areas. We dedicated our first attempt to all the voices we could represent knowing there were those whose stories we could not elevate. In many regards, *Shifting the Mindset: Socially Just Leadership Education* is both a widening and deepening of what we aimed to accomplish in *Changing the Narrative: Socially Just Leadership Education*. Here, you will find more, and different accounts of identities, dynamics, and contexts not included in our previous work; including perspectives from oft-neglected areas like the armed forces traditions and agricultural leadership education environments. We also sought to prominently feature campus populations—like student athletes, international-status students, and LGBT-identified individuals—who can no longer go underserved by a field claiming to prepare all students for success in a complex and dynamic world. Finally, we included even more practical recommendations for educators striving to incorporate ethics, intersectionality, and civic responsibility into their leadership praxes.

Designed to continue *Changing the Narrative: Socially Just Leadership Education* (Guthrie & Chunoo, 2018), *Shifting the Mindset* does not assume readers are well-versed in our previous attempt at framing and engaging this work. If this is where you have come to find us for the first time—welcome, and we look forward to the journey with you. For those who have been with us from our earlier days, welcome back and let's keep going. Before progressing any further; however, it may benefit us to reorient around the foundational ideas we used to chart the path forward.

(RE)ORIENTING SOCIALLY JUST LEADERSHIP EDUCATION

Socially just leadership education exists at the convergence of two adaptive imperatives: preparing people to lead and creating a fairer world for everyone. In roles such as teacher, advisor, mentor, supervisor, and guide, socially just leadership educators accomplish their goals, in part, by encouraging students to develop voice and agency along the way to becoming social critics and active agents of positive and sustainable change. As we move through these experiences together, we become more impactful activists for causes, groups, and reforms we care for deeply as well as stronger advocates for the organizations, associations, and relationships necessary for those who are different from us to thrive. By building robust networks of similar and dissimilar others, we improve everyone's chances of living fuller and more meaningful lives in a society truly characterized by liberty and justice for all.

Important distinctions abound related to leadership education, social justice allyship, followership, and our roles in drawing them all into closer contact. We envision leadership education as any human activity designed to create, maintain, or improve leadership identity, capacity, motivation, efficacy, and/or enactment. Leadership learning occurs across contexts, between disciplines, and over the lifespan. Social justice education is preparation to craft a society that is, "equitable and [where] all members are physically and psychologically safe and secure" (Adams et al., 2007, p. 1). Learning to be an ally of this nature requires extensive personal commitment, enhanced collaborative potential, and a keen awareness of the mechanisms behind social structures, social movements, and social change. Successful teaching at the intersection of leadership and allyship goes beyond subject knowledge of each area. Socially just leadership educators develop a mindset attuned to the integrative, holistic, and complex interactions between students, information, and context to maximize their productive influence. In these ways, leadership learning for social justice is rooted in vulnerability, morals, ethics, critical thinking, deep reflection, creativity, practical experience, and substantive feedback in all directions.

We know more now than we did before; both as an editorial team for this text and as members of a field that is improving incrementally. We honor the work of John Dugan (2017) and his associates (Dugan et al., 2017b) in advancing critical perspectives in our field. We value Guthrie and Jenkins' (2018) emphasis on transformational learning in leadership education. We appreciate Volpe White et al.'s (2019) thoughtful advice related to reflection and metacognition's impact on leadership learners. We have found Priest and Jenkins' (2019) work around becoming and being leadership educators as both a warm introduction for newcomers and a fair, but firm, reminder of shared responsibilities among continuing educators. We have been enlightened to the differential ways varied academic disciplines frame, embody, and enact leadership development due to the efforts of Sowcik and Komives (2020). Finally, we are reminded of the worth of activism in leadership learning by Martin et al. (2019). A comprehensive review of the relevant scholarship in the time between our previous book and now would be far beyond manageable. However, these works (among many others) continue to shape our thinking around the interplay of identities, contexts, and social forces, as well as their integrated impact on our daily realities; professional and personal.

The year 2020 will also see a new version of the National Leadership Education Research Agenda published before its closing. Although the inaugural 2013 version (Andenoro et al., 2013) may have been limited in scope and focus, it nonetheless established the foundation for a national dialogue about priorities among those studying the educational mechanisms, players, and paradigms in leadership learning. The updated agenda is poised to influence, at minimum, the next 5 years of scholarship around these same factors, and many more, with a distinctly clear focus on reducing oppression, increasing inclusion, and moving toward a more just future. We are proud to have played a role in advancing such an agenda, and to recommitting our scholarship and practice to its recommendations, suggestions, and admonitions. The ideas presented by our authors and their teams in this compilation complement those priorities in ways we could not have known when we began, but are grateful for having.

SHIFTING THE MINDSET

In partnership with our authors, this text intends to shift the mindset of leadership education toward approaches which center identities, contexts, and influences that can no longer be overlooked in our courses, programs, and initiatives. After a brief introduction in this chapter and the next, we organize our contributors' ideas into two parts, the first of which raises the prominence of student social identities not otherwise well-represented in leadership education publications, while the second portion highlights leadership learning contexts too often rendered invisible through inattention. Each chapter in every section contains specific questions, resources, considerations, challenges, and/or action steps educators can leverage as they enhance equity and justice in leadership teaching and learning.

As a continuation of this introduction, in the next chapter Michael Promisel takes us on a brisk walk through the history of social justice. His careful review of the historical roots, influential individuals, and dramatic turning points details a moral arc from 19th century Europe to the global community of today. This historical account frames the almost 200-year legacy of social justice (as we have come to know it) as a living, thriving, and ongoing commitment to improving conditions for all of humankind. At the end of his review, he lays bare our clear responsibility to cultivate socially just leaders and leadership for the next 200 years and beyond.

Shifting the Mindset around Student Identities

Chapters 3 through 13 ground socially just leadership education recommendations and practices in the best knowledge available regarding the experiences of students from diverse populations and backgrounds. While far from a comprehensive record of the lived histories and contemporary realitics faced by all undergraduates, these chapters continue demystifying the nature of our students with the intent of broadening our individual and collective horizons on who we teach, how they show up, and what really matters in their leadership learning. We still need more and different voices in the chorus of socially just leadership education, and look forward to additional opportunities to build upon what is presented here.

In Chapter 3, Symphony Oxendine and Deborah Taub deconstruct the treatment of Native students in postsecondary environments, drawing a sharp focus on the mismatches between dominant ways of leading and Native ways of knowing. They advocate awareness around and application of Indigenous Knowledge Systems to provide nuanced and authentic leadership learning. Next, Valerie Luutran and Jessica Chung bravely confront their personal histories with societal structures and cultural pressures as they describe socially just leadership learning for Asian American students. They directly confront the model minority myth that plagues members of these communities, while challenging notions of what counts as leadership, to help students lead from in-between in Chapter 4.

In Chapter 5, Darren Pierre and Jonathan Okstad tackle socially just leadership learning for lesbian, gay, and bisexual students. Alex Lange and Kieran Todd, in Chapter 6, center transgender students in leadership learning through illustrative and reflexive vignettes. Taken together, these chapters offer a wealth of perspectives and challenges for leadership educators who want to make a different among students who identify with gender- and sexuality-minority communities. Christopher Travers and John Craig, in Chapter 7, alongside the trio of Julie Owen, Brittany Devies, and Danyelle Reynolds in Chapter 8, continue to highlight the intersections of gender dynamics and leadership in their writings on masculinity and feminism in social justice; moving us from "adding women and stir" toward love and healing.

In Chapter 9, Spencer Scruggs and Sally Watkins challenge the ableist assumptions underpinning leadership education, with a keen focus on the experiences of students with disabilities. David Gray, Dan Marshall, and David Dixon lift the veil on leader identity development in the U.S. Army Officer Corps in Chapter 10. Readers may be surprised to learn of the striking similarities among civilian and soldier leader development. Chapter 11 finds Amie Runk and Becca Piers' robust connections between socially just leadership education and career readiness among employed students. Ben Cecil and Pei Hu, in Chapter 12, apply a global lens to leadership learning by redefining engagement among international students. In the final chapter of this part, Kacy King and Cathy Badger deeply dive into the world of student athletics and shift our mindset beyond competition, encouraging the socially just leadership development of student-athletes.

Leveraging Context to Shift Mindsets

Chapters 14 through 21, the second part of our text, expand contextual considerations related to socially just leadership education. Ranging from the intrapsychic influences of intersectionality to the sociopolitical impacts of White guilt, our contributors rigorously examine important elements of various leadership learning environments to deepen our personal and professional awareness of the implicit and explicit forces shaping socially just leadership education. Together, these chapters encourage nuanced and thoughtful exploration of what it means to be leadership educators in challenging times and under strained conditions. The recommendations put forth in these areas move social justice praxes from surviving to thriving.

Susan Jones and Adrian Bitton apply the intersectional model of multiple dimensions of identity to guide leadership educators toward social justice in Chapter 14. Their focus on the interlocking dynamics of social identity and social location reveal innovative pathways toward enacting critical tenets in leadership education. In Chapter 15, Jasmine Collins and Shane Whittington deftly weave personal narratives into a meaningful discourse on the ethical aspects of leadership education. The original theoretical framework they developed and described is brought to life through relevant and relatable use of case study pedagogy.

In chapter 16, Michaela Shenberger and Kathy Guthrie advocate for leader activists by connecting leadership learning to student resistance. V. Chunoo and Greg French operationalize the culturally relevant leadership learning model (Guthrie et al., 2016) to make it imminently implementable for socially just leadership educators in Chapter 17. Their approach to making theoretical concepts actionable involves expanding and reframing essential elements of the framework itself. Chapter 18 finds Julie LeBlanc and Kathy Guthrie's recommendations regarding critical community engagement to move leadership education beyond the campus footprint.

Katherine McKee and Jackie Bruce advocate for the use of project-based learning within communities of practice to aid leadership learners in agricultural education contexts. In Chapter 20, Kirstin Phelps boldly guides us through the next frontier of social justice—virtual and online leadership learning contexts. Cameron Beatty, Amber Manning-Ouellette and Erica Wiborg, in Chapter 21, provide their insights on addressing White fragility in making leadership education more anti-racist and socially just. Finally, in Chapter 22, we share some thoughts on where we go next in collaborative and productive ways.

We ended *Changing the Narrative* with an imperative for action, claiming calls to action were no longer enough. They still are not. If we have learned anything from recent history, it is how the social fissures which have historically swallowed whole people, their groups, and some communities have now become gaping societal chasms. For much too long, far too many of our elected and appointed officials have been able to maintain their intentional ignorance of the injustices deeply rooted in our society, which threatens the health, prosperity, and well-being of its members. Now, more than ever, the demand for justice, fairness, and equity must be met with bold, creative, and compassionate leadership. We get to decide on which side of history we will stand. *Shifting the Mindset* is our invitation for you to stand with us.

REFERENCES

Andenoro, A. C., Allen, S. J., Haber-Curran, P., Jenkins, D. M., Sowcik, M., Dugan, J. P., & Osteen, L. (2013). *National leadership education research agenda 2013-2018: Providing strategic direction for the field of leadership education.* http://leadershipeducators.org/ResearchAgenda

Adams, M. E., Bell, L. A. E., & Griffin, P. E. (2007). *Teaching for diversity and social justice.* Routledge/Taylor & Francis Group.

Dugan, J. P. (2017). *Leadership theory: Cultivating critical perspectives.* Jossey-Bass.

Dugan, J. P., Turman, N. T., & Barnes (2017). *Leadership theory: A facilitator's guide for cultivating critical perspectives.* Jossey-Bass.

Guthrie, K. L., & Chunoo, V. S. (Ed.). (2018). *Changing the narrative: Socially just leadership education.* Information Age.

Guthrie, K. L., & Jenkins, D. M. (2018). *The role of leadership educators: Transforming learning.* Information Age.

Guthrie, K. L., Bertrand Jones, T., & Osteen, L. (Eds.). (2016). *New Directions for Student Leadership, No. 152. Developing culturally relevant leadership learning.* Jossey-Bass.

Martin, G. L., Linder, C., & Williams, B. M. (Eds.). (2019). *New Directions for Student Leadership, No. 161. Leadership learning through activism.* Jossey-Bass.

Priest, K. L., & Jenkins, D. M. (Eds.). (2019). *New Directions for Student Leadership, No. 164. Becoming and being a leadership educator.* Jossey-Bass.

Sowcik, M., & Komives, S. R. (Eds.). (2020). *New Directions for Student Leadership, No. 165. How academic disciplines approach leadership development.* Jossey-Bass.

Volpe White, J. M., Guthrie, K. L., & Torres, M. (2019). *Thinking to transform: Reflection in leadership learning*. Information Age.

CHAPTER 2

PRIESTS, PROGRESSIVES, AND A MIRAGE

A Short History of Social Justice

Michael E. Promisel

The ideas behind social justice can be polarizing. While some consider it of paramount importance, others associate it with actions, commitments, and policies they oppose. Conflicting ideologies around social justice serve as the heart of many political divisions. Our relationship with these ideas, against the backdrop of a national presidential election in the United States, renders socially just leadership education unavoidable. This state of affairs provides both a challenge and an opportunity for educators. The challenge is to remain honest and forthcoming about the nature and scope of social justice—to avoid the politicization of a moral value for one's own purposes. The opportunity is to provide students a robust vision for promoting the common good—the true end of social justice.

An honest reflection concerning the nature and scope of socially just leadership education, therefore, must seriously contend with the ends it seeks. What is education, other than the training and guidance of students toward certain goals? It would be folly to hire a guide who will not

Shifting the Mindset: Socially Just Leadership Education
pp. 9–21
Copyright © 2021 by Information Age Publishing
All rights of reproduction in any form reserved.

(or cannot) specify the destination. It would be foolish to seek out a teacher (even more so, a teacher of teachers) who is not explicit and forthright in specifying the ends of education. In observance of these prerequisites, I begin by documenting the history of social justice. In practice, social justice takes on a number of meanings, and its use in educational contexts is often a cover a host of other values (Novak & Adams, 2015). There are good reasons for this; social justice is an umbrella under which other values find comfortable homes. Nonetheless, the standards of social science demand clear and concise descriptions to make this concept operable.

I begin by providing a brief history of social justice. The way forward, I argue, is clearest to those who understand the traditions of thought that have shaped this value. The next section proposes an operable definition of social justice. This definition draws on the earliest roots of social justice to revitalize its integrity for the practice of leaders. I conclude by offering guidance for developing an education that cultivates socially just leadership.

A SHORT HISTORY OF SOCIAL JUSTICE

Social justice is an abstract concept with a winding history. The term was first coined around the 1840s by two Italian Catholic priests, Antonia Rosmini Serbati (1797–1855) and Luigi Taparelli d'Azeglio (1793–1862; Kraynak, 2018). Although each independently developed the term (*la giustizia sociale*), it was Fr. Taparelli's conception that gained the most traction (Behr, 2005; Paulhus, 1987). Writing during the extremes of individualism and collectivism that characterized 19th century European politics, Taparelli used the term, "to characterize the rights and duties between different levels of all of the intermediary associations that every society above a limited size comprises" (Behr 2005, p. 6). Every association—from the church and the chess club to charter schools and corporations—has its own purposes and distinct common good. For Taparelli, social justice described the social conditions and civic habits which encourage people and groups to freely pursue their purposes while maintaining subsidiarity and solidarity.

While Taparelli's conception of social justice is little known, his students (among them Gioacchino Pecci, also known as Pope Leo XIII) secured its central position in the modern social teaching of the Roman Catholic Church (Burke, 2010). In fact, the religious heritage of this term was well recognized by early 20th century figures who sought to adopt the concerns of social justice to mainstream politics. While campaigning in 1932, Franklin D. Roosevelt quoted *Quadragesimo Anno*—the papal

Figure 1.   Prominence of social justice historically.

encyclical establishing social justice a central value—suggesting it was "one of the greatest documents of modern times" (Rosenman, 1938, p. 738).

As Roosevelt's endorsement suggested, the progressive movement of the 1930s introduced social justice into mainstream American politics. According to Google's n-gram tool—an imperfect but helpful representation of published material in English—this decade was the moment when social justice rose to prominence in popular nomenclature. Figure 2.1 demonstrates this rise and continued prominence of "social justice" following the 1930s.

Generally speaking, it was progressives who invoked "social justice" in secular politics after World War II. While the term rose to prominence in popular discourse, it was generally unheralded in academic discussion. Some argue John Rawl's (1971) *Theory of Justice* introduced social justice into mainstream discussion in academic circles (Bankston, 2010). This monocausal account is almost certainly incomplete, but it is evident by the 1970s social justice was established as an emerging value of progressives, both lay and academic (Miller, 1999).

This characterization is confirmed in one of the most famous commentaries on the subject: F.A. Hayek's (1976) *The Mirage of Social Justice*. In that work, he deemed social justice, "the new religion of our time," "the most widely used and most effective argument in political discussion," and "the distinguishing attribute of the good man" (Hayek, 1976, pp. xii, 65–66). For Hayek, this was a problem: "Scarcely anyone doubts that the expression has a definite meaning, describes a high ideal," yet scarcely anyone can delineate the precise bounds of social justice. Consequently, nearly any perceived grievance can be denounced as a breach of social justice, especially those that require government intervention to rectify.

This led Hayek to a dramatic conclusion: "'social justice' is at present probably the gravest threat to most other values of a free civilization" (pp. 65–67). For those who remain sympathetic to Hayek's argument, issues of social justice are categorically bemoaned.

What is the status of social justice today? Is Hayek's characterization fair to contemporary proponents? In one recent attempt to document social justice's contemporary meanings, Novak and Adams (2015) discern six consistent goals associated with concept:

1. *Distribution:* the fair distribution of advantages and disadvantages in society;
2. *Equality:* the impetus to rectify and eliminate inequalities, especially systemic and identity-based inequalities;
3. *Common good:* the conditions of social life that facilitate the flourishing of individuals and social groups;
4. *Progressivism:* the improvement of the human condition through rigorous social reform;
5. *Empowering underserved identity groups;* and
6. *Compassion:* deep concern for the marginalized and the underserved (Novak & Adams, 2015, pp. 29–36).

This list exhibits a progressive bias; indeed, social justice and progressivism are often conflated. However, the value need not exclude nonprogressive principles. People of all political persuasions are concerned with distribution, equality, the common good, and compassion for the marginalized.

Thus, even those sympathetic to Hayek's critiques are not bound to concur with his conclusion that social justice is "empty and meaningless." As I hope to demonstrate, social justice does not necessitate progressive policies or top-down rectifications of injustice. In fact, social justice can and should be a value all aspire to, like freedom or virtue. The next section proposes such an understanding by arguing for a return to its original principles.

A RETURN TO THE ROOTS

If we wish to counter the polarizing politization of social justice, we ought to heed Hayek's critique. The concept must be defined and limited. If social justice is a superficial substitute for partisan causes, it threatens to replace education with indoctrination. If we cannot agree on the concept's definition, how can we form leaders who seek it?

I do not highlight these questions to suggest the impracticality of developing a curriculum for socially just leaders. Instead, I encourage educators to begin by considering three questions:

1. *Definition:* Does social justice admit of clear and consistent principles by which we understand its distinct meaning?
2. *Scope:* To what extent does social justice "compete" with other values (e.g., subsidiarity, individual rights) in the realization of the common good? In other words, what is the proper scope of social justice?
3. *Openness:* Does social justice permit a genuine diversity of viewpoints concerning the purposes and policies appropriate to realizing the common good?

It is only after we understand the nature, scope, and openness of social justice that we are in a position to bring about its education. The task of this section is to propose an understanding of social justice that meets these criteria.

We can find such an understanding of social justice, I argue, by returning to its original introduction into philosophical discourse. As detailed above, social justice was introduced by Fr. Luigi Taparelli in response to the extremes of oppressive collectivism and individualism prominent in the 19th century. More specifically, Taparelli conceptualized social justice as a particular form of justice that exists "to protect and promote the exercise of rights and the fulfillment of the duties of others in society" (Behr, 2019, p. 149). While there are multiple species of justice (e.g., distributive, commutative), *social* justice pertains to the social flourishing of individuals *and* entities that are neither the individual nor the state—what we might associations (Hittinger, 2008). These associations are "beings" of social life that form "the heart and soul of personal identity"; intermediaries between the citizen and the state (Behr, 2005, pp. 6–7).

Social justice, therefore, concerns the protection (respecting others' rights) and the promotion (fulfilling social responsibilities) of both individuals and associations to pursue the common goods of social life. This form of justice is called *social* for three reasons. First, social justice concerns rights and responsibilities situated within a particular social order. Social responsibilities are not abstract; we strive to fulfill them in relation to a particular network of relations. Similarly, breaches of rights are most evocative when seen firsthand. The primacy of one's social position renders this form of justice uniquely relational.

> Social justice seeks to equalize actual persons, as well as their various associations, with respect to the freedom to fulfill their duties of self-preservation,

social order, and pursuit of the truth and happiness, in light of the natural, finite, and temporal goods available in society. (Behr, 2019, p. 152)

Second, social justice concerns the rights and responsibilities of associations as well as individuals. Associations inhere authority and responsibility best understood outside of the individual-state dichotomy. These associations, or intermediaries, provide the space to exercise our rights and entail responsibilities to others in our community. Social justice describes the civic habits and social conditions that facilitate the flourishing of these intermediary associations that breathe meaning into our rights and responsibilities.

Finally, social justice is social by its relation to the common good. While each political community has a distinct common good, so too do the many associations that constitute it. The religious communities, universities, families, and other associations that populate a society all have their own common goods. Social justice pertains to the ordering of various common goods to facilitate the common good of all while retaining each group's distinct identity and purpose.

With these considerations in mind, we can distinguish social justice from other forms of justice with which it is commonly associated. Traditionally, justice is understood to take three forms: legal (or general), commutative, and distributive (Pieper, 1966, pp. 70–75). Each form applies justice—to render each his due—to a particular subject. Legal, or general, justice governs community members' relation to the political community (Aristotle, 2011, pp. 104–105). To disobey the law, therefore, is to disrupt one's relationship to the political whole. This may result in politically binding punishment (e.g., a fine or jail time). But injustice may take other forms. Commutative justice governs relations between individuals. It is unjust for me to break a promise or contract I have formed with another private individual. There may be legal consequences for this act, but the object of my injustice is not the political community—it is a particular person. This difference is reflected in the separation of criminal and civil law in the American code.

Finally, distributive justice orders the relations between the political community and its members (Aristotle, 2011, pp. 94–95; Fleischacker, 2004, pp. 19–27). Distributive justice is achieved through the appropriate allocation of community goods (e.g., authority, wealth, resources). Figure 2.2 illustrates the traditional tripartite division of justice (Pieper, 1966, p. 113).

What is the place of social justice in this traditional division? As mentioned above, each form of justice is distinguished by its subject. The subject of social justice is neither the political community as such nor a particular individual. Taparelli introduced social justice precisely to dis-

Figure 2.2.   Traditional tripartite division of justice.

rupt the individual-state dichotomy. Instead, social justice pertains to the multitude of subjects, both individual and corporate, that constitute social life within a particular context (Novak & Adams, 2015, pp. 21–28). Social justice may therefore be understood as:

1. *Social justice:* the civic habits and social conditions that facilitate individual and corporate flourishing;
2. *Distributive justice:* the equitable distribution of goods;
3. *Commutative justice:* the rights and responsibilities of contractual relations; and
4. *Legal justice:* the adjudication of positive law.

After grasping the proper subject of social justice, we can offer positive statements concerning its nature. For Taparelli, social justice was "first and foremost a personal virtue with regard to the disposition to protect and promote the exercise of rights and the fulfillment of the duties of others in society" (Behr, 2019, p. 149). Recent conceptions of social justice as a virtue can also be found in Novak and Adams (2015), who argued "*social justice is first of all a virtue,* that is, *a habit* or *disposition* making it easier to perform certain social actions well, as if by second nature" (p. 273, emphasis original).

What does it mean to call social justice a virtue? This is not as foreign as it may seem. After all, we consider justice both an individual characteristic and the ideal of a community. We describe people as just or unjust in the same way we describe social conditions. Social justice shares this multidimensional depth. To understand social justice as primarily an individual virtue—a disposition to act in a certain way—recognizes how it places demands upon each one of us. More specifically, social justice inclines us to engage in common, associational life and to direct its various entities (e.g., a family, business, or congregation) to embrace healthy "direction, purpose, scope, and inner drive" (p. 274). The local newspaper does not write itself, nor does the soup kitchen self-generate food. We cultivate the habits that facilitate a vibrant civic life. The intermediary institutions that constitute social life are maintained by the virtue of social justice.

These intermediary associations connect the virtue of social justice to the common good of the entire political community. Citizens do not contribute to an abstract "common good" any more than volunteers aid "humanity." Social justice and virtue manifest in particular actions with particular objects; they are not aloof ideals. Every member of a community is connected to a distinct network of individuals and associations. The virtue of social justice facilitates individuals' discernment and promotion of the common good according to the tasks they are positioned to address. Social justice, in other words, describes the habits of civic association that promote the flourishing of the communities we touch.

While understanding social justice as an individual characteristic may make its realization more practicable, some may find it unsatisfying. In contemporary parlance, social justice is often invoked to counteract systemic, macrolevel, injustices. A discriminatory criminal justice system, we might say, is socially unjust. How, then, does the conception of social justice as an individual virtue pertain to systematic levels of analysis?

One commentator of Taparelli affirms this level of analysis is evident in the original conception. "Secondarily, the term can be meaningfully used as a characterization of a socioeconomic and political order, the actual arrangement of institutions, laws, and policies that operate to protect and promote the same exercise of rights and duties of individuals who make up that society" (Behr, 2019, pp. 149–150). Thus, social justice might be said to have two levels of operation: the individual virtue and the conditions conducive to flourishing communities. While social justice is realized through the individual practice of the virtue, the sum total of the conditions and order of a society may be accord in varying degrees with standards of social justice (Stoner & James, 2015). Importantly, even in this macroanalysis, social justice retains focus on the "exercise of rights and duties of individuals." This is social justice's chief concern.

The sketch of social justice outlined above may now be summarized according to the criteria specified above:

1. *Definition:* Social justice is a "personal virtue with regard to the disposition to protect and promote the exercise of rights and the fulfillment of the duties of others in society" (Behr, 2019, p. 149).

- Social justice facilitates the common good, especially through the promotion of healthy intermediary associations (e.g., the family, local community, or business)
- While social justice is fundamentally an individual virtue, like justice, it also describes a set of social conditions conducive to flourishing. Both levels of analysis are necessary for a complete understanding

2. *Scope:* Social justice is distinguished from other forms of justice according to its subject matter: the rights and duties of individuals and associations to promote the common good.

    - The realization of rights and duties depends on the conditions of the society in question

3. *Openness:* The realization of social justice does not require practitioners' adherence to a particular political platform. Progressives and conservatives exhibit and seek social justice.

One final point should be made regarding the "openness" of the aforementioned conception of social justice. This conception of social justice may disappoint those who want the value to represent a host of causes. But social justice must admit of some boundaries. The just distribution of goods is not inconsequential; indeed, it is a condition of a flourishing society. However, this is the concern of distributive, not social, justice. By circumscribing the scope of social justice, we make it more practicable and open to a multiplicity of manifestations.

SOCIALLY JUST LEADERSHIP AND ITS EDUCATION

So far, the topic of leadership has made little appearance in this chapter. With social justice properly bounded, we can finally identify guiding principles for the leadership appropriate to it. Three layers of leadership education emerge from the conception of social justice above: (1) appreciation for the rights *and* responsibilities of individuals and associations, (2) commitment to communities and associations within which leaders act, and (3) cultivation of the individual virtue of social justice. For each layer, I propose three questions educators (and students) can use for developing concrete educational practices. These questions might be the minimum threshold—the lowest common denominator—that can unite a diversity of educational approaches.

Appreciation for Social Rights and Responsibilities

Social justice, I have argued, principally concerns the protection and promotion of individual and group rights and responsibilities. Any socially just leader, therefore, is well versed in understanding what this means—in theory and practice.

Socially just leadership education equips leaders to understand what rights and responsibilities are and why they are important. The topics and conversations conducive to this appreciation may be largely theoretical; however, education should not stop there. Too often, conversations of rights devolve into turf battles over what is *mine*, *yours*, and *"the state's."* This renders the topic far too political. Instead, I propose beginning from the starting point of any constructive, liberal discourse: every human being is the bearer of unalienable dignity and rights demanding respect and recognition.

Rights also entail responsibilities. The two ideals cannot be separated. To acknowledge one's rights necessitates the responsibility of exercising those rights in a way that respects others'. Rights and responsibilities are the two wings upon which social justice soars—we ensure leaders grasp the importance of both.

I offer these guiding questions to reflect:

- What philosophical principles are necessary to recognize the inherent dignity and unalienable rights possessed by every individual?
- What responsibilities follow from the recognition and exercise of individual rights?
- What are the rights and responsibilities of associations (nonprofit, corporate, state based, and familial)?

Commitment to Communities

While the first layer of socially just leadership education is rather abstract, the next requires a rigorous engagement with the particular. Leadership is actualized amidst specific and nuanced contexts. Effective leaders appreciate the demands of the political community, the purposes of local stakeholders, the particulars of place, and the timing it takes to build sustainably community. To engage these layers takes time and commitment. Socially just leaders are not consultants; they are committed members of a community—aware of its history, values, and struggles. Take, for example, a nonprofit working to providing pro bono legal defense for a particular community. To be effective, the leaders are conversant with the many rings of society they operate amidst. They know the relevant federal, state, and local laws. They understand (not impose, but truly comprehend) the needs and wishes of those they serve. They grasp the problems particular to the local community. They are also be cognizant of the many other efforts working to help the same communities—that is, their unique contribution.

We equip socially just leaders by educating them to be capable of identifying and understanding the multitudinous communities their actions touch. While we cannot tailor education to every context, we can do two things: study the history and values of the broader communities we are part of (e.g., our nation and state) and equip students to immerse themselves amidst those they serve. This requires genuine engagement with history, social science, and public policy.

I offer these guiding questions to reflect:

- How do we identify and understand the many communities touched by a particular issue of social justice?
- What guiding principles can inform the resolution of conflicts between various communities, both horizontally (those with differing purposes) and vertically (those with overlapping purposes and jurisdictions)?
- How can we engage particular cases (both successful and unsuccessful) to inform our own work in different contexts?

Cultivating the Virtue of Social Justice

The central contention of this chapter is that social justice is first and foremost a virtue of the individual. To educate socially just leaders means to study and practice the habits conducive to social flourishing. What are these habits? Justice is classically considered as the virtue that disposes us to treat others according to their due. This general virtue has many aspects. *Social* justice, we have seen, is a disposition to protect and promote the rights and responsibilities of others within a particular social order. More specifically, it is the capacity whereby the intermediary associations of civic life thrive and contribute to the common good.

Cultivating social justice requires practicing the habits that contribute to flourishing associational life. Many such habits come to mind. Socially just leaders are humble to ensure serving others is placed above themselves (Keys, 2008). They are gentle in restraining their frustrations. They are tolerant without being obsequious (Avramenko & Promisel, 2018). They are truthful while remaining witty and civil (Lombardini, 2013). They are also prudent in discerning the most practicable avenue for realizing their purposes (Pieper, 1966).

The lofty aims of this list may give socially just leadership the appearance of an unattainable ideal. But we should not let such aspirations desensitize us to an elementary intuition: without character, leadership lacks its central wellspring. Social justice will not be incorporated into our society until its constitutive habits are instilled into our hearts. A socially just society is nonsensical without individuals animated to populate, sustain, and nourish it. For what is social justice other than respect and recognition for those we encounter in social life?

Fortunately for us, the cultivation of leadership virtue is not a new demand. In fact, one of the longest standing genres of political thought—the mirror for princes genre—embraces the ideal of exposing leaders to virtuous models for imitation. We would do well to head the insights of this genre. These texts were written for, and read by, actual leaders. They are called "mirrors" because they depicted the ideal virtues (e.g., prudence, moderation, justice, courage) that rulers should embody—as if they were peering into an ideal version of themselves. Contrary to conventional wisdom, mirrors were neither an exclusively western phenomenon (Blaydes et al., 2018) nor exclusive to male leaders (Forhan, 2002).

These mirrors operate by not only reflecting upon the ideal virtues of leadership—and the corresponding vices to be avoided—but also the lessons of history that provide practical wisdom to practitioners. Aspiring leaders are presented with ideal character traits to strive for and practical lessons from history to better realize their purposes. This tradition also educates leaders in their community's history. Armed with this knowledge we can better understand the traditions and values that inform our fellow citizens. In sum, the mirror genre, at its best, is an exercise of liberal arts leadership education—an examination of values, the striving for ideals, and the cultivation of appreciation for history and culture.

Thus, while cultivating the virtue of social justice may be a lofty ideal, we would do well to heed the models and the history of educators who have already blazed this trail, such as the authors of princely mirrors. The practice of studying exemplary models of socially just leadership may be just as powerful as any handbook of techniques.

I offer these guiding questions to reflect:

- What exemplars are most relevant to our leadership aspirations?
- How should we balance the demands of effective leadership with the values of social justice and the communities we serve?
- What are the limits of what socially just leadership can achieve?

REFERENCES

Aristotle. (2011). *Aristotle's Nicomachean ethics* (R. C. Bartlett & S. D. Collins, Trans.). University of Chicago Press.

Avramenko, R., & Promisel, M. (2018). When toleration becomes a vice: Naming Aristotle's third unnamed virtue. *American Journal of Political Science, 62*(4), 849–860.

Bankston, C. L. I. (2010). Social justice: Cultural origins of a perspective and a theory. *The Independent Review, 15*(2), 165–178.

Behr, T. (2005). Luigi Taparelli and social justice: Rediscovering the origins of a 'hollowed' concept. *Social Justice in Context, 1*, 3–16.

Behr, T. (2019). *Social justice and subsidiarity: Luigi Taparelli and the origins of Modern Catholic social thought*. Catholic University of America Press.

Blaydes, L., Grimmer, J., & McQueen, A. (2018). Mirrors for princes and sultans: Advice on the art of governance in the medieval Christian and Islamic worlds. *Journal of Politics, 80*(4), 1150–1167.

Burke, T. P. (2010). The origins of social justice: Taparelli d'Azeglio. *Modern Age, 52*(2), 97–106.

Fleischacker, S. (2004). *A short history of distributive justice*. Harvard University Press.

Forhan, K. L. (2002). *The political theory of Christine de Pizan*. Ashgate.

Hayek, F. A. (1976). *Law, legislation and liberty (Vol. 2): The mirage of social justice*. Routledge & Kegan Paul.

Hittinger, R. (2008). The coherence of the four basic principles of Catholic social doctrine: An interpretation. *Pontifical Academy of Social Sciences, Acta 14*.

Keys, M. M. (2008). Humility and greatness of soul. *Perspectives on Political Science, 37*(4), 217–222.

Kraynak, R. P. (2018). The origins of 'social justice' in the natural law philosophy of Antonio Rosmini. *The Review of Politics, 80*(1), 3–29.

Lombardini, J. (2013). Civic laughter: Aristotle and the political virtue of humor. *Political Theory, 41*(2), 203–230.

Miller, D. (1999). *Principles of social justice*. Harvard University Press.

Novak, M., & Adams, P. (2015). *Social justice isn't what you think it is* (First American ed.). Encounter Books.

Paulhus, N. J. (1987). Uses and misuses of the term 'social justice' in the Roman Catholic tradition. *The Journal of Religious Ethics, 15*(2), 261–282.

Pieper, J. (1966). *The four cardinal virtues: Prudence, justice, fortitude, temperance* (1st ed.). Notre Dame University Press.

Rawls, J. (1971). *A theory of justice*. Belknap Press of Harvard University Press.

Rosenman, S. I. (Ed.). (1938). *The public papers and addresses of Franklin D. Roosevelt*. Random House.

Stoner, J. R., & James, H. (Eds.). (2015). *The thriving society: On the social conditions of human flourishing*. The Witherspoon Institute.

PART I

SOCIAL IDENTITY AND SOCIALLY JUST LEADERSHIP EDUCATION

CHAPTER 3

REFRAMING LEADERSHIP EDUCATION AND DEVELOPMENT FOR NATIVE COLLEGE STUDENTS

Symphony D. Oxendine and Deborah J. Taub

Indigenous students seek higher education to better serve their communities by "gaining access to power, authority, and an opportunity to exercise control over the affairs of everyday life" (Kirkness & Barnhardt, 1991, p. 14). Native college students are called to prepare themselves to be the next generation of leaders in tribal communities (Minthorn et al., 2013). Education is one way tribal communities are addressing challenges and engaging in the process of nation-building to strengthen their communities regarding issues of economic development, health and wellness, cultural preservation and revival, legal and political practices, educational development, and spiritual processes (Brayboy et al., 2012).

There are numerous terms for the Indigenous people of the Americas (i.e., Native American, Alaska Native, American Indian, Native, Indigenous). Throughout this chapter, we use the term Native for consistency unless otherwise referenced from the literature. Before we proceed further, there is a significant consideration that we must provide. As a result of the colonization of North American, identity for Indigenous peoples is

Shifting the Mindset: Socially Just Leadership Education
pp. 25–37
Copyright © 2021 by Information Age Publishing

a liminal space encompassing both a legal/political aspect and an identity as a racialized group (Brayboy, 2013). Therefore, one cannot equate Native identity with other racial/ethnic identities. "We share common experiences of colonization, similarities in our worldview and thus common epistemologies" (Waterman & Bazemore-James, 2019, p. 159). Indigenous knowledge systems (IKS) refer to "specific systems of values, knowledge, understandings, and practices developed and accumulated over millennia, by a group of human beings in a particular region, which may be unique to that group or region" (Thaman, 2006, p. 176). At the core of IKS are the elements of:

- community and community survival;
- lived experience as important knowledge;
- relationality, respect, and reciprocity; and
- importance of land, space, and location (Brayboy et al., 2012)

It is important to keep in mind, though, that Indigenous peoples are not a monolithic group with one culture or identity; the diversity of peoples, nations, languages, cultures, and experiences is vast and complex. In this brief chapter, we can only present a very general overview of common Indigenous values and experiences; in practice, it is important to understand the more specific values and experiences of members of individual tribes.

NATIVE STUDENTS PARTICIPATION IN HIGHER EDUCATION

Many higher education professionals have been shielded from considering how their institutions in the past *and present* benefit from educational and governmental policies of forced removal, assimilation, and oppression. All U.S. institutions of higher education exist on dispossessed Indigenous land. "The truth is—if it were not for the loss of land by Indigenous peoples, American colleges and universities would not exist" (Red Shirt-Shaw, 2020, p. 2). Land-grant institutions benefited in particular from the Morrill Act of 1862, which dispossessed Indigenous people of their land which was sold by the states to support the establishment of colleges. The U.S. government expropriated 80,000 parcels of land, which totaled 11 million acres, from more than 250 tribes to broaden access to higher education through the first Morrill Land Grant Act of 1862 (Lee & Ahtone, 2020). This dispossession of land benefits all institutions of higher education in the United States to this day, with special gains for land-grant schools.

It may be comforting to think of such actions as purely historical events typically taught in "history of higher education" courses; events that beneficently increased access to higher education. However, institutions continue to profit from the colonizing impacts of the Morrill Act:

> Our data shows how the Morrill Act turned Indigenous land into college endowments. It reveals two open secrets: First, according to the Morrill Act, all money made from land sales must be used in perpetuity, meaning those funds still remain on university ledgers to this day. And second, at least 12 states are still in possession of unsold Morrill acres as well as associated mineral rights, which continue to produce revenue for their designated institutions. (Lee & Ahtone, 2020, para. 6)

Western/Eurocentric institutional education, in practice and in theory, for Native people since colonization has been aimed at assimilation, Christianization, civilization, and eradication with the goal of "kill the Indian, save the man" (Brayboy, 2013; Faircloth & Tippeconnic, 2015). It is critical for higher education professionals to understand the historical and present-day realities of Native people's experiences with education and policies that have sought to eradicate IKS and the resulting trauma that continues to impact Native people.

According to the U.S. Department of Education and National Center for Education Statistics (2019), in fall 2018 approximately 133,800 Native students were enrolled in degree granting postsecondary institutions in the United States. Native students accounted for .68% of all students enrolled; the majority of whom were enrolled at nonnative colleges and universities. Although the reported volume of Native students is small compared to their peers, we place importance on the justification of actions or inactions that resulted in such underrepresentation, since

> numbers often equate to power, influence and control. For many American Indians, their small population size has been used to argue against prioritizing their concerns ... treated only as an aside in discussions of educational practices, conditions and subsequent attainment. (Faircloth & Tippeconnic, 2015, p. 130).

College leadership education is but one of many ways Native students have been neglected in postsecondary practices. It is too simple to assume Native student participation is low when Native students are either not present in analyses or not disaggregated from an overall sample. The impetus for us to explore leadership for Native students was driven by the incorrect assumptions made from the national enrollment data. In particular, due to the small proportion of Native students relative to the overall enrollment of all postsecondary students, Native students are typically not included in analysis or disaggregated from large-scale data sets, such as the Multi-Institutional Study of Leadership (see also: www.leadership-study.net).

There have been studies that have sought to explore Native student leadership in higher education through a quantitative approach that centered the perspectives of Native students. Using data drawn from the Multi-Institutional Study of Leadership, we explored the impact of leadership development experiences and involvement in campus organizations on Native students' leadership efficacy and leadership capacity. Overall, approximately one quarter of Native students had ever participated in any leadership opportunity. The findings identified Native students who were involved in leadership opportunities had increased leadership efficacy and leadership capacity. However, the leadership opportunities that were short-term or one-time opportunities or those that were part of major requirements (i.e., business leadership) were those that Native students participated in most frequently. Stewart (2018) explored predictors of leadership skills among Native college students using data from the Cooperative Institutional Research Program and the College Student Survey interpreted through the lens of the social change model.

From on our analysis of responses from Native students on the 2012 and 2015 Multi-Institutional Study of Leadership, we observed participation of Native students in leadership development activities is low (Oxendine & Taub, 2018). In general, Native students participated most frequently in short-term experiences and least frequently in those experiences requiring longer term commitment. Their participation in formal leadership education experiences (e.g., a leadership major or minor) was very low when compared to their otherwise equivalent peers as well. We attribute these occurrences, at least in part, to mismatches between expectations of leadership learning environments and Native students' ways of leading. We highlight the latter in the next section.

CHARACTERISTICS OF NATIVE LEADERSHIP

To improve socially just leadership learning for native students, we begin with an overview of the various ways that leadership is identified, characterized, and perceived within Native communities. It is critical to keep in mind; however, just as there is no monolithic "Native" identity or culture, there is no singular "Native leadership" approach either. Faircloth and Tippeconnic (2015) illustrated this by showcasing how "we also know that the way in which this leadership is conceptualized and practiced will differ according to tribe, community, and place" (p. 131). Furthermore, leadership for Native people is neither separate nor distinct from the cultural values inherent to Native nations and IKS, including community, collaboration, relationality, responsibility, and reciprocity (Salis Reyes & Taula, 2019; Waterman & Bazemore-James, 2019). For many Indigenous cultures, this means "we are, we know, and we do through our relationships with not only other people but the natural and spiritual worlds" (Salis Reyes & Taula, 2019, p. 47). The IKS and worldviews, though encompassing diverse Indigenous nations, have some common epistemologies to frame how Native peoples relate to the world.

There is an abundance of leadership theories, models, and approaches from a variety of disciplines. Within higher education, numerous social, corporate, and community leadership theories have been adapted for college students, as well as new theories and models developed specifically for postsecondary contexts. However, most if not all of these models reflect Western/Eurocentric perspectives, and suffer from research failing to address the intersections of identity, culture, and leadership (Faircloth & Tippeconnic, 2015; Minthorn & Chávez, 2014).

Leadership for Native people within higher education has been largely drawn from the Tribal college and university setting; primarily from professionals in administrative/presidential roles or within educational leadership programs preparing Native school leaders (Faircloth & Tippeconnic, 2015; Minthorn & Chávez, 2014). Robin Minthorn and Alicia Fedelina Chávez's (2014) *Indigenous Leadership in Higher Education* provided autobiographical narratives of 22 Indigenous leaders within higher education. The editors leveraged themes from their authors to create an Indigenous leadership model. The Indigenous Leadership Model is a circle, similar to a medicine wheel, comprising four quadrants identifying the tenets of leadership as "who we are, what we strive to embody, what is known, and what we do" (Minthorn & Chávez, 2016, p. 8).

These four tenets are described:

> Leadership occurs in the context of the importance and wisdom of Elders, leading within and understanding that adaptability and tradition are essential and part of our history, that committed relationships are critical to deep transformation, and that we are strengthened with and by the collective. (p. 8)

In reviewing literature on leadership from Native/Indigenous perspectives, several elements consistently surface; including: collective/communal orientation, shared vision and responsibility, humility, service/serving, commitment, collaboration, balance, cultural competence/cultural knowledge, and understanding history and traditions of communities (Badwound & Tierney, 1988; Faircloth & Tippeconnic, 2015; HeavyRunner & DeCelles, 2002; Jules, 1999; Minthorn, 2014; Minthorn & Chávez, 2014; Tippeconnic, 2006; Warner & Grint, 2006).

Native college student leadership literature also has greatly increased in the last decade. Williams (2012) described how leadership education and corresponding models and theories used at nonnative colleges and universities were devoid of Native values and conceptualizations of leadership. Native students bring leadership values from their respective communities, and socially just leadership educators include Indigenous leadership concepts, since non-Indigenous students benefit from them as well. Minthorn et al. (2013) described an example of a leadership education opportunity: the Oklahoma Native American Students in Higher Education (Minthorn et al., 2013). Centering the experiences and needs of Native students is imperative for any leadership education or development.

> If we are to develop our Native students as future leaders we must first empower them. The experience of Native students in education often is one of being silenced or overlooked, an experience that is counter to the concept of empowerment.... Native students should be reassured that their voice matters, that they matter. (Minthorn et al., 2013, p. 70)

The Oklahoma Native American Students in Higher Education provided an opportunity for Native students to have an active role in planning and implementing the conference based on their own needs, priorities, and values. Also, the conference focused on providing attending students with interactions to build community and a support system, exposure to Native role models, and developing a positive self-image (Minthorn et al., 2013).

The dichotomy between Western/Eurocentric and Indigenous concepts of leadership, and the failure of current campus leadership education to engage Native students, illustrates the critical importance of reframing college leadership education. It is past time that "leadership education makes space for genuine self-examination, critical exploration, and opportunities to learn from comparing and contrasting Indigenous and Western thought where both are regarded with equal esteem and both regarded as fully legitimate ways of knowing" (Cross et al., 2019, p. 105). Envisioning and creating a future of leadership education as a relevant opportunity for Native students in higher education is incumbent on leadership educators, now more than ever.

HOW COLLEGE LEADERSHIP EDUCATION MISSES THE MARK

First, we want to be clear that providing data on the low rates of participation of Native students in leadership education opportunities (Oxendine & Taub, 2018) does not indicate there is a problem with Native students, per se, because they are not taking advantage of these opportunities. We offer this information to motivate leadership educators in their interrogation of systemic barriers to participation. Identifying how leadership education has been structured to exclude Native students is an important step toward social justice.

One barrier to Native participation in college leadership education is related to mismatches between underlying models of leadership used in programs and Natives' ways of leading. For example, the social change model of leadership development (Higher Education Research Institute, 1996), which is one of the most popular models in collegiate leadership learning (Komives & Sowcik, 2020). The social change model of leadership development is built around seven values (the "Seven C's"), which are organized into three groups: individual values (consciousness of self, congruence, commitment), group values (collaboration, common purpose, controversy with civility), and societal/community values (citizenship). Although the model suggests one can enter at any point, it may not always be taught from such a perspective. "Recent research supports the value of developmental sequencing of each of the dimensions of the model, in which capacity in the individual domain precedes capacity with group values, which precedes society/community (Dugan, Bohle, Woelker, & Cooney, 2014)" (Skendall, 2017, p. 20). Despite alluding to a sequential orientation to the values of the social change model of leadership development, Dugan et al. (2014) did not provide demographic information about the racial/ethnic identification of their participants in the study cited; however, the proportion of Native student participants was likely quite low.

Recommendations like these, when generalized to college students en masse, may not yield the benefits expected at best, and may hinder the leadership learning of students from under- or unrepresented groups, like Native students, at worst. When developmental sequencing begins with considerations of the self, it contradicts Indigenous ways of knowing and associated values, such as collective/communal orientation, shared vision and responsibility, humility, and service (Salis Reyes & Taula, 2019; Waterman & Bazemore-James, 2019). As the Indigenous leadership model (Minthorn & Chavez, 2016) highlights, one tenet of Indigenous leadership is "who *we* are" (p. 8, emphasis added); a focus on the group and not on the individual. Therefore, although popular approaches to the social change model of leadership development frequently "begin[s] with the self", this may not be the most appropriate sequencing for leadership development among Native students.

Many of the ways college leadership programs are missing the mark with Native students can be found in recruitment and selection processes for leadership positions. Specifically, the problem of *redundancy* may be a barrier facing Native students' opportunities to lead. Redundancy (Barker & Gump, 1964) exists when the number of people in a setting exceeds the number of opportunities for meaningful involvement. Each organization can have only a few positional leaders. Therefore, when the pool of potential participants in a leadership education opportunity (e.g., training, classes, professional development workshops, etc.) is limited to those with leadership roles in organizations, the opportunities for involvement for all students—not just Native students—is limited. Opportunities for involvement are even more restricted when the pool of leadership learners is exclusive to presidents of organizations. Redundancy also may create barriers in more specialized leadership education offerings. For example, if those to be invited to a multicultural leadership retreat are the officers of multicultural organizations on campus, the number of Native students eligible to participate is quite low. Not many campuses have even a single Native American Student Organization; those that do are unlikely to have more than one despite heterogeneity among Native students. This is unlikely to be as acute a problem with other cultural-affinity organizations. Thus, leadership education can impose a filtering effect on those Native students who could gain the most from those opportunities.

Nominations processes for leadership development opportunities also can be problematic due to the impact of selection biases. A particularly challenging dynamic on many college campuses occurs when the same few students [seem to] get nominated for everything. The underlying systemic obstacle is the basis on which these nominations are made. If faculty and administrators, when asked to nominate students for leadership development opportunities, default to customary and familiar leadership characteristics or behaviors to make their endorsements, they de facto exclude Native students from consideration. Given the notable differences between Western/Eurocentric versions of leadership, and those of Native peoples, Native ways of leading will largely be overlooked and undervalued in nomination processes.

Open applications might appear to have the fewest difficulties as a recruitment and enrollment strategy. However, to nominate oneself for a leadership development program requires one to identify oneself as a leader or potential leader. Again, this is contradictory to many Native cultural values as "leaders were not elected or appointed through a formal process, but rather were recognized or chosen inasmuch as other people looked to them for leadership" (Jules, 1999, p. 44). The self-aggrandizement required by self-nomination runs counter to the cultural value of humility (Bryant, 1996).

RETHINKING OUR PRACTICES

Given our understanding of Native views of leadership and how current leadership education programs may be missing the mark, there are a number of ways socially just leadership educators (re)evaluate their current practices to be more inclusive of Native students. Below, we outline some suggestions to guide this rethinking.

First, look for what already is working, should such pathways exist. Currently, where are Native students engaged in leadership activities or leadership education in and around your context? Invite these students to share their stories about leadership, their life experiences, and their reasons for choosing these venues as opposed to other available opportunities. Reflect on how to leverage this knowledge to illuminate current practices and guide future processes. We strongly advise against putting the burden of how to "fix" programs onto the Native students.

Second, socially just leadership educators strive to possess, "a philosophy and practice of life-long learning and professional development" (Council for the Advancement of Standards in Higher Education, 2006, p. 2). It is imperative to learn more about Native people in general, Native students' learning preferences in particular, as well as IKS, and Indigenous worldviews. Such learning is essential to learning that is inclusive and affirming for Native college students. Cross and colleagues (2019) identified the following recommendations for decolonizing education for Native student leaders:

- recognizing, affirming, and legitimizing Indigenous ways of knowing;
- incorporate responsive instruction for Native learning styles;
- small group learning;
- using narrative;
- mutuality and respect between faculty and students;
- Freedom to explore in safety;
- instructor openness and directness; and
- student autonomy and influence.

Additionally, socially just leadership educators examine underlying leadership development model(s) being used on campus, during programs, and in courses. As Cross et al. (2019) described,

> leadership education itself ... grew out of the same unified national culture of education established by the founding fathers long ago. Along with the entire higher education curriculum, leadership education risks continuing a paradigm which is no longer relevant in a multicultural society. (p. 108)

We suggest examining how current models in use can be adapted and expanded to reflect IKS and Indigenous ways of knowing. Perhaps a truly decolonizing approach to leadership education would embrace multiple models and reflect the diversity of Native worldviews.

Finally, we empower the interrogation and interruption of policies and practices which serve as barriers to Native student participation. Here are some changes to consider:

- Is it necessary to require a minimum number of students to create an organization? Question how this disproportionately disadvantages the smaller populations on campus. Recognize how different it is to require a minimum of 10 students from among a potential pool of 26,000 from requiring that same minimum from a group of less than 100 students. In such cases (based on actual enrollment data at one institution), a requirement of 10 students represents approximately 10% of the Native student population; the equivalent 10% of all students would be 2,600. Would you reasonably expect a minimum of 2,600 students to be able to form an organization?

- When soliciting nominations, how, if at all, is leadership defined? Consider including a description of leadership extending beyond Western/Eurocentric leadership ideals. Take this opportunity to educate and broaden perspectives about leadership among those you turn to for nominations. Encourage them to consider students other than the "usual suspects."

- Look beyond positional leaders. Besides holding an elected office, what other students are demonstrating leadership? Consider the students organizing protests, those staffing the campus food pantry, and student employees. Front desk workers, food service workers, and the students driving campus shuttles demonstrate leadership.

- Leadership does not occur only on campus. Rather than, or in addition to, involvement on campus, Native students may be engaged and display leadership off campus. Stewart (2018) found participating in volunteer work during college was a significant predictor of developing leadership skills among Native students.

- Relabel leadership education. The word "leadership" itself may be off-putting to students from collectivist cultures, such as Native students. What words fit better for your students given the context, location, and values of the tribes represented on your campus? Just as there is no monolithic Native culture; there is no magic word with universal appeal.

CONCLUSION

As we observed at the beginning of this chapter, higher education plays an important part in addressing the challenges to, and in securing, the futures of tribal communities (Brayboy et al., 2012). As Native college students are called to be the next generation of leaders in their communities (Minthorn et al., 2013), college leadership education can contribute in important ways to Native nation-building. Actualizing this potential requires leadership educators to include IKS and to enact more inclusive policies, programs, and practices that embrace Native ways of leading.

REFERENCES

Badwound, E., & Tierney, W. G. (1988). Leadership and American Indian values: The tribal college dilemma. *Journal of American Indian Education, 28*(1), 9–15.

Barker, R. G., & Gump, P. V. (1964). *Big school, small school: High school size and student behavior*. Stanford University Press.

Brayboy, B. M. J. (2013). Tribal critical race theory: An origin story and future directions. In M. Lynn & A. D. Dixson (Eds.), *Handbook of critical race theory in education* (pp. 88–100). Routledge.

Brayboy, B. M. J., Fann, A. J., Castagno, A. E., & Solyom, J. A. (2012). Postsecondary education for American Indian and Alaska Natives. *ASHE Higher Education Report, 37*(5), 1–140. https://doi.org/10.1002/aehe.3705

Bryant, M. T. (1996, October 25–27). *Contrasting American and Native American views of leadership*. Paper presented at the annual meeting of the University Council for Educational Administration, Louisville, KY. https://files.eric.ed.gov/fulltext/ED402691.pdf

Council for the Advancement of Standards in Higher Education (Ed.). (2006). CAS characteristics of individual excellence for professional practice in higher education. In *CAS professional standards for higher education* (6th ed.). https://www.cas.edu/files/IndividualExcellence.pdf

Cross, T. L., Pewewardy, C., & Smith, A. T. (2019). Restorative education, reconciliation, and healing: Indigenous perspectives on decolonizing leadership education. In B. A. Nagda & L. D. Roper (Eds.), *New Directions for Student Leadership: No. 163. Centering dialogue in leadership development* (pp. 101–115). https://doi.org/10.1002/yd.20350

Faircloth, S. C., & Tippeconnic, J. W., III. (2015). Leadership development for schools serving American Indian students: Implications for research, policy, and practice. *Journal of American Indian Education, 54*(1), 127–153.

HeavyRunner, I., & DeCelles, R. (2002). Family education model: Meeting the student retention challenge. *Journal of American Indian Education, 41*(2), 29–37.

Higher Education Research Institute. (1995). *A social change model of leadership development: Guidebook version III*. National Clearinghouse for Leadership Programs.

Jules, F. (1999). Native Indian leadership. *Canadian Journal of Native Education, 23*(1), 40–56.

Kirkness, V. J., & Barnhardt, R. (1991). First Nations and higher education—The four R's—Respect, relevance, reciprocity, responsibility. *Journal of American Indian Education, 30*, 1–15.

Komives, S. R., & Sowcik, M. (2020). The status and scope of leadership education in higher education. In M. Sowcik & S. R. Komives (Eds.), *New Directions for Student Leadership: No. 165. How Academic Disciplines Approach Leadership Development* (pp. 23–36). Jossey-Bass.

Lee, R., & Ahtone, T. (2020, March 30). Land-grab universities. *High Country News, 52*(4). https://www.hcn.org/issues/52.4/indigenous-affairs-education-land-grab-universities

Minthorn, R., & Chávez, A. F. (Eds.). (2014). *Indigenous leadership in higher education*. Routledge.

Minthorn, R. W. (2014). Perspectives and values of leadership for Native American college students in non-Native colleges and universities. *Journal of Leadership Education, 13*(2), 67–95.

Minthorn, R. W., Wanger, S., & Shotton, H. J. (2013). Developing Native student leadership skills: The success of the Oklahoma Native American students in higher education (ONASHE) conference. *American Indian Culture and Research Journal, 37*(3), 59–74.

Oxendine, S. D., & Taub, D. J. (2018, December 9–11). *Missing the mark: Native student involvement in leadership experiences and campus organizations* [Conference session]. Leadership Educators Institute, Orlando, FL, United States.

Red Shirt-Shaw, M. (2020). *Beyond the land acknowledgement: College "land back" of free tuition for Native students* [Policy Brief]. ACCEPT: Admissions Community Cultivating Equity & Peace Today & RISE Center at Colorado State University. https://hackthegates.org/wp-content/uploads/2020/08/Redshirt-Shaw_Landback_HTGreport.pdf

Salis Reyes, N. A., & Tauala, M. (2019). Indigenous paradigms: Decolonizing college student development theory through centering relationality. In E. S. Abes, S. R. Jones, & D. L. Stewart (Eds.), *Rethinking college student development theory using critical frameworks* (pp. 45–54). Stylus.

Skendall, K. C. (2017). An overview of the social change model of leadership development. In S. R. Komives & W. Wagner (Eds.), *Leadership for a better world* (2nd ed., pp. 17–40). Jossey-Bass.

Stewart, T. J. (2018). Predictors for American Indian/Alaska Native student leadership. In R. S. Minthorn & H. J. Shotton (Eds.), *Reclaiming Indigenous research in higher education* (pp. 88–106). Rutger University Press.

Thaman, K. H. (2006). Acknowledging Indigenous knowledge systems in higher education in the Pacific Island region. In V. L. Meek & C. Suwanwela (Eds.), *Higher education, research, and knowledge in the Asia Pacific region* (pp. 175–184). Springer. https://doi.org/10.1057/9780230603165_9

Tippeconnic, J. (2006). Identity-based and reputational leadership: An American Indian approach to leadership. *Journal of Research on Leadership Education, 1*(1), 1–3. https://doi.org/10.1177/194277510600100115

U.S. Department of Education & National Center for Education Statistics. (2019). *Total fall enrollment in degree-granting postsecondary institutions, by level of enroll-ment, sex, attendance status, and race/ethnicity or nonresident alien status of student: Selected years, 1976 through 2018.* https://nces.ed.gov/programs/digest/d19/tables/dt19_306.10.asp

Warner, L. S., & Grint, K. (2006). American Indian ways of leading and knowing. *Leadership, 2*(2), 225–244. https://doi.org/10.1177/1742715006062936

Waterman, S. J., & Bazemore-James, C. M. (2019). It's more than us. In E. S. Abes, S. R. Jones, & D. L. Stewart (Eds.), *Rethinking college student development theory using critical frameworks* (pp. 158–170). Stylus.

Williams, R. S. (2012). *Indigenizing leadership concepts through perspectives of Native American college students* [Doctoral dissertation, Oklahoma State University]. ProQuest Dissertations and Theses Global.

CHAPTER 4

LEADING FROM IN BETWEEN

Asian American Student Leadership

Valerie Luutran and Jessica Chung

"Don't cause trouble." "Go help with the dishes." "It doesn't matter whose mess it is, you clean up for your family." "Don't work too much, you need time for family." "Why not 100%?" "Don't speak up too much." These are just some messages characteristic of our separate, yet parallel, upbringings that influence the ways we saw ourselves as leaders (or not) in a predominantly White, middle-class, cis-male society.

Asian Americans are often left out of the discourse on race in America—our oppression minimized by perceived economic prosperity, our cultural values of community and humility painted as the ideal follower, our positionality in between the Black-White racial binary. This tenuous position carries over into the conceptualization of Asian Americans as leaders.

AUTHOR ACKNOWLEDGEMENT

We acknowledge the limitations of our lenses as two cis-female educators who are children of immigrants. As a Chinese American and a Vietnamese American, neither of us can speak firsthand to the experiences of the

Shifting the Mindset: Socially Just Leadership Education
pp. 39–52
Copyright © 2021 by Information Age Publishing

larger range of "Asians," such as Desi Americans or Pacific Islanders. Nonetheless, we do our best to share our perspective, histories, research contexts, then suggest how to apply a culturally relevant approach to working with students from the Asian diaspora. We lean into the existing literature and our own personal experiences to scratch the surface, in hopes this chapter leads to further conversation and research about our incredibly diverse community.

A NOTE ABOUT LANGUAGE

Language describing members of this vast population has evolved from Asian American to Asian American Pacific Islander to Asian Pacific Islander Desi American. Since the term "Asian American" often conjures images of East Asians, specifically naming Desi helps acknowledge Indian identities (Chowdhury, 2017). Recognizing our specific positionality, we will be using Asian American in this chapter.

CONTEXT: DISMANTLING THE MONOLITH

In indirect and high context cultures like ours, telling a story includes sharing detail and backdrop. In parallel, an exploration of Asian American leadership requires embracing the complexity of intersecting identities and cultural history, as well as reevaluating foundational student development assumptions.

Model Minority Myth and the "Oppression Olympics"

Asian Americans have long been positioned as financially stable, hardworking, docile, and non disruptive—the example for how all minoritized persons should defer to authority and assimilate to Western norms to succeed. William Peterson was the first to coin the term "model minority" to describe this in his 1966 *New York Times* article, "Success Story, Japanese-American Style." This myth raises questions like: if Asians are successful despite a history of oppression (e.g., Japanese internment camps), why cannot Black people? Since Asians were accepted as less threatening to the White status quo, alongside our tendencies toward lighter complexions, we are often labeled "White adjacent." This was not an elevation of Asians, but an anti-Black oppression tactic, still operating in facets of the Asian community today.

The presumed success of East Asians was the reward for aligning with Whiteness while distancing from the harsh realities faced by members of Black and Brown populations. This fueled historical and modern anti-Blackness in our communities, including reactions to the killing of George Floyd and Breonna Taylor, among others. This resulted in a range in how Asian Americans see themselves and are seen by others as people of color. Some argue the oppression faced by Asian Americans is "not as bad" as the oppression faced by other people of color in the United States. Asian Americans may internalize this and see ourselves ranging from being White to simply "not Asian" to the "perpetual foreigner" who never belongs.

This external erasure was institutionalized by the first iteration of affirmative action regulations, which did not include Asian Americans as a protected minority group (Suzuki, 2002). Many colleges and universities continue to exclude Asian Americans in their classifications of minority students (Chung, 2014); research and university demographics often lump Asian American students with White peers, separating them from other students of color. In institutional discussions about race, we are often left out.

Internally, Asian American students and leaders may experience self-erasure in their identity development through passive and active White identification (Kim, 2012). We make ourselves racially invisible by assimilating to Whiteness, subsequently falling behind our peers of color in developing our racial identity salience.

Russell Jeung, a professor of Asian American studies at San Francisco State University, explained this in the context of the 2020 Black Lives Matter movement, saying "Asian Americans find it difficult to find their position in American society, and so when they address Black Lives Matter they don't know if they are White or Black … they have to recognize that there's another positioning of Asians in the American racial dynamic, and that's whether we're outsiders or insiders" (Delaney, 2020). This positioning as outsiders or insiders changes often depending on context.

Between the varying impacts of stereotypes, "not so bad" disparities, and the constantly shifting positionality of Asian Americans, it is exhausting to figure out where we stand. This makes it easier for Asian Americans to ignore systemic issues and disengage from political discourse because of the internal and external messages that say, "We don't have any problems." This, in conjunction with other systemic barriers, relates to our community having one of the lowest voting registration and turnout rates among voting-age Americans—rendering us voiceless in our democracy as well (Lien et al., 2001).

American social structures focus narrowly on civil rights and racial discrimination as Black and White. Asians and Asian Americans have contributed greatly but are featured in the background—minoritized beyond the minorities; more hidden than the hidden figures. Many learn about the 1954 Brown versus the Board of Education of Topeka as a landmark case for civil rights challenging the "separate but equal" doctrine. However, 27 years earlier, a Chinese citizen brought a similar case to the supreme court (*Gong Lum v. Rice*, n.d.). In another example, because the workforce responsible for the Central Pacific Railroad was 90% Chinese, they were not allowed to attend the railroad's completion celebration (Asian American History, n.d.).

Without mainstream representation, students feel they are great followers for others' success, rendering their significant contributions invisible. The lack of acknowledgment as active contributors carries on in the media and in our families from generation to generation.

Presently, the impacts of the model minority myth manifest in higher education through affirmative action. The 2019 *Students for Fair Admissions v. Harvard* case argued non-Asian racial minorities were "preferred" and admitted more frequently than Asian Americans with stronger scores, grades, and involvement. The Harvard case is just one example of how Asian Americans are still co-opted as tools to uphold oppressive systems at the expense of other members of communities of color.

The erasure of our position in the racial history of and modern discourse of this country has direct implications for our complicated position in student leadership learning.

Cultural Values and Disposition

Growing up Asian American can feel like living in two worlds: one governed by the norms and values of our families' home country, and another governed by those of the United States. This creates dissonance between "at-home values" like prioritizing the group over the self, deference to authority, humility, and harmony (Yammarino & Jung, 1998) and "outside values," such as assertiveness, decisiveness (Zane et al., 1991), and self-confidence (Astin, 1993). Some of our students are children of refugees; those whose parents experienced upheaval or unrest in their motherlands and saw firsthand how divisive political and socioeconomic issues could be (like the Chinese Cultural Revolution) before immigrating to the United States (Delaney, 2020). The effects of this trauma is seen in Asian Americans' political disengagement, and is aligned with the cultural value of maintaining harmony or not wanting to "rock the boat" with strong opinions.

How we were taught to be respectful was often regarded as ideal follower traits once we left our homes. This is one example of how code-switching manifests in the Asian diaspora; performing to different expectations to avoid disappointing people in different contexts.

Asian culture is typically implicit or learned through immersion. Western culture is explicit, where norms are clearly explained. Our implicit culture also features an indirect communication style that prioritizes harmony and public maintenance of others' honor, meaning there is often subtext to someone's words. For students, this can be experienced as being too soft or passive in the U.S. context while being too wild and blunt in the Asian context—not a suitable "wife" for a Chinese family and not enough of a "leader" in an American organization.

If organizations are oriented toward these individualistic cultural values, there are direct impacts on the cultivation of Asian American leaders.

INTERSECTIONS OF IDENTITY

We complicate our understanding by adding layers of intersection. This section is limited in scope; we do not explore the nuanced challenges that exist for Asian Americans who identify as LGBTQ+, are transracial adoptees, experience mental health issues, or many other intersecting identities. We shed light on just a few that are most salient to us and hope this opens the door to ask questions for further exploration: ethnicity, gender, class, and immigration status.

Ethnicity is closely entwined with tradition and is often an entry point to racial consciousness for Asian Americans (Accapadi, 2012). The broad "Asian" classification usually equates to East Asians, and inadequately captures the richness and diversity of practices, beliefs, and cultures from Thai to South Indian, to Indonesia to mainland China. While there is often one overarching Asian American student organization on any given college's campus, Asian students are able to associate with additional ethnicity-specific clubs (such as Chinese American Student Organizations, Filipino American Student Associations, Korean American Student Associations, Vietnamese Student Associations, among others).

Another major intersection is gender. Patriarchal gender norms and roles are a common feature in many Asian cultures. Many female Asian Americans find validation in and define themselves through serving other people. According to the servant leadership model, this is a desirable orientation. However, this preference may be perceived as pandering, being a doormat, or not being assertive/decisive enough. Further, when family issues arise, women in Asian families are expected to pick up home responsibilities, which can hinder involvement in campus leadership opportunities. By contrast, men in these communities typically support their homes financially through jobs, which may improve their market-ability in college and beyond.

Outside the home, Asian women are fetishized and hypersexualized by U.S. media. Plays like Madame Butterfly and Miss Saigon portray Asian women as damsels in perpetual distress, eternally grateful to their White male saviors. Conversely, Asian men have been sidelined and emasculated by stereotypes including the nonsexual nerd, intense martial artist, and rarely, the romantic lead. These stereotypes may influence how we view Asian Americans as authors of their own story, or as effective leaders.

Our identities are also inextricably connected to social class. A common misperception exists of Asian Americans have a higher average household income than Whites. However, rigorous studies reveal Asian American families tend to have more earners per household than White families, translating to multiple lower wage jobs per household than one or two six-figure salaries (Suzuki, 2002). The poverty rate for Asian Americans is still higher than Whites, in addition to a lack of upward job mobility. When compared to individuals with similar education, Whites are still likely to have a higher average income than Asian Americans (Suzuki, 2002). While highly educated Asian Americans are able to enter well-paying career fields, the leaders in these fields remain predominantly White. This "bamboo ceiling" phenomenon was first described in Jane Hyun's (2005) book on career strategies for Asians.

These data suggest using socioeconomic status to determine oppression is a deeply flawed approach. Personal experience tells us this is harmful and leads to more feelings of internalized oppression in Asian Americans. For example, when I (Valerie) began exploring how systems of oppression impacted me, there were few times I was ever lacking in privilege if I considered my experiences through a lens of class alone. I struggled with feeling that racism I faced as an Asian American was "not as bad" because it was not overtly compounded with class issues.

The last intersection we discuss is immigration status. Recent U.S. immigration discourse focuses primarily on Latinx populations; however, more Asian immigrants have arrived in the United States than Hispanic immigrants in most years since 2009 (Budiman, 2020). We also acknowledge as of 2017, Asian immigrants accounted for nearly 16% of the undocumented immigrant population in the United States (Ramakrishnan & Shah, 2017). Challenges specific to immigrant students, both documented and undocumented, are necessary for educators to recognize as domestic-born and immigrant Asian students intermingle closely on our campuses.

For children of immigrants, there is a foreignness of culture (see Aparicio & Tornos, 2017 for a study on this topic, although conducted in Madrid with non-Asian participants) that makes it harder to create the 'Asian Pride' needed to combat the White assimilation expectations. When these expectations are brought home to immigrant parents or families, the mismatch leads to lack of interest in cultures of origin, thereby creating disconnections between generations. This dissonance compounds itself as students face resistance from their families, as they may not understand the implicit values behind expectations, yet still feel compelled to meet them. This tension is ever-present as we strive to fully belong somewhere, while not quite belonging anywhere.

Asian values prioritize the collective over the individual; this orientation is compounded for children of immigrant parents. The incredible and tragic persistence to create new lives in a foreign place for their children is a powerful foundation for us to navigate our own stories. This creates a sense of duty to make our families and parents' sacrifice worthwhile. This level of responsibility is notable, yet not always labeled as leadership.

Despite the volumes left unsaid here, the breadth of this population is undeniable. When compared to this entire group, we personally and professionally have faced many of the stereotypes we have unpacked. The internalization of these implicit biases leads to doing, or not doing things because you are afraid of either upholding a stereotype or not upholding one.

CONTEMPORARY ASIAN AMERICAN DEVELOPMENT MODELS

Widely used student development models view independent decision-making as a sign of maturity and self-authorship. However, studies show Asian American students are more likely to have interdependent relationships for a variety of cultural and contextual factors (Kodama & Maramba, 2017). For Asian American students' development, family members are more of an internal consideration, not an external one as typically defined by traditional models (Kodama & Maramba, 2017). This pervasive predilection requires greater exploration to ascertain its impact on student and leadership development.

Student Development

Many Asian American students' family members expect them to pursue lucrative career fields or academic accolades. These students tend to prioritize academic and career pursuits over interpersonal and social pursuits (Kodama & Maramba, 2017). Traditional development models would suggest interdependent decision-making styles are antithetical to a "developed" student. However, they fail to recognize the cultural importance of interdependence and familial relationships in a collectivist context.

With this understanding, Maekawa Kodama and colleagues (2002) proposed a model of psychosocial development to describe how Asian Americans navigated college experiences in between an adopted individualistic society and an interdependent community of origin (Kodama & Maramba, 2017). We challenge educators to examine the assumptions they have about who is developed, who is not, and the differences between the two.

Leadership Development

The bamboo ceiling, in similar fashion to the glass ceiling faced by women, has meaningful implications in fields like higher education, where fewer Asian Americans inhabit leadership roles than any other racial group, dominant or marginalized (Assalone & Fann, 2017). In 2016, Asian Americans made up 9.8% of the federal professional workforce, but only 4.4% of top management positions (Gee & Peck, 2018). Since socially just leadership educators know the importance of representation on leadership self-efficacy, it is no surprise that the lack of Asian American leaders on college campuses contributes to students struggling to see themselves in leadership roles.

Next, we advocate for socially just leadership educators to examine their assumptions about Asian Americans and, ultimately, dismantle this oppressive mold to make room for a more inclusive future.

STRATEGIES FOR SOCIALLY JUST LEADERSHIP EDUCATORS

We all have influence to create accessible and equitable leadership learning spaces as educators. We encourage all educators to reflect on this chapter and use the ideas it contains to continue examining their implicit biases about Asian student leaders. We challenge you to interrogate where those biases show up as systemic barriers in your organizations.

As described in the culturally relevant leadership learning model, students' experiences in broader contexts impacts their leadership learning (Guthrie et al., 2016). With that in mind, we use the domains of the culturally relevant leadership learning model to guide our recommendations for educators: identity, efficacy, and capacity. Although we may be focusing on how we guide the work with students, it is just as important to apply the ideas to ourselves.

Leader Identity: Reframing Leadership

Student leader identity development requires understanding the complex layers of social identity construction (Bertrand Jones et al., 2016).

Socially just leadership educators encourage students to consider how various intersecting identities impact their leadership experiences and behaviors. For Asian American students specifically, many aspects of their culture are implicit, so it will be difficult to explicitly name these values.

For many Asian Americans, our values shape the ways we lead. However, in Western contexts, these qualities may be viewed more as deficiencies than assets, fueling arguments our values are explicitly incompatible with those of good leaders (Chung, 2014). Since Western leadership philosophies prioritize individual values over the collective (Dugan, 2017), connecting students to their social identities can reframe their conceptualization of themselves as valuable leaders. For example, reframing indirect communication as having consideration and respect for the honor of the people around you, or deferring to others as being inclusive of all opinions to seek workable consensus. Highlighting and rewarding the use of supportive skills like listening, strategizing, and researching as leadership also helps. Reimagining what felt like deficits as strengths can bolster leader identity in Asian American students. For example, it took many years of deconditioning for me (Jessica) to reframe messaging that I was a doormat for others and unwilling to take hard stances to being able to consider many perspectives and a deep listener—a valuable leadership skill.

As leader identity development continues, highlight diverse leader profiles or diversify information sources. When discussing Malcom X's leadership in the Civil Rights Movements, consider also discussing Yuri Kochiyama—a Japanese American activist who fought alongside Freedom Riders and helped achieve the signing of the Civil Liberties Act. In contemporary contexts, consider Golden Globe winner Sandra Oh, comedians Hasan Minhaj and Ali Wong, politicians like Andrew Yang, and social activists like Grace Lee Boggs and Jameela Jamil.

Socially just leadership educators bring these stories out of hiding into the public leadership discourse—they are not just for Asian Studies classes! When students see themselves represented as prominent leaders in diverse fields, it cracks the bamboo ceiling and furthers leader identity gains.

Leader Capacity: We Have Been Leading

We are well positioned to pave pathways for students to integrate their leadership knowledge, skills, and attitudes in meaningful ways—having influence on and being influenced by their leadership capacity (Guthrie et al., 2016).

Assuming Asian Americans can be heavily involved in their own communities and families, highlight these transferable skills as leadership. College and university contexts can narrow definitions of leadership skills to merely being in a position of authority in a club or a formal job; however, students with family responsibilities have similar skills that translate across contexts. Making that connection explicit can further affirm their skills.

In learning spaces, there is a power dynamic between facilitators and participants. The value of respect for authority can make it hard for Asian American students to engage the ways we hope; take care to ask open-ended questions and wait for the response, to build personal levels of trust, and be aware of how much of our directions can seem declarative rather than genuinely inviting. With obedience being a rewarded behavior (especially with Asian women), explicitly inviting challenges to dominant systems and contributions without negative consequence from Asian American students is critical to empowering emerging learners.

The wide range of Asian American experiences means many Asian American students want to focus on their own accomplishments and skills outside of a racial justice lens. Encourage students' involvement in these conversations as participants with valid perspectives as whole people; not just tokenized for a singular Asian perspective they can bring. This invites Asian American students, regardless of racial salience, into sociocultural conversations with peers, which is one of four high-impact experiences identified by the Multi-Institutional Study of Leadership (MSL) as capacity-building (Guthrie et al., 2016).

Mentoring relationships, community service, and membership in off-campus organizations are also identified by the MSL as high-impact capacity-building experiences (Guthrie et al., 2016). Socially just leadership educators meaningfully initiate these mentoring relationships by acknowledging potential hesitancy to seek help, recognizing a cultural deference to authority, and offering guidance on creating strong relationships.

Regarding student organizations, Asian American cultural groups exist on many college campuses; both more widely encompassing Asian American groups and ethnicity-specific groups. There is a strong relationship between involvement in these organizations and students' racial identity salience and understanding of Asian American issues (Inkelas, 2004), promoting a greater sense of common identity amongst Asian American students, which may later develop into leadership roles to support their communities and long-term civic engagement even beyond college (Inkelas, 2004). This all can build overall leadership capacity in socially just ways.

Asian American students may also be involved in organizations entirely unrelated to their racial or ethnic identities. Socially just leadership educators are those who take note of how Asian American students are (un)able to attain leadership positions within these organizations and engage in dialogue about differential leadership styles and their value. In our own organizations, we examine who gets to be named positional leaders and how that happens.

Leader Efficacy: See Your Students, Motivate Your students

Asian American student leaders have high capacities for leadership skills and behaviors; however, their motivations are rooted in a strong sense of self-efficacy. Defined as the belief in their ability to be successful, students' self-efficacy is influenced by the messages they receive about leadership expectations, affirmations, or discouragement (Bertrand Jones et al., 2016). We have the power and influence to shape those messages by expanding the definition of desirable and effective leadership traits, what "counts" as leadership experience, and what will be successful in a given context. We can model the way in student leader selection, training, hiring, classes, and workshops when we highlight different kinds of successful leader behaviors and emphasize the value of relationship-building skills, listening, and consensus building.

These insights expand the qualities and skills we knowingly and unknowingly validate in students. Despite desires toward flattened hierarchies, we, as practitioners, are still the formal authority, which carries influence; students take their cues from what we focus on, what or who we reward, what or who we critique, what or who gets encouraged and discouraged. Highlighting diverse ways of leading can increase students' confidence which motivates them to lead more.

Knowing it can be hard to go against the value of humility and modesty, we can build these skills into criteria used for hiring, assessment, performance reviews, and more to affect the change through systemic reward. For example, in hiring processes we can ask about general experiences that have transferable skills to the leadership work. Students with family responsibilities likely have mentorship qualities and a sense of responsibility that is not typically recognized on a resume. These roles are often expected of children, and often go unrecognized as anything notable, which then can go without recognition in interview settings. Changes must go beyond our personal understanding of our biases and interpersonal relationships: it must be changed in our systems as well.

CONCLUSION

We must notice how, even in writing this chapter, we grappled a lot with our individual duty to the collective, struggling with how to best honor the vast array of stories in our larger groups. It continues to reveal the work we all have to do as educators to keep learning and doing our own work. We wrote and posed a lot of controversies and we can make sense of them through our own work, lived experiences, research of others, and the stories of our students.

As young women in the profession, we found ourselves looking to the research and wondering why we would be writing or what new ideas we had to share. Our imposer syndrome was in full force even as credentialed professionals, and we must wonder if our students feel it as deeply as we did when writing this. Thanks to support from one another and the authors that have gone before us coaching us through the process, we are more able to own our expertise and practice the skills of translating our stories and histories into practice in a way that honors our growing branches and our grounding roots. We hope that, as educators, we can similarly coach and inspire our students to overcome these barriers.

REFERENCES

Accapadi, M. M. (2012). Asian American identity consciousness: A polycultural model. In D. Ching & A. Agbayani (Eds.), *Asian Americans and Pacific Islanders in higher education* (pp. 57–93). NASPA.

Aparicio, R., & Tornos A. (2017). National identity and the integration of the children of immigrants. In C. Bolzman, L. Bernardi, & J.M. Le Goff (Eds.), *Life Course Research and Social Policies: Vol. 7. Situating children of migrants across borders and origins* (pp. 215–230). Springer. http://doi.org/10.1007/978-94-024-1141-6_11

Asian American History. (n.d.). *Japanese American Citizens League*. https://jacl.org/asian-american-history/

Assalone, A. E., & Fann, A. (2017). Understanding the influence of model minority stereotypes on Asian American community college students. *Community College Journal of Research and Practice*, *41*(7), 422–435.

Astin, A. W. (1993). *What matters in college? Four critical years revisited*. Jossey-Bass.

Bertrand Jones, T., Guthrie, K. L., & Osteen, L. (2016). Critical domains of culturally relevant leadership learning: A call to transform leadership programs. In K. L. Guthrie, T. Bertrand Jones, & L. Osteen (Eds.), *New Directions for Student Leadership: No. 152. Developing culturally relevant leadership learning* (pp. 9–21). Jossey-Bass.

Budiman, A. (2020, August 20). *Key findings about U.S. immigrants*. Pew Research Center.https://www.pewresearch.org/fact-tank/2020/08/20/key-findings-about-u-s-immigrants/

Chowdhury, P. (2017) "I am Desi": (Re)claiming racialized narratives of being Asian in White America, *The Vermont Connection*, *38*(1), 9.

Chung, J. Y. (2014). Racism and Asian American student leadership. *Equity & Excellence in Education*, *47*(2), 117–132. https://doi.org/10.1080/10665684.2014.900392

Delaney, R. (2020, June 15). Black Lives Matter movement reveals divides among Asian-American community. *South China Morning Post*. https://www.scmp.com/news/china/article/3089169/black lives matter-movement-reveals-divides-among-asian-american

Dugan, J. P. (2017). *Leadership theory: Cultivating critical perspectives.* Jossey-Bass.

Gee, B., & Peck, D. (2018). Asian Americans are the least likely group in the U.S. to be promoted to management. *Harvard Business Review.* https://hbr.org/2018/05/asian-americans-are-the-least-likely-group-in-the-u-s-to-be-promoted-to-management

Gong Lum v. Rice (n.d.) *Education Law.* https://usedulaw.com/309-gong-lum-v-rice.html

Guthrie, K. L., Bertrand Jones, T., & Osteen, L. (Eds.). (2016). *New Directions for Student Leadership: No. 152. Developing culturally relevant leadership learning.* Jossey-Bass.

Hyun, J. (2005). *Breaking the bamboo ceiling: Career strategies for Asians.* HarperCollins.

Inkelas, K. K. (2004). Does participation in ethnic cocurricular activities facilitate a sense of ethnic awareness and understanding? A study of Asian Pacific American undergraduates. *Journal of College Student Development*, *45*, 285–302. https://doi.org/10.1353/csd.2004.0037

Kim, J. (2012). Asian American racial identity theory. In C. L. Wijeyesinghe & B.W. Jackson, III (Eds.), *New perspectives on racial identity development: Integrating emerging frameworks* (2nd ed., pp. 138–160). New York University Press.

Kodama, C. M., & Maramba, D. C. (2017). Reconsidering Asian American student development. In D. C. Maramba & C. M. Kodama (Eds.), *New Directions for Student Services: No.160. Bridging research and practice to support Asian American students* (pp. 25–37). Jossey-Bass.

Lien, P., Collet, C., Wong, J., & Ramakrishnan, S. (2001). Asian Pacific-American public opinion and political participation. *PS: Political Science and Politics*, *34*(3), 625–630.

Maekawa Kodama, C., McEwen, M. K., Liang, C. T., & Lee, S. (2002). An Asian American perspective on psychosocial student development theory. In M. K. McEwen, C. Maekawa Kodama, A. N. Alvarez, S. Lee, & C. T. H. Liag (Eds.), *New Directions for Student Services, No. 97. Working with Asian American college students* (pp. 45–60). Jossey Bass.

Peterson, W. (1966, January 9). Success story, Japanese-American style. *New York Times*.

Ramakrishnan, K., & Shah, S. (2017). One out of every 7 Asian immigrants is undocumented. *AAPI Data.* https://aapidata.com/blog/asian-undoc-1in7/

Suzuki, B. H. (2002). Revisiting the model minority stereotype: Implications for student affairs practice and higher education. In M. K. McEwen, C. Maekawa Kodama, A. N. Alvarez, S. Lee, & C. T. H. Liag (Eds.), *New Directions for Stu-*

dent Services, No. 97. Working with Asian American college students (pp. 21–32). Jossey Bass.

Yammarino, F. J., & Jung, D. I. (1998). Asian Americans and leadership: A levels of analysis perspective. *Journal of Applied Behavioral Science, 34*, 47–68.

Zane, N. W. S., Sue, S., Hu, L., & Kwon, J. H. (1991). Asian American assertion: A social learning analysis of cultural differences. *Journal of Counseling Psychology, 38*, 63–70.

CHAPTER 5

DEVELOPING LESBIAN, GAY, AND BISEXUAL STUDENT LEADERS IN AND OUT OF THE CLASSROOM

Darren E. Pierre and Jonathan J. Okstad

Within leadership development, as in other areas of higher education, lesbian, gay, and bisexual (LGB) students have been underrepresented and in some cases systemically excluded (Roberts, 2007). This chapter explores intersecting socially just leadership and sexual orientation. We begin by presenting an overview of the theories that gave birth to the field of leadership development. We highlight these theories to provide context for understanding leadership learning and shed light on the inherently heterosexist paradigms that guided early leadership theories. We then discuss sexual identity development theories to offer insight into the experiences of LGB student leaders. We conclude by discussing implications and offering recommendations, with the goal of advancing a more inclusive leadership praxis.

LEADERSHIP OVERVIEW

A variety of approaches and descriptions have been offered to explain the complexities of leadership (Northouse, 2018). Over the years, leadership

Shifting the Mindset: Socially Just Leadership Education
pp. 53–64
Copyright © 2021 by Information Age Publishing
All rights of reproduction in any form reserved.

theories have evolved to honor the role environments play in students' leadership development, capacity, and efficacy (Guthrie & Chunoo, 2018). Today's conversations on leadership are, in many ways, a departure from those of the past; honoring and incorporating the ways in which socially constructed identities influence leadership development. Historically, leadership was understood to be based on power (Northouse, 2018). Over time this belief has changed, as authentic, spiritual, servant, and adaptive approaches, just to name a few, emerged to offer more nuanced understandings of leadership.

Exclusionary Assumptions of Leadership

An exclusionary approach to leadership development characterized its early beginnings, defining traits and prototypes of what a leader "should be," which were inherently problematic and left deep imprints on who identified (and did not identify) as a leader. Implicit leadership theory (ILT) examines how unconscious assumptions and expectations influence who we define or identify as a leader. Derived from cognitive psychology, this approach uncovers the subjective views shaping our definitions of "good" and "bad" leaders (Tsai et al., 2017). Terms like "strong" and "charismatic" gained prominence to identify the traits of a good leader (Northouse, 2018). Today, we recognize the need to critically interrogate many of those earlier assumptions (Dugan, 2017).

In relation to the LGB community, ILT promotes heteronormative performativity. According to ILT, cisgender men who present in a traditionally masculine manner are viewed as having greater leadership capacity than cisgender men who present in a more historically feminine manner, or than women who present in either fashion (Stock & Özbeck-Pothoff, 2014). In truth, early theories of leadership were grounded in exclusionary notions on the basis of sexual orientation, and on the bases of gender, race, among other minoritized identities. As leadership educators and consumers, constructors, and interrogators of leadership theories past and present, we must recognize and challenge the lasting impact of the inherently biased assumptions characterizing the early history of leadership development.

Four Domains of Leadership Development

Dugan (2017) identified four leadership development domains: leadership capacity, enactment, motivation, and efficacy. The first domain, capacity, "reflects an individual or group's overarching knowledge, skills, and abilities related to the leader role or group leadership process" (Dugan, 2017, p. 24). Capacity speaks to a person's belief in their leadership abilities and is one of the first domains of leadership development.

Leadership enactment captures an individual's willingness to act upon capacity. However, enactment does not necessarily indicate one's leadership capacity. As ILT clarifies, some individuals who lacked genuine leadership capacity have nevertheless enacted leadership by displaying superficial traits; aligning with latent biases, accepted as truth, about what a leader should be. Examples of this implicit leadership bias include: being male, able-bodied, White, cisgender, and charismatic, among others. Conversely, those who had leadership capacity have been unable to enact leadership because—in their own eyes or the eyes of others—they did not possess innate leader characteristics.

The third domain, leadership motivation, represents the space between capacity and enactment. Put differently, it is an individual's desire to transform leadership potential into action. The fourth domain, efficacy, measures the belief in one's own ability to effectively transform capacity into behavior. Collectively, these four domains align with ILT to offer a contextual understanding for why some people are (and others are not) welcomed to the leadership development process. A contextual understanding of ILT, complemented by an appreciation of the four domains, offers a foundation for fostering an environment to enhance leadership learning.

Culturally Relevant Leadership Learning

While ILT provides context, culturally relevant leadership learning offers a framework for leadership education initiatives. Culturally relevant leadership learning is comprised of five domains: historical legacy, compositional diversity, psychological dimensions, behavioral dimensions, and organizational structural dimensions (Guthrie et al., 2016; Guthrie & Chunoo, 2018). The first domain, *historical legacy* honors the traditions of inclusion and exclusion existing within colleges and universities. Socially just leadership educators routinely consider the policies, practices, and traditions that have afforded opportunity to some, while limiting opportunities for others. From a place of privilege, it is easy to allow exclusionary norms to persist. Growth-oriented educators ask who has not been included, what remnants of those exclusionary traditions persist today, and what changes are needed—or should be maintained or accelerated—to advance fair and just leadership learning.

Compositional diversity refers to who is and is not represented demogrpahically and the roles those individuals play in a leadership context. In our leadership development programs and services, how are we representing LGB leaders? Are we using literature written by LGB authors and activists in our leadership education? Are we including figures such as Harvey Milk and Alice Walker as leadership examples in the same ways we include Bill Gates and Jeff Bezos? A diverse representation of leadership is not only important for LGB students, but for all students in dismantling ill-informed, out-dated assumptions of who is a leader. Note, the biases about leadership we hold as educators can only be changed by offering, alongside old prototypes, new and diverse depictions of what it means to lead.

Increasing compositional diversity supports development in the third domain, *psychological dimensions*. At the institutional level, psychological dimensions captures how diverse communities view the larger community's response and commitment to diversity and inclusion. In determining psychological dimensions, a review of the historical legacies of inclusion and compositional diversity are considered in concert with perceptions of inclusion by members within the community.

In the fourth domain, *behavioral dimensions*, educators consider how opportunities are constructed to engage students across difference. LGB students are often targeted by bullying in ways that are unique to members of this community. Thus, socially just educators remain mindful in crafting intentional interactions among students not to elicit unintentional harm. This work must be done and this vigilance maintained on an ongoing basis.

The fifth domain, *organizational/structural*, honors the practice of embedding culturally inclusive practices in the day-to-day operations of the organization. Transforming the exclusionary legacy of practices in higher education surrounding sexual orientation into a standard of inclusion cannot be achieved quickly or with a one-off program. Instead, this vital work must be embedded in the very fabric of our practice. Despite the numerous forms of leadership and the many ways in which it is described, the following common characteristics apply to the majority of leadership frameworks: (1) leadership is a process, (2) leadership involves influence, (3) leadership occurs in groups, and (4) leadership involves common goals (Komives et al., 2013).

LGB OVERVIEW

While this chapter addresses LGB students specifically, we will also use the terms "queer" to refer to this community. At times, the term LGBTQ (lesbian, gay, bisexual, transgender, and queer) will be used when the source's terminology or how participants were defined in a particular research study was presented in that manner. We feel it is important to note that while sexual orientation and gender identity will be spoken to in a related terms at times, the two aspects of identity differs in a number of ways (Bornstein, 2016).

Queer theory specifically addresses societal power structures associated with sexuality, gender, and their relationship with other forms of identity (Kasch, 2013). Queer theory underscores the role of context in development, gender performativity, and the fluid nature of identity development (Kasch, 2013). Utilizing queer theory, we will discuss how LGB students navigate the journey through higher education, manage the process of coming out, persist despite barriers, and develop a leadership identity.

Inherent heterosexism has underpinned and reproduced heteronormativity within leadership and across social institutions, including academia. *Heteronormativity* is the assumption heterosexuality is the norm, from which LGB people deviate (Smith & Ingram, 2004). Events such as the Stonewall Riots in New York City in June 1969 instigated a national movement for gay rights. What began as a demonstration against police brutality and oppression became a movement protesting the hegemonic, heterosexist, and homophobic culture the queer community constantly encountered (Carter, 2004). Half a century later, LGB people continue to confront these issues as a result of their sexual orientation.

Sexual Identity Formation

One cannot speak thoughtfully about LGB leadership without understanding sexual identity development. The Kinsey Scale "marking sexuality" points to the beginnings of our understanding of sexual identity development. While the Kinsey Scale assessed behaviors, subsequent research would interrogate Kinsey's centering of sexual identity on behaviors in favor of an emphasis on "orientation" (Hunter, 2007; McWhirter et al., 1990).

The early models of LGB development were linear, conceptualizing sexual identity formation as a series of stages (Bilodeau & Renn, 2005). Vivienne Cass's (1984) theoretical model of sexual identity formation is among one of the most recognized stage models of identity development (Hunter, 2007). Cass proposed a linear model of sexual identity development with six stages: identity confusion, comparison, tolerance, acceptance, pride, and synthesis (Patton et al., 2016). Each stage moves in a progressive fashion from a limited awareness of one's sexual identity, to a position of exploration, finally moving into sexual identity acceptance and integration with other aspects of life.

Lesbian and Gay Identity Development

Stage models have largely been replaced by conceptualizations of identity development as fluid and occurring longitudinally (D'Augelli, 2012). D'Augelli (2012) proposed a model of six interactive processes of sexual identity development in which each "process" functioned independently, rather than progressing in the ordered fashion of stages. D'Augelli's (2012) model showcased holistic development as sexual orientation exploration occurs. The model's six processes included: exiting heterosexual identity, developing a personal LGB identity status, developing an LGB social identity, becoming an LGB offspring, developing an LGB intimacy status, and entering an LGB community (Bilodeau & Renn, 2005).

Later, Dillon et al. (2011) developed a parallel structured process model of sexual identity development. Similar to those later models, Dillon et al. (2011) used statuses instead of stages to describe identity development. The first of the five statuses, *compulsory heterosexuality*, described assumption of universal heterosexual identity forming the basis of identity development. From the early assumption of heterosexual orientation, the model proposed a shift toward *active exploration* or *diffusion*. The model also showcased the opportunity to achieve a *deepening and commitment* to sexual identity exploration. The final status is *synthesis*; integrating one's sexual identity with other aspects of one's self-concept. This model emphasized how individuals can recognize their sexual orientation and choose to explore those identities more fully.

Bisexual Identity Development

Klein (as cited by Fox, 1995) proposed bisexual identity development processes as distinct from gay or lesbian identity construction. Klein argued bisexuality takes one of four forms: transitional, historical, sequential, or concurrent (as cited by Fox, 1995). In this model, *transitional* bisexuality represents D'Augelli's (1994) characterization of a "phase" in the process of coming out as gay or lesbian. *Historical* bisexuality refers to a previous experience of both same- and opposite-sex attraction, which is not necessarily ongoing. *Sequential* bisexuality describes the experiences of those who date both men and women in the past, but not at the same time. Finally, *concurrent* bisexuality encompasses those who have dated both men and women simultaneously (Fox, 1995).

Although each model contributes to understanding LGB development, all sexual identity development models are subject to limitations. In particular, one cannot speak about sexual orientation without recognizing other intersecting identities' (gender, race, class, ability status, religion, and others) influence over how one views and explores their sexual orientation

(Denton, 2016). Furthermore, sociopolitical systems, culture, and other contexts all influence the construction and understanding of sexual identity.

For many LGB student leaders, college is where sexual identity exploration accelerates (Patton et al., 2016). Recognizing the role of colleges and universities play in supporting sexual identity formation is critical for holistically supporting the leadership development of LGB students. Socially just leadership educators reflect regularly on how LGB identities are represented in our leadership learning initiatives; asking questions like: How are LGB authors represented in the text used to teach our programs/courses? Are we taking an intersectional approach to examining LGB leadership? It is vital that sexual orientation is not considered in isolation; rather, it must be discussed in conjunction with other socially constructed identities.

Knowledge of sexual identity development is key for leadership educators supporting LGB students. Sexual identity formation has become understood less in terms of stages and more as an identity constructed over the life span (D'Augelli, 2012). Students may have an awareness of their LGB identity, yet actively choose not to explore or disclose this orientation. LGB identity development is best fostered in inclusive environments like those many colleges are poised to offer. Finally, socially just leadership educators are mindful that LGB identity is best understood when considering students' various other intersecting identities (Abes et al, 2007; Crenshaw, 1989). These considerations are vital for leadership educators who are committed to supporting leadership development for all students.

BARRIERS TO SOCIALLY JUST LEADERSHIP

LGB students, as they explore their sexual identity, face barriers when navigating involvement and leadership development opportunities in college. Leadership educators have opportunities to respond through intentional programming grounded in equitable and socially just leadership practices. These practices support students by building affinity within the campus community, broadening their understanding of leadership, and fostering spaces for safe exploration of their intersectional socially constructed identities.

Coming Out

Not all LGB faculty and staff feel professionally and/or personally safe "coming out" within the classroom or in other spaces on a university campus; particularly within the context of a heterosexist and homophobic society (Orlov & Allen, 2014). LGB higher education professionals play important roles in the identity development of sexual minority students. Research has demonstrated the powerful influence of a professor's disclosure of their LGB sexual orientation on teaching, learning, student support, and societal change on college campuses (Orlov & Allen, 2014). Disclosing sexual identity supports students' identity development as they see themselves reflected in faculty and staff leadership roles.

Many LGB students expect to come out during their college years. They navigate a complicated process of making intentional decisions about disclosing their sexual identity to, or concealing it from, family, friends, and others with whom they interact (Strayhorn, 2012). Sexual minority college students are more likely to leave school or have difficulty learning when faced with the chronic stress of discrimination and harassment (Blumenfeld, 2012; Sanlo, 2004).

This prejudice still exists on college and university campuses (Blumenfeld, 2012). In one study "a significant number of participants talked about encountering peers (including gay or same race) and faculty members who held negative beliefs and perceptions about gays and lesbians" (Strayhorn, 2012, p. 43). As a result, participants reported feeling uncomfortable, unwelcome, unsupported, threatened, and insecure at their institution. It is unrealistic to expect robust student development, including growth in leadership, to occur under threatening conditions.

Given the importance of one's sexual orientation intersecting with other elements of identity, it is unsurprising that "gay men of color experience 'coming out' in different ways, markedly different from what's been written about the 'coming out' experience(s) of gays in general" (Strayhorn, 2012, p. 41). Gay men of color confront additional societal barriers and discrimination compared to their White counterparts. Moreover, bisexual students are often excluded from research and positive narratives, as they are seen only as "experimenting" during their college years or are viewed as yet not "fully gay." These deficit mindsets preclude students from obtaining the full benefits of their colleges and hinders their overall leadership learning.

Engaging LGB students in socially just programs supports their identity development and connection to a university community, and makes the campus environment more welcoming and accepting. When LGB students come out and achieve a sense of belonging at their institution, they are more likely to "be high achievers, involved student leaders, and very likely to 'intend to stay' in college" (Strayhorn, 2012, p. 47). Additionally, feeling valued, respected, and needed by others on campus resulted in LGB students improving their grades, increasing their involvement, and elevating their aspirations (Strayhorn, 2012), including their ambitions as leaders.

Institutional Policies, Practices, and Culture

LGB students are more likely to consider leaving an institution if they perceive the campus to have a "chilly" climate. Studies have shown that while the majority of campus communities support the rights of LGB students, and desire to make the campus more welcoming for LGB people, hostility and anti-LGB prejudice persist nationwide (Yost & Gilmore, 2011). Creating an inclusive campus climate for LGB students and employees through changes in institutional policy, practice, and climate supports the retention and overall well-being of LGB students, faculty, and staff at their institutions.

Persistent and entrenched homophobia, transphobia, and heterosexism lead to discrimination, harassment, and even violence; as well as to more subtle incidents of exclusion, marginalization, and silencing (Dilley, 2002; Zemsky & Sanlo, 2005). In response, scholars have researched LGB students (and to a lesser extent transgender students) and university administrations have developed task forces and centers to address these issues.

Results have included changes in institutional nondiscrimination policies, many of which encompass sexual orientation, gender identity and expression, domestic partner benefits (prior to the legalization of same-sex marriage in the United States), inclusion of LGBT issues in campus diversity initiatives, and the development of queer studies programs. Additionally, LGBTQ/sexuality student centers have been established, policies and procedures have been revised within student affairs divisions to reflect equity, and additional programming has been developed to educate students about diverse sexual identities (Zemsky, 2004).

LGB students with intersecting marginalized identities encounter different barriers, and experience campus environments differentially (Denton, 2016). Research indicates first-generation LGB students experience a more hostile campus climate than legacy students, and classroom climate plays a large role in students' perceptions of the broader campus community (Garvey et al., 2015). In addition, many religiously affiliated institutions represent additional barriers and obstacles for LGB students (Marine, 2011). Although each institution is different, and religiously affiliated institutions exist on a continuum of inclusion, there is limited research on how these institutions support LGB students and employees (Love, 1998).

Recognizing how student success and retention are directly related to students' campus engagement and campus culture itself, institutions have created programs designed to positively affect the experiences of LGB students (Tinto, 1993). Programs such as the Safe Zone project, trainings for student affairs professionals and others in student-facing roles, curriculum revisions undertaken with faculty, the availability of mentoring and peer counseling, lavender graduation celebrations, leadership training programs, and other initiatives influence both campus climate and individual students' experiences on campus (Sanlo et al., 2002).

A PATHWAY FORWARD

Socially just leadership educators devote attention to developing collaborative partnerships with colleagues across various units and divisions. Leadership does not occur in isolation; it happens in intercultural affairs, residence life, fraternity and sorority life, classrooms, and a host of other spaces, both in and out of the classroom. These leadership educators support faculty in developing inclusive classroom environments for LGB students. Sexual orientation is only one of a college student's identities; thus, best practices in serving students require embracing an intersectional approach to programs, policies, and leadership learning.

Finally, the study of identity development among college students is ongoing. As educators, it is our responsibility to remain abreast of the literature as these conversations continue to evolve. Concepts, such as Abes et al.'s (2007) reconceptualized model of multiple dimensions of identity, offers insight into the importance of context in identity salience. Again, we encouraged educators at all levels and contexts to engage conversations about sexual identity beyond the oft-cited establishment of an LGBT resource center or similar space. We implore pursuing partnerships with identity-focused centers to ensure LGB representation and advocacy are deeply embedded into the frameworks of all leadership development initiatives.

LGB individuals have played a formidable role in the leadership narrative. From cinema to the front lines of the civil rights movement of the 1960s, the LGB community has always been part of the force toward societal reform. This community has fought for inclusion, been ambassadors of authenticity, and champions for justice. As educators, we now more than ever are charged with inviting LGB students to the table of leadership, and reminding them they have always deserved a place at that table. In doing so, we continue the tradition of supporting the holistic development of the next cohort of leaders who represent our diversity, work toward positive change, and lead with an enduring sense of hope.

REFERENCES

Abes, E., Jones, S., & McEwen, M. (2007). Reconceptualizing the model of multiple dimensions of identity: The role of meaning-making capacity in the construction of multiple identities. *Journal of College Student Development*, *48*(1), 1–22.

Bilodeau, B., & Renn, K. (2005). Analysis of LGBT identity development models and implications for practice. In R. Sanlo (Ed), *New Directions for Student Services: Vol 111. Gender identity a sexual orientation: Research, policy, and personal* (pp. 25–39). Jossey-Bass.

Bornstein, K. (2016). *Gender outlaws: On men, women and the rest of us* (revised and updated, 2nd ed.). Vintage Books.

Blumenfeld, W. J. (2012) LGBTQ campus climate: The good and still the very bad. *Diversity & Democracy*, *15*(1). https://www.aacu.org/publications-research/periodicals/lgbtq-campus-climate-good-and-still-very-bad

Carter, D. (2004). *Stonewall: The riots that sparked the gay revolution*. Macmillan.

Cass, V. (1984). Homosexual identity formation: Testing a theoretical model. *The Journal of Sex Research*, *20*(2), 143–167.

Crenshaw, K. (1989). Demarginalizing the intersection of race and sex: A Black feminist critique of antidiscrimination doctrine, feminist theory, and antiracist politics. *University of Chicago Legal Forum*, *1989*(1), 139–168.

D'Augelli, A. R. (1994). Identity development and sexual orientation: Toward a model of lesbian, gay, bisexual development. In E. J. Trickett, R. J. Watts, & D. Birman (Eds.), *Human diversity: Perspectives of people in context* (pp. 312–333). Jossey Bass.

D'Augelli, A. R. (2012). Restoring lives: Developmental research on sexual orientation. *Human Development*, *55*(1), 1–3.

Denton, J. M. (2016). Critical and poststructural perspectives on sexual identity formation. In E. Abes (Ed.), *New Directions for Student Services: Vol. 154. Critical perspectives on student development theory* (pp. 57–69). Jossey-Bass.

Dilley, P. (2002). 20th century postsecondary practices and policies to control gay students. *Review of Higher Education*, *25*(4), 409–431.

Dillon, F. R., Worthington, R. L., Moradi, B. (2011). Sexual identity as a universal process. In S. J. Schwartz, K. Luyckx, & V. L. Vignoles (Eds.), *Handbook of identity theory and research* (pp. 649–669). Springer.

Dugan, J. P. (2017). *Leadership theory: Cultivating critical perspectives*. Jossey-Bass

Fox, R. (1995). Bisexual identities. In A. D'Augelli & C. Patterson (Eds.), *Lesbian, gay, and bisexual identities over the lifespan psychological perspectives* (pp. 48–86). Oxford University Press.

Garvey, J. C., Taylor, J. L., & Rankin, S. (2015). An examination of campus climate for LGBTQ community college students. *Community College Journal of Research and Practice*, *39*(6), 527–541.

Guthrie, K. L., & Chunoo, V. S. (Eds.). (2018). *Changing the narrative: Socially just leadership education*. Information Age.

Guthrie, K. L., Bertrand Jones, T., & Osteen, L. (Eds.). (2016). *New Directions for Student Leadership: No. 152. Developing culturally relevant leadership learning*. Jossey-Bass.

Hunter, S. (2007). *Coming out and disclosures: LGBT persons across the life-span*. Haworth Press.

Love, P. G. (1998). Cultural barriers facing lesbian, gay, and bisexual students at a Catholic college. *The Journal of Higher Education*, *69*(3), 298–323.

Kasch, D. (2013). Queer theory. In R. Jones & E. Abes (Eds.), *Identity development of college students: Advancing frameworks for multiple dimensions of identity* (pp. 191–212). Jossey-Bass.

Komives, S. R., Lucas, N., & McMahon, T. (2013). *Exploring leadership for college students who want to make a difference* (3rd ed.). Jossey-Bass.

Marine, S. B. (2011). Stonewall's legacy: Bisexual, gay, lesbian, and transgender students in higher education. *ASHE Higher Education Report, 37*(4), 1–145.

McWhirter, D., Sanders, S., & Reinisch, J. (1990). *Homosexuality/heterosexuality?: Concepts of sexual orientation*. Oxford University Press.

Northouse, P. G. (2018). *Leadership: Theory and practice* (8th ed.). SAGE.

Patton, L. D., Renn, K. A., Guido, F. M., & Quaye, S. (2016). *Student development in college: Theory, research, and practice* (3rd ed.). John Wiley & Sons.

Orlov, J. M., & Allen, K. R. (2014). Being who I am: Effective teaching, learning, student support, and societal change through LGBQ faculty freedom. *Journal of Homosexuality, 61*(7), 1025–1052.

Roberts, D. (2007). *Deeper learning in leadership: Helping college students find potential within*. Jossey-Bass.

Sanlo, R. L. (2004). Lesbian, gay, and bisexual college students: Risk, resiliency, and retention. *Journal of College Student Retention: Research, Theory & Practice, 6*(1), 97–110.

Sanlo, R. L., Rankin, S., & Schoenberg, R. (2002). *Our place on campus: LGBT services and programs in higher education*. Greenwood.

Smith, N. G., & Ingram, K. M. (2004). Workplace heterosexism and adjustment among lesbian, gay, and bisexual individuals: The role of unsupportive social interactions. *Journal of counseling psychology, 51*(1), 57–67.

Strayhorn, T. L. (2012). *College students sense of belonging: A key to educational success for all students*. Routledge.

Stock, R., & Özbeck-Pothoff, G. (2014). Implicit leadership in a intercultural context: Theory extension and empirical investigation. *The International Journal of Human Management, 25*(12), 1651–1668

Tinto, V. (1993). *Leaving college: Rethinking the causes and cures of student attrition* (2nd ed.). University of Chicago Press.

Tsai, C., Dionne, S., Wang, A., Spain, S., Yammarino, F., & Cheng, B. (2017). Effects on relational schema congruence on leader-member exchange. *The Leadership Quarterly, 28*(2), 268–284.

Yost, M. R., & Gilmore, S. (2011). Assessing LGBTQ campus climate and creating change. *Journal of Homosexuality, 58*(9), 1330–1354.

Zemsky, B., & Sanlo, R. L. (2005). Do policies matter? In R. Sanlo (Ed), *New Directions for Student Services: Vol 111. Gender identity a sexual orientation: Research, policy, and personal* (pp. 7–15). Jossey-Bass.

CHAPTER 6

TRANSGENDER STUDENTS AND SOCIALLY JUST LEADERSHIP LEARNING

Alex Lange and Kieran Todd

Throughout history, transgender communities show up and agitate for change in a host of societal contexts (Stryker, 2017). Marsha P. Johnson, Miss Major Griffin-Gracy, and Sylvia Rivera all advocated for trans people's dignity and right to exist, fighting against police brutality while critiquing the White-centric nature of LGBTQ social movements. Individuals like Jennicet Gutiérrez, Janet Mock, Angelica Ross, Alok Vaid-Menon, and Raquel Willis challenge individual and institutional reproduction of gender normativity as a form of violence upon, and erasure of, trans communities. On campuses, students like Kye Allums and Calliope Wong disrupt institutional policies excluding transgender students from full and equitable participation in college life (Steinmetz, 2014b; Wong, 2014).

It is important to note positive social change for transgender people never came about by the work of individuals in isolation. Johnson, Griffin-Gracy, and Rivera worked together to advocate for homeless queer and trans youth. It has been Gutiérrez, Mock, Ross, Vaid-Menon, and Willis collectively challenging modern-day movements to better advocate for *all* members of transgender communities. Similarly, ordinary trans-

Shifting the Mindset: Socially Just Leadership Education
pp. 65–74
Copyright © 2021 by Information Age Publishing

gender people each day push against the boundaries of society as it currently stands, both on and off-campus through collective action. Indeed, researchers suggest committing to challenging transphobia and genderism serves as a key vector of transgender identity development (Bilodeau, 2005). Whether or not they desire to do so, transgender students engage in socially just leadership practices. Key to the goal of this volume, transgender students deserve intentional, educator-facilitated opportunities to further discuss, cultivate, and nurture their socially just leadership capacities.

This chapter provides examples of socially just leadership learning for transgender students. We use two vignettes from our experiences working together as student (Kieran) and advisor (Alex) during our time together at Michigan State University. Specifically, we chose examples where we both played a role and worked together to exercise positive change for queer students broadly and trans students specifically. We argue trans students focus socially just leadership efforts through collecting action which seeks to address and dismantle multiple, intersecting systems of oppression while building up community with and for one another.

TRANSGENDER IDENTITES: ON AND OFF CAMPUS

While certain narratives would have us believe transgender communities have reached peak visibility and acceptance (Steinmetz, 2014a), transgender individuals and collectives have long existed (Stryker, 2017). It may be more apt to say transgender people more recently received more formal recognition from cisgender individuals and institutions (Children of the House of "Pay It No Mind," 2018; Spade, 2015). This recognition and visibility come with costs (Gossett et al., 2017). For higher education educators, this recognition means the collection of meaningful gender identity data to provide an empirical window into the lives of transgender college students (Garvey, 2019; Greathouse et al., 2018; Lange et al., 2019). Over the last 15 years, research on transgender college students has ballooned. While *transgender* serves as a broad term for a variety of identities, researchers find it remains important to study transgender students' experiences both broadly and specific to particular subidentities (Dugan et al., 2012; Greathouse et al., 2018; Nicolazzo, 2017).

Transgender students appear more connected and involved with campus-based LGBTQ resource centers (Brazelton et al., 2013). Not only do these students utilize campus-based resources to a greater degree than their cisgender peers, they also form kinship networks as a way to practice resilience and navigate hostile, genderist campus climates (Nicolazzo, 2016, 2017; Nicolazzo et al., 2017). Though there is scant research on transgender students' leadership development, Jourian and Simmons (2017) argued trans leadership may present as "activism and resistance against oppressive and exclusionary structures and practices than as positional leadership" (p. 64). Given these findings, we posit trans students' leadership efforts in higher education happen through collectivist structures, and promoting community-based social change goals. The exemplars provided below bolster this framing of transgender student leadership.

WHO WE ARE

Before delving into our vignettes, we share more about us as individuals and our relationship with one another, over time. Alex identifies as a genderqueer, queer, White-passing multiracial, temporarily able-bodied, and neuro-typical person. Kieran identifies as a Black, queer, nonbinary transmasculine disabled person. Alex was first hired as assistant director to the LBGT Resource Center at Michigan State in the summer of 2014. In that role, cultivated leadership and community between and within the 10+ LGBTQ student organizations on campus. Alex most directly advised the Alliance of Queer and Ally Students (AQAS).

In 2015, Kieran enrolled at Michigan State University as a transfer student and quickly became involved in a number of organizations, including the then-named Queer and Trans People of Color Coalition (QTPOCC) and later became chair of AQAS. Alex and Kieran met through their involvement as advisor of, and student in, these groups respectively. Kieran would often spend time in the center outside of student responsibilities where they developed a relationship with Alex. We engaged in the leadership process: we spent a great deal of time together discussing our individual lives, the needs of queer and trans students on campus, and the ways we could change campus policies, practices, and procedures for better lives and livelihoods for transgender college students. After Alex's time at Michigan State University, Kieran and Alex remained in contact and call one another close friends.

VIGNETTE #1: BLACK TRANS LIVES MATTER EVENT

Before joining AQAS, Kieran cochaired QTPOCC. As a student group with minimal resources, the LBGT Resource Center ensured QTPOCC had access to resources and funding typically reserved for university-sanctioned marginalized student groups like AQAS. The leaders of QTPOCC planned a program to center and celebrate the lives of Black transgender folks. To do so, they needed to secure partnerships with larger organizations on campus with resources, access, and leverage to secure funding and space. In addition to their support from the resource center, QTPOCC formed partnerships with leaders in the Black Student Alliance (BSA) and AQAS. The leaders of both BSA and AQAS, being entirely cisgender, exercised solidarity by working with the leaders of QTPOCC to access funding closed off to almost all other groups: an intersections fund. While working together had their own challenges (e.g., the Whiteness of AQAS, the heteronormativity of BSA), the three groups came together to plan the event.

However, the student affairs administration created an oversight dynamic that undermined the agency of the Black queer and trans students who attempted to put on the Black Trans Lives Matter (BTLM) event. The chief administrator who controlled the necessary funds for the event required QTPOCC leaders to prove they held meetings with both the Black Student Alliance and AQAS; failure to demonstrate this meant the funds would not be disbursed, including payment for speakers already secured for the event. Additionally, the administrator required supplementary explanations about how the event spoke to multiple identities. Though the students met many times prior to the administrator's absurd request, the groups worked together to further document meetings while ensuring all groups involved had a hand in the planning and implementation of the event.

Key Lesson: The Power of Collective Leadership

Cultivating collective leadership among college student leaders proved critical to helping these students envision a just world. Student leaders who advocate for marginalized communities within this collectivist model also acknowledge the varying experiences of folks in their community. When QTPOCC, AQAS, and BSA came together for the BTLM event, members of each group discussed their learning edges and competencies related to Black transgender people's experiences in the United States, both on and off campus. Much of the labor of education fell on the members of QTPOCC to help both BSA and AQAS understand how their organizations differentially supported Black transgender students. This demonstrated the power of collective leadership while recognizing how opportunities to harm and erase the experiences of folks who exist in multiple marginalized identities are also present. Effective advising of trans students allows for these leaders to navigate conceptions of identity, relationships, and beliefs with other leaders, and recognizes when to step in and advise more directly to reduce harm. Alex and Kieran worked together with the BSA advisor to help instill this understanding in both that organization and AQAS, which Alex advised.

Key Lesson: Intersectionality as a Framework for Socially Just Leadership

The leaders of QTPOCC modeled an understanding of intersectionality in their organizing of BTLM. In working to access funds for the group, money they could not otherwise have accessed because of student organization rules, required the QTPOCC leaders to work with students in more umbrella student organizations. The largely cisgender and heterosexual students from BSA and the entirely White members of AQAS failed to acknowledge this particular intersection of identity and the overlapping forms of oppression these particular students experienced. Additionally, the administrator in charge of the fund required an explanation as to why BTLM met the requirements of the fund. Said otherwise, both administrators and students lacked an understanding of the experiences of Black transgender students and why such an event should exist in the first place. Kieran and the other QTPOCC leaders worked with Alex to strategize a way to fund and support the BTLM event in the face of erasure of experience from upper level administrators. While barriers to funding should not have existed in the first place, the intersectionally minded leaders of QTPOCC ensured that Black transgender students would be better represented on campus and in the minds of leaders with the BTLM event.

VIGNETTE #2: ALLIANCE OF QUEER AND ALLY STUDENTS ACCOUNTABILITY MEETING

The AQAS operated primarily from the work of its executive board. Given the labor fell to the collective membership of the executive board, when a task was not accomplished, someone would first try and reach out to the responsible party. However, when communication became stagnant and members did not reach out to declare why they missed meetings, the work still needed to be done. During Kieran's term as chair, they and Alex noticed how much of the burden for accomplishing the organization's goals was placed primarily on Kieran; the only executive board member of color. They planned to address these dynamics at the next regular executive board meeting. That evening, the executive board met in the LBGT resource center. Alex and the graduate coadvisor facilitated the conversation at Kieran's request. The conversation began with a discussion of how members felt about the productivity and process of the board. Both

Kieran and the vice-chair spoke first. Kieran and the vice-chair shared their perceptions that too much of the labor fell on them to get the organization's work done, with Kieran picking up much of the slack for others and the racialized dimension of the imbalance.

As the meeting progressed, those who felt targeted by the comments explained feeling caught off guard by the topic of the meeting. One member began to cry uncontrollably at the thought of taking advantage of Kieran's time, labor, and friendship. Another member expressed both anger and responsibility; acknowledging work did not get done and how members were insensitive to the ways the executive board functioned. In particular, the member noted a lack of understanding for members of the board with disabilities. At times, they explained, members of the executive board may be so infirm they could not communicate as neuro-typical members could. Through the two hour conversation, members of the executive board felt exhausted, concluded greater understanding existed on multiple sides, and identified ways to move forward.

Key Lesson: Accountability in Collective Leadership

Transgender students and collectives repeatedly prove group-based leadership and decision-making is possible (Jourian & Simmons, 2017; Sylvia Rivera Law Project, 2013). Practicing generative, ongoing accountability is vital to this collective leadership style. Rather than being grounded as a form of punishing one another, dialogue becomes the medium through which problems are examined and new and alternative paths forward are generated. In this situation, honest appraisals of the organization from multiple members helped determine the way forward. One way forward was developing several check-in points with at least one other member of the board. This diffused the responsibility of the chair being in touch with all leaders at all times and created a networked system of communication. Accountability at this moment required everyone to share their past, current, and future capacities and how they fit into the scale of tasks the organization took on for the rest of the school year. Rather than prioritizing burn out, AQAS came back to the goals they set for themselves to determine how they would move forward in the best interests of one another and the communities they served.

Key Lesson: Holding Multiple, Conflicting Truths in Organizations

Part of the success of a membership-led organization lies in its ability to address multiple needs and realities of members through dialogue and discourse. What became clear over the course of AQAS's conversation was students' wrestling with how to deal with different members' needs and the inequitable division of labor. On one hand, much of the organization's operating status quo privileged students who were able-bodied or neurotypical. On the other hand, the racialized dynamics of labor could not be ignored. Rather than these needs and realities being in opposition to one another, they existed simultaneously. Though difficult, it became important to frame the conversation as one where these tensions could be addressed in conjunction with one another, rather than opposition.

LESSONS LEARNED AND MOVING FORWARD

As these vignettes demonstrate, transgender students work toward socially just leadership with and without the accompaniment of leadership educators. These students demonstrated the power of collective leadership models, the importance of intersectional thinking, how leaders can hold one another accountable, and enacting a form of leadership that holds multiple and often conflicting truth in collectives and organizations. Based on our individual and collective experiences, we offer suggestions for leadership educators to create environments where transgender students can best learn leadership and pose questions for leadership educators to reflect on as they meaningfully engage with transgender students on their own campuses.

First, leadership educators providing examples of socially just leadership learning may turn to the examples of the figures we discussed at the beginning of this chapter. While representation and visibility are the most basic forms of inclusion, they remain an important foundation to build future efforts. How might the grassroots organizing of Marsha P. Johnson and Sylvia Rivera inform students' thinking about collaborative efforts? How could the advocacy efforts of Gutiérrez and Willis disrupt ideas of how we engage in social change, particularly in light of mainstream organizations' avoidance and neglect of multiple marginalized communities? These individuals, among others, serve as excellent lessons in teaching all students, not just transgender students, the power of socially just leadership practices.

CALL TO ACTION

In terms of cocurricular development, we urge leadership educators to cultivate opportunities for students that do not require particular roles. At Michigan State University, Alex created a community leadership retreat for LGBTQ students. While the resource center invited all student organization leaders to attend, we also opened the event to any member of the community who wished to cultivate their leadership capacities. This allowed different collectives and kinship networks of transgender students to come together and participate in the day as a collective. Creating a leadership retreat concerning community development, rather than positional leader development, allowed nonuniversity sanctioned groups to participate and highlight those working toward social change on campus.

Within these community leadership retreats, attendees focused on forwarding social change while challenging dominant ways of organizing oneself in an organization or collective. For instance, through the aforementioned retreat, attendees discussed ways to consider more collective leadership structures that moved away from a president/vice-president/secretary/treasurer formation of executive leadership and toward those where organizations leveraged a collective leadership decision-making process. Attendees examined potential impacts on social change work in their organizations. During the retreat, we also discussed how individuals could practice accountability, particularly with members who shared an identity with them. Given that college provides an opportunity for transgender students to meet others like them for the first time, in our experience, many do not wish to challenge or criticize their peers and do not know how to do so without harming the relationship. Socially just leadership educators teach transgender students generous accountability practices, allowing them to advocate for themselves and their viewpoints within collective structures.

As we close, we challenge leadership educators to reflect on the following questions as they begin or continue to work with transgender students.

- While we wish this did not have to be our first question, our experiences point it to being one of the least considered questions by many professionals: Are the places where you host education opportunities equipped with restroom facilities for transgender students? A lack of such spaces sends implicit signals of the value of transgender identities to these students.

- How might you develop relationships with key administrators and institutional stakeholders for whom you can better translate the needs of transgender students? Repeatedly in our work together, we learned Alex's work with administrators helped these administrators better understand transgender students' needs.

- When you teach about socially just leadership practices, is your analysis of oppression from a single- or multiple-identity vantage

point (e.g., able to think of students' multiple identities simultaneously)?

We hope these suggestions and questions transform approaches into
interventions that benefit a more expansive set of today's college students.
After all, our students deserve a generation of leaders who attend to the
needs of all of their social identities, not just some.

REFERENCES

Bilodeau, B. L. (2005). Beyond the gender binary: A case study of two transgender
students at a Midwestern university. *Journal of Gay and Lesbian Issues in Education, 3*(1), 29–46.

Brazelton, G. B., Renn, K. A., & Woodford, M. (2013, November). *LGBTQ gendered participating with campus resources.* Paper presented at the Association for
the Study of Higher Education Annual Meeting, St. Louis, MO.

Children of the House of "Pay It No Mind." (2018). Refuting contemporaneity:
Trans* experiences in, out, and beyond higher education. In M. Gasman & A.
C. Samayoa (Eds.), *Contemporary issues in higher education* (pp. 119–134). Rout-
ledge.

Dugan, J. P., Kusel, M. L., & Simounet, D. M. (2012). Transgender college students: An exploratory study of perceptions, engagement, and educational
outcomes. *Journal of College Student Development, 53*(5), 719–736.

Garvey, J. C. (2019). Queer quantitative query: Sexual orientation in higher education surveys. *Journal of College Student Development, 60*(4), 495–501.

Gossett, R., Stanley, E. A., & Bruton, J. (2017). *Trap door: Trans cultural production
and the politics of visibility.* MIT Press.

Greathouse, M., BrckaLorenz, A., Hoban, M., Huesman, R., Jr., Rankin, S., &
Stolzenberg, E. B. (2018). *Queer-spectrum and trans-spectrum student experiences
in American higher education: The analyses of national survey findings.* Tyler Clem-
enti Center.

Jourian, T. J., & Simmons, S. L. (2017). Trans* leadership. In D. Tillapaugh & P.
Haber-Curran (Eds.), *New Directions for Student Leadership: No. 154. Critical
perspectives on gender and student leadership* (pp. 59–69). Jossey-Bass.

Lange, A. C., Duran, A., & Jackson, R. (2019). The state of LGBT and queer
research in higher education revisited: Current academic houses and future
possibilities. *Journal of College Student Development, 60*(5), 511–526.

Nicolazzo, Z. (2016). "Just go in looking good": The resilience, resistance, and
kinship-building of trans* college students. *Journal of College Student Development, 57*(5), 538–556.

Nicolazzo, Z. (2017). *Trans* in college: Transgender students' strategies for navigating
campus life and the institutional politics of inclusion.* Stylus.

Nicolazzo, Z., Pitcher, E. N., Renn, K. A., & Woodford, M. (2017). An exploration
of trans* kinship as a strategy for student success. *International Journal of
Qualitative Studies in Education, 30*(3), 305–319.

Spade, D. (2015). *Normal life: Administrative violence, critical trans politics, and the limits of law* (2nd ed.). Duke University Press.

Steinmetz, K. (2014a, May 29). The transgender tipping point. *TIME*. http://time.com/135480/transgender-tipping-point

Steinmetz, K. (2014b, October 28). Meet the first openly transgender NCAA Division I athlete. *TIME*. https://time.com/3537849/meet-the-first-openly-transgender-ncaa-athlete/

Stryker, S. (2017). *Transgender history: The roots of today's revolution*. Seal Press.

Sylvia Rivera Law Project. (2013). *From the bottom up: Strategies and practices for membership-based organizations*. https://srlp.org/wp-content/uploads/2013/05/SRLP_From_The_Bottom_Up.pdf

Wong, C. (2014, March 10). Thank you [web log post]. *Transwomen @ Smith*. https://calliowong.tumblr.com/post/45074030481/thank-you

CHAPTER 7

EXPLORING THE INTERSECTION OF LOVE, HEALING, AND LEADERSHIP AMONG MEN OF COLOR

Christopher S. Travers and John P. Craig

In the summer of 2015, I (Chris) was invited to serve as a faculty member for the inaugural all-African American Male LeaderShape Institute. Twenty fifteen was the first year the institute attempted to create a population-specific leadership community (i.e., Black men). I was the youngest and least experienced professional of all the faculty who were invited. In fact, I was just finishing up my first year of doctoral studies in higher education and student affairs and wondered what exactly I had to offer to a leadership space given how young I was at the time. I spent hours and hours digesting the Leader-Shape curriculum and talked with several leadership experts within my professional network to soak up as much information as I could before starting the institute. Despite all the LeaderShape training, what I realized at the end of that experience was that the students in my leadership cluster family were mostly drawn to my authenticity, vulnerability, and willingness to love them. And this is a lesson that I have continued to learn even as a faculty member and coordinator of a master's program, advisor to various student organizations, and in my current role, as a director of young adults in a Baptist

Shifting the Mindset: Socially Just Leadership Education
pp. 75–88
Copyright © 2021 by Information Age Publishing
All rights of reproduction in any form reserved.

church. In leadership education with men of color, learning what it means to love yourself and love others unconditionally and to prioritize that over any leadership tool, technique, or outcome has taken me farther as a leader than any other leadership skill or gift I possess.

In late 2016, I (John) joined a local chapter of Black Youth Project 100 (BYP100), a membership-based youth organization that operates from a Black, queer, feminist standpoint. Coming from a military family where the decision-making hierarchy was top down, this was my first time witnessing the intentional dismantling of patriarchal leadership. While BYP100 has a national director and chapter cochairs, chapters operate fairly autonomously within a leader-full structure, encouraging leadership and collaboration to emerge from any chapter member at any time. This kind of trusting and affirming leadership development was initially unnerving because of my own uncertainties leading as a masc-assumed nonbinary queer person. However, as I grew with this community, I witnessed Black youth with minoritized identities—myself included, walk fully supported into leadership roles and practice care, humility, and community accountability. Witnessing and experiencing this has shown me that meaningful interrogations of dominant leadership values can generate greater opportunities for minoritized youth to see themselves as always-already leaders.

INTRODUCTION

Despite changes in the fabric of higher education, one recurring core tenet is developing students into responsible effective leaders (Guthrie & Osteen, 2016). Under the guise of patriarchy, much of what has historically been labeled "effective" leadership within Western contexts are traditional and hegemonic masculine principles (e.g., assertiveness, strength, control) in disguise. Yet, leadership literature has only recently documented connections between leadership education and masculinity among young boys and college men (e.g., Beatty & Tillapaugh, 2017). Additional scholarly focus on men of color and leadership is a worthy and necessary endeavor for several reasons: First, men of color remain underrepresented and underserved within American higher education (Brooms et al., 2018; Travers, 2019). Second, within an imperialist White-supremacist capitalistic patriarchal society, all men of color negotiate privileged (i.e., gender) and minoritized (e.g., race) identities (hooks, 2004b). Thus, when thinking about bridging leadership and social justice, it is paramount to address the topic of men and masculinity. Last, conforming to traditional patriarchal masculine ideals among college student leaders is not gender exclusive and therefore, has significant implications for *all* student leaders in higher education. Although we use terms like "men," "male," and "masculine" throughout this chapter, we believe gender to be a spectrum and not a binary. We resist the myth that gender can only be defined as man or woman and believe that gender identity and expression exist on a spectrum of many possibilities.

Presently, men of color-based leadership learning opportunities within higher education abound. For instance, several institutions have developed Black male initiatives, masculinity-based programming, and male-based leadership courses (Brooms et al., 2017; Spencer, 2018). Within many of these, curricula is situated between principles of manhood and effective leadership. In other words, how men of color should be responsible, strong, hard-working, and service-oriented leaders. However, we believe the concepts of love and healing (hooks, 2004a) are missing from both theory and practice at the intersection of men of color, masculinity, and leadership education. While under ubiquitous assault by patriarchal masculinity and racism, men of color have learned to conceal pain and fear, which we believe can serve as significant roadblocks in developing men of color as thoughtful and engaged social justice leaders. In her book, *The Will to Change: Men, Masculinity, and Love*, bell hooks (2004a) writes, "The truth we do not tell is that men are longing for love" (p. 4). hooks continues, "men want to know love and they want to know how to love" (p. 10). Under the backdrop of socially just leadership, it is critically important to incorporate love and healing practices within leadership education among men of color in college. Building on the work of hooks (2004a), Page (2010), Ginwright (2015), Okello and Quaye (2019), and Okello and Travers (n.d.), we offer embodied autocritography to bring love and healing into male-focused leadership learning.

BACKGROUND LITERATURE

In order to ground our approach, we highlight the experiences of men of color in higher education. Then, we document themes from extant literature on manhood and masculinity among men of color. Finally, we offer some literature on male-based leadership programs.

Men of Color in Higher Education

Much has been written on the academic and social experiences of men of color in higher education. Some scholars focus on the varying experiences students have across multiple institution types; like predominantly White institutions, minority serving institutions, and community colleges (e.g., Harper, 2012; Sáenz et al., 2013; Strayhorn, 2008). Another set of authors illuminate how environmental factors, such as campus climate may serve as a barrier to, or instrument of, the success of men of color. Other investigators emphasize the role of psychosocial contributors or identity-based factors to help men of color succeed (e.g., Sanchez, 2019). Across much of the research conducted in the last two decades, a strong body of evidence suggests men of color are more likely to be successful when they are engaged, connected and supported by peers and faculty/ staff, and feel like they belong on their respective campuses (Brooms, 2017; Harper, 2012; Strayhorn, 2008).

Masculinities Among Men of Color

More recently, scholars have explored the gendered experiences of men of color. While there is a great deal of attention on Black men specifically, this scholarship has offered insight regarding how men of color: define their manhood on college campuses (Dancy, 2012; Edwards & Jones, 2009; Saenz et al., 2017); make decisions regarding social experiences and career choices (Harris, 2010; Harris et al., 2011); and make meaning of their masculinity in light of varying intersecting social identities (Chan, 2017; Strayhorn & Tillman-Kelly, 2013).

For instance, Edwards and Jones (2009) conducted a grounded theory study on 10 college men's experiences with gender identity and found participants consistently described a tension between adhering to society's standard of normative masculinity versus walking in authenticity. Participants compared the daily performance of living up to traditional masculinity to wearing a mask. In another study focused on Black college men specifically, Harris et al. (2011) found participants associated their masculinity with toughness, stoicism, strength, material success, and responsibility. These definitions of masculinity led to associations among: leadership and student success, homophobia and fear of femininity, and sexist relationships with women.

Beyond definitions of masculinity, men of color also make decisions regarding their academic, social, and career experiences based on ideas of what it means to be a man. In one study, Harris (2010) identified participants who endorsed patriarchal ideals of masculinity tended to pursue majors leading to wealthier career options. They also expressed expectations that men should be in leadership positions on campus. Similar to Edwards and Jones (2009), gay, bisexual, and queer Filipino college men in Chan's (2017) study also referenced an internal tension of pressure to conform to patriarchal masculinity, while also staying true to themselves regarding the fluidity of gender and sexual identity.

Leadership Spaces for Men of Color

The experiences of men of color broadly within leadership education is an underdeveloped area of scholarship; however, a few studies have been focused on Black men specifically (e.g., Beatty et al., 2010; Harper & Quaye, 2007; Sutton & Terrell, 1997), and some on both Black and Latino college men collectively (Brooms et al., 2017). For example, Beatty et al. (2010)'s exploration of the experiences of Black student leaders within student organizations found supportive relationships and social climate are both critically important to how students experience leadership. In a study conducted with Black and Latino college men by Brooms et al. (2017), participants expressed the importance of developing strong peer relationships (i.e., brotherhood) and how these "brotherly ties" aided in personal growth, masculine development, and overall understanding of leadership.

In our review of the literature related to men of color, leadership, and masculinities, words like "peer connection," "belonging," "support," and "brotherhood" are ever present. At the core of these concepts is the desire among men of color to love and be loved. We hope through this chapter, we can extend thinking and acting around men and masculinity leadership education for men of color to explicitly incorporate love and healing practices.

THEORIZING LOVE AND HEALING

We are guided by the knowledge of and contributions by Black women in organizing our framework of love and healing for men of color in leadership education. As one of the most minoritized groups in society, we argue bridging the gap between leadership and social justice is to also borrow from the thinking, writing, and lived experience of Black women. It is important to note, in addition to invoking a love and healing framework, we also invite leadership educators to consider what it means to encourage college men of color to develop *feminist masculinities*. In the words of Black feminist writer bell hooks (2004a), "Feminist masculinity presupposes that it is enough for males to *be* to have value, that they do not have to *do*, to 'perform' to be affirmed and loved" (p. 117). Since patriarchal masculinity is based on the principles of domination and submission, consequently there is no love in patriarchy. In other words, "Males cannot love themselves in patriarchal culture if their very self-definition relies on submission to patriarchal rules" (p. 123). Alternatively, when men of color begin to define themselves outside of patriarchal boundaries, they develop the emotional awareness to learn to love. While some think of love as a noun, we think of it as a verb. As Peck (1978) describes, love is:

> the will to extend one's self for the purpose of nurturing one's own or another's spiritual growth.... Love is as love does. Love is an act of will—namely, both an intention and an action. Will also implies choice. We do not have to love. We choose to love. (p. 85)

Love has the power to lead to healing and it is critically important to the link between leadership education and social justice. Based in the teaching of Black feminisms, "without love, struggle is fruitless and justice is out of reach" (Baszile, 2018, p. 266).

Engaging in authentic giving and receiving of love means men of color must understand and address the trauma and pain of growing up in a patriarchal world. hooks (2004a) advised, "To heal, men must learn to feel again. They must learn to break the silence, to speak the pain" (p. 142). In a White supremacist, patriarchal world, men of color are taught to disregard pain and silence fear. In response, we offer healing justice to help college men of color bear witness to this silencing. Black queer feminist cultural worker Cara Page described healing justice as a holistic intervention "on generational trauma and violence" (2010, para. 5), which demands "collective practices that can impact and transform the consequences of oppression on our bodies, hearts, and minds" (para. 5). Ginwright (2015) uncovered healing justice in Black youth movements as a having three key features: (1) restoration of collective meaning and wellness, (2) resistance to oppressive hegemonic ideas, and (3) reclamation of future possibilities (p. 38). Invoking healing justice includes acknowledging manhood and masculinity as historically and presently oppressive experiences for racialized people. Healing justice uplifts these experiences, from personal narratives to collective inherited memory, to articulate and transform the tensions and harms of patriarchal masculinity.

Embodied Autocritography as a Tool

Inspired by autocritographic (McGuire et al., 2014) writing principles that channel authenticity, self-reflection, and vulnerability, we offer what Okello and Quaye (2019) outlined as *embodied autocritography* as a tool for men of color in leadership learning. In embodied autocritography, the body becomes the primary site for meaning-making, and aims to uncover the lived experiences of self and others. As noted in Okello and Travers (n.d.), "embodied autocritography emphasizes mutual vulnerability and witnessing as necessary to its love politics." The notion of mutual vulnerability and sharing is accomplished as each participant makes a commit-ment to each other, emphasizing "nobody means more to me than you" (Nash, 2018, p. 116). In the tradition of autocritography, this exchange moves beyond simply listening to the stories of others; it is also about wit-nessing through the body.

Grounded in a dialogic exchange, embodied autocritography invite participants to engage by asking several questions like: What is being said? What is not being said? What am I feeling as I engage in dialogue with my brother? In what ways does my brother's experience resonate with me? What is my brother's body doing as he engages in dialogue with me?. This technique also shares some of the elements of intergroup praxis (Buckley & Quaye, 2016). To effectively engage in this practice, partici-pants must be present and maintain a willingness to disconnect them-selves from distractions (Okello & Quaye, 2019).

We believe embodied autocritography maps on to our framework of love and healing for men of color and how they can develop within lead-ership learning. Recall, there are three key features of Ginwright's (2015) healing justice framework: (1) restoration of collective meaning and well-ness, (2) resistance to oppressive hegemonic ideas, and (3) reclamation of future possibilities. The notion of collective meaning is connected to the ongoing dialogic exchange that takes place between a pair of students. It is not solely based on the individual, but meaning is also derived and exchanged through the process of giving and receiving each other through the body. Through engaging in an authentic and vulnerable form of counterstorytelling, embodied autocritography helps men of color push against oppressive hegemonic ideas toward their own personal definitions of self, as both men and leaders. As engaging the body and each other through dialogue invokes healing, we believe that new possi-bilities of what it means to be both a man and leader within a White-supremacist, patriarchal world can be imagined and attained.

CONNECTING LOVE AND HEALING WITH LEADERSHIP LEARNING

Learning to wear a mask (that word already embedded in the term "mascu-linity") is the first lesson in patriarchal masculinity that a boy learns. He learns that his core feelings cannot be expressed if they do not conform to the acceptable behaviors sexism defines as male. Asked to give up the true self in order to realize the patriarchal ideal, boys learn self-betrayal early and are rewarded for these acts of soul murder. (hooks, 2004b, p. 153)

Leadership learning is defined as the means by which individuals understand the process of leadership (Guthrie et al., 2013). We chose to focus specifically on two concepts often discussed in leadership learning literature, particularly for students of color: leader identity and leader capacity. While leader identity focuses on how students see themselves as a leader (Day et al., 2009), leader capacity is all about the learning and doing of leadership (Spencer, 2018). The challenge for those socialized toward performative masculinity is that both leadership identity and capacity become rooted within the limits of patriarchal masculinity. Several dangers are connected to patriarchal leadership models: First, when men of color subscribe to patriarchal leadership, they are more likely to hold misogynistic ideals; leading to a devaluation of women and characteristics traditionally associated with femininity (e.g., consensus, compassion, empathy, care). Moreover, men of color guided by patriarchy also operate from a domination-subordination paradigm, where cis-straight men are held at the top and all others are positioned at the bottom, including queer and trans people and people with disabilities. This approach to leadership poses concern for men of color who also sit at the intersections of other minoritized social identities, and it may also present challenges in terms of how they relate to and lead other men of color, women, or gender nonbinary people with various minoritized identities.

Situated within a White-supremacist, patriarchal society where men of color are often made to believe they have to acquiesce to the contours of heteronormative masculinity to be accepted as legitimate, love and healing is useful in reimagining leaders who are engaged in social justice. In the next section, we outline how through embodied autocritography, men of color can grow in their leader identity and capacity; through engaging directly with love of self, love of others, and love in action.

A few things are important to note before detailing how embodied autocritography might be a useful technique to employ in leadership education spaces among college men of color. First, invoking this affective form of dialogue is best practiced in leadership learning contexts where men of color consistently connect with each other in community throughout the academic year. Embodied autocritography as a technique requires time and strong rapport among those involved. We recommend incorporating embodied autocritography after at least two to three initial gatherings. It is crucial for students to build trust prior to engaging in these exercises. Also, literature on social learning (Bandura, 1976) suggests one of the best ways to help students grow more confident is for them to watch teachers or facilitators engage. We believe students will be more comfortable being vulnerable and transparent when they see their leaders modeling it. We firmly recognize complete healing and liberation within a White-supremacist world may not be fully accomplished within the scope of leadership learning spaces for men of color. Rather, we hope those environments become spaces for male student leaders of color to begin this process and carry it with them into other collegiate contexts and beyond.

Self-Love

The first, and arguably most important, form of love we wanted to discuss is self-love and its connection to leadership identity. To us, self-love is personally held acceptance in spite of perceived flaws or mistakes. Acceptance of self for men of color transcends how they see themselves as men toward whether they feel comfortable displaying their true and honest self. Self-love means recognizing we are all on a journey of self-improvement and maintaining a healthy level of kindness, compassion, and patience with myself as I continue to move through that journey. Part of the challenge for men of color to consistently engage in the practice of self-love are the myriad of negative messages from society through the media suggesting there is something wrong with us. Beyond what the media portrays, many men of color also struggle with the desire to just "be" out of pressure to "do" and perform patriarchal masculinity (Edwards & Jones, 2009; Harris et al., 2011; hooks, 2004). Questions related to self-love which might be useful for students to consider include: In what ways are you kind to yourself and in what ways are you not? Do you struggle with loving yourself, and if so why? What do you like most about yourself? What do you dislike? How are you patient with yourself? How do you affirm yourself?

During a meeting of male leaders, students pair up and each spends a few minutes responding to each question. While the first student is responding, others focus on being present and engaged, taking note of what they are experiencing and what they notice from their bodies and presentation of their partner. At the end of the session, each student journals separately about their experience before dialoging with each other. They might use a few of the following questions as journaling prompts: What is being said? What is not being said? What was I feeling as I engaged in dialogue with my brother? In what ways did my brother's experience resonate with me? What was my brother's body doing as he engages in dialogue with me? Finally, each student shares their reflections, highlighting what was said during the dialogue, and how it felt to be in the dialogue itself. Self-awareness and self-interrogation, combined with having someone give back to you what you have given to them through dialogue, is helpful for men of color unlearning patriarchy and relearning who they are as leaders.

Love Between Men

In the 2002 book, *Communion*, bell hooks explored the meaning of love and freedom for women and how this journey can be taken up and supported in, and through, community. In one of the chapters, hooks wrote about the importance of intimate friendships between women. While hooks was focused primarily on women in this text, we believe this is also paramount to the development of men of color as both men and leaders; for them to be engaged in healthy and authentic relationships with one another. Some of the major questions surrounding current college men of color who have been socialized under patriarchy is: "Where do they go to be built up or cared for?" and "Where are the spaces for men of color to just be, with no expectation, performance, or posturing?" The messages outlined earlier related to self-love can also be applied to love between men. Love between men is something often discussed in extant literature, even when it is not explicitly named. When themes related to the importance of peer connection, bonding, brotherhood, and belonging are reported in articles, love between men is at the core. We encourage men of color leadership education spaces to consider what it means to build programs and initiatives that invite men to feel and experience love from each other.

Here are a set of questions related to love between men that we believe might be useful for students to respond to as they engage in embodied autocritography with each other: When was the first time you told another man you love them? What was it like? What makes it challenging to engage in loving friendships with other men? How do you show compassion to other men? What does it feel like when you hear another male friend tell you they love you? A similar approach as the one outlined in the "self-love" section would also be applied here following the initial questions. Love between other men is directly connected to leadership capacity. Moving beyond patriarchal practices and engaging in true, honest, and loving friendships with other men elevates the longevity of leaders and elevates rapport and camaraderie among those who work with leaders.

Love in Action

We firmly believe love is what it does. Similar to Fromm, we think of love as a verb; something that can be felt and received. Here is where we see the clearest connections to how healing and love can end up facilitating the bridge between leadership education and social justice for men of color. As men of color move along their journey of love and healing, it is also important for them to recognize what it means to show up with and for people at the margins of society. As men, there is inherent privilege that students hold, so beyond recognizing how to show up on behalf of those who are oppressed, students must also consistently reflect on what it means to be aware of one's privilege, while also being committed to forging meaningful ties with those who are often silenced or invisible and amplifying their voices. Socially just leadership educators include service or field experiences for students to apply various lessons in love as they engage in community with others who hold various minoritized identities. Shifting from simply discussing leadership education to realizing the call to social justice, there is a requirement of action. We also recommend as students engage in various field experiences; they also continue to engage in embodied autocritography with their partners.

Here are a set of questions related to love in action we believe might be useful for students to respond to as they engage in embodied autocritography with each other: In what ways do you reflect on your privilege as a man? How do you create space for women and other minoritized people in society? What prevents you from speaking up and/or advocating for minoritized students? What does being a socially just leader mean to you? Just like in the previous two sections, students would answer each of the questions in back and forth dialogue and then end with journal reflection responding to following prompts:

- What is being said? What is not being said?
- What am I feeling as I engage in dialogue?
- In what ways does my brother's experience resonate with me?

CONCLUSION

Leadership is something with both formal and informal designations. Some men of color currently occupy leadership positions on campus, while others might be leaders in their families or communities. Some leaders step up in the lab as leaders in the classroom, while others are actively engaged in student leader activist roles. No matter how formal or informal, it is important for leadership educators who work with men of color on college campuses to be aware of just how tightly connected leader identity and capacity among men of color can be to masculinity. Given how deeply White-supremacist patriarchal ideals are rooted within the fabric of the United States, men of color must move through the process of healing and love (hooks, 2004a) in order to develop into the sound, effective, and transformative social justice-oriented leaders they have the potential to be. What we offered in this chapter is one technique, embodied autocritography, we believe can be significantly useful in the development of men of color as social justice leaders.

REFERENCES

Bandura, A. (197). *Social learning theory (Vol. 1).* Prentice Hall.

Baszile, D. T. (2018). Another lesson before dying. In O. N. Perlow, D. I. Wheeler, S. L. Bethea, & B. M. Scott (Eds.), *Black liberatory pedagogies: Resistance, transformation, and healing within and beyond the academy* (pp. 265–280). Palgrave MacMillan

Beatty, C. C., Bush, A. A., Erxleben, E. E., Ferguson, T. L., Harrell, A. T., & Sahachartsiri, W. K. (2010). Black student leaders: The influence of social climate in student organizations. *Journal of the Student Personnel Association at Indiana University,* 48–63.

Beatty, C. C., & Tillapaugh, D. (2017). Masculinity, leadership, and liberatory pedagogy: Supporting men through leadership development and education. In D. Tillapaugh & P. Haber-Curran (Eds.) *New Directions for Student Leadership: No. 154. Critical perspectives on gender and student leadership* (pp. 47–58). Jossey-Bass.

Brooms, D. R., Clark, J., & Smith, M. (2018). Being and becoming men of character: Exploring Latino and Black males' brotherhood and masculinity through leadership in college. *Journal of Hispanic Higher Education, 17*(4), 317–331.

Buckley, J. B., & Quaye, S. J. (2016). A vision of social justice in intergroup dialogue. *Race Ethnicity and Education, 19*(5), 1117–1139.

Chan, J. (2017) "Am I masculine enough?": Queer Filipino college men and masculinity. *Journal of Student Affairs Research and Practice, 54*(1), 82–94.

Dancy, T. E. (2012). *The brother code: Manhood and masculinity among African American males in college.* Information Age.

Day, D. V., Harrison, M. M., & Halpin, S. M. (2009). *An integrative approach to leader development: Connecting adult development, identity, and expertise.* Routledge.

Edwards, K. E., & Jones, S. R. (2009). "Putting my man face on": A grounded theory of college men's gender identity development. *Journal of College Student Development, 50*(2), 210–228.

Ginwright, S. (2015). Radically healing Black lives: A love note to justice. In M. P. Evans & K. Knight Abowitz (Eds.), *New Directions for Student Leadership: No. 148. Engaging youth in leadership for social and political change* (pp. 33–44). Jossey-Bass.

Guthrie, K. L., Bertrand Jones, T., Osteen, L., & Hu, S. (2013). Cultivating leader identity and capacity in students from diverse backgrounds: *ASHE Higher Education Report, 39,* 4.

Guthrie, K. L., & Osteen, L. (Eds.). (2016). *New Directions for Higher Education: No. 174. Reclaiming higher education's purpose in leadership development.* John Wiley & Sons.

Harper, S. R. (2012). *Black male student success in higher education: A report from the National Black Male College Achievement Study.* University of Pennsylvania,

Graduate School of Education, Center for the Study of Race and Equity in Education.

Harper, S. R., & Quaye, S. J. (2007). Student organizations as venues for Black identity expression and development among African American male student leaders. *Journal of College Student Development, 48*(2), 127–144.

Harris, F., III. (2010). College men's meanings of masculinities and contextual influences: Toward a conceptual model. *Journal of College Student Development, 51*(3), 297–318.

Harris, F., III, Palmer, R. T., & Struve, L. E. (2011). "Cool posing" on campus: A qualitative study of masculinities and gender expression among Black men at a private research institution. *The Journal of Negro Education, 80*(1), 47–62.

hooks, b. (2002). *Communion: The female search for love*. Perennial.

hooks, b. (2004a). *The will to change: Men, masculinity, and love*. Beyond Words/Atri Books.

hooks, b. (2004b). *We real cool: Black men and masculinity*. Psychology Press.

McGuire, K. M., Berhanu, J., Davis, C. H. F., III, & Harper, S. R. (2014). In search of progressive Black masculinities: Critical self-reflections on gender identity development among Black undergraduate men. *Men and Masculinities, 17*(3), 253–277.

Nash, J. C. (2018). *Black feminism reimagined: After intersectionality*. Duke University Press.

Okello, W. K., & Quaye, S. J. (2019). Reimagining dialogue-based praxis. In D. Tillapaugh & B. McGowan (Eds.), *Men and masculinities on campus: Theoretical foundations and promising practices* (pp. 131–146). Stylus.

Okello, W. K., & Travers, C. S. (n.d.). Love lifted me: Toward an anti-heteronormative love ethic.

Page, C. (2010). Reflections from Detroit: Transforming wholeness and wellness. https://incite-national.org/2010/08/05/reflections-from-detroit-transforming-wellness-wholeness/

Peck, M. S. (1978). *The road less traveled: A new psychology of love, traditional values, and spiritual growth*. Simon & Schuster.

Sáenz, V. B., Lu, C., Bukoski, B. E., & Rodriguez, S. (2013). Latino males in Texas community colleges: A phenomenological study of masculinity constructs and their effect on college experiences. *Journal of African American Males in Education, 4*(2), 82–102.

Sanchez, M. E. (2019). Perceptions of campus climate and experiences of racial microaggressions for Latinos at Hispanic-serving institutions. *Journal of Hispanic Higher Education, 18*(3), 240–253.

Spencer, D. (2018). The world is yours: Cultivating Black male leadership learning. In K. L. Guthrie & V. S. Chunoo (Eds.) *Changing the narrative: Socially just leadership education* (pp. 109–126). Information Age.

Strayhorn, T. L. (2008). The role of supportive relationships in facilitating African American males' success in college. *NASPA Journal, 45*(1), 26–48.

Strayhorn, T. L., & Tillman-Kelly, D. L. (2013). Queering masculinity: Manhood and Black gay men in college. *Spectrum: A Journal on Black Men, 1*(2), 83–110.

Sutton, E. M., & Terrell, M. C. (1997). Identifying and developing leadership opportunities for African American men. *New Directions for Student Services, 1997*(80), 55–64.

Travers, C. (2019). Theorizing manhood, masculinities, and mindset among Black male undergraduate students. *The Journal of Negro Education, 88*(1), 32–43.

CHAPTER 8

GOING BEYOND "ADD WOMEN THEN STIR"

Fostering Feminist Leadership

Julie E. Owen, Brittany Devies, and Danyelle J. Reynolds

This chapter takes an interrogatory approach to offer critical questions that challenge how existing systems and structures constrain women's experience of leadership. Critical feminist theory and the culturally relevant leadership learning (CRLL) model serve as our frameworks. Critical scholars accept that knowledge is situated in the larger social and political world and think that it is dangerous to ignore that embeddedness. As a response, we would like to briefly introduce ourselves as authors, learners, and knowers. We share this information to describe some of our own positionalities, identities, and epistemologies and how these facets shape our views of gender, leadership, and our contribution to this volume.

As a team we each hold multiple privileged identities; we are currently-able, cisgender, heterosexual women with advanced academic degrees working in the academy. We hold multiple identities around race (Black, White), social class (working class and middle class), and generation status. Each of us works to be critically conscious of the way our multiple privileged and marginalized identities shape our gender identity and

Shifting the Mindset: Socially Just Leadership Education
pp. 89–99
Copyright © 2021 by Information Age Publishing
All rights of reproduction in any form reserved.

expression, as well as our approaches to leadership. We are committed to considering our own socialization of gender and leadership from the perspectives of our communities, faith traditions, and our embeddedness in racist, colonizing, and patriarchal institutions. We use our voices to advocate for positive social change leading to more equitable leadership for all, and to consider how these identities and social power shape our practice.

We have had sustained authentic conversations where we worked to identify areas of ideological commonalities and distinctions in our beliefs about leadership and gender. We take an intersectional approach in our thinking and writing which includes honest conversations about how power and privilege shape the world, as well as challenging dominant approaches which only serve narrow interests. We are committed to radical inclusion, equity, and justice, and challenging spaces that reify exclusionary narratives. Finally, we seek to move beyond a 'add women and stir' framework where educators sprinkle in a few ideas related to gender into existing programs or reducing gender to essentialist notions. Instead we seek to analyze, critique, and reconstruct programs so that they challenge the sexist, racist, classist structures that shape student leadership learning.

FRAMING

This chapter explores the CRLL model through a critical feminist theory lens, offers questions that will further illuminate aspects of the CRLL, and highlights specific implications for leadership practice. The following propositions frame our approach.

Gender and Leadership are Socially Constructed

We acknowledge concepts of gender and leadership as socially constructed. To say something is socially constructed indicates that its meaning is determined through social interactions; the things we do and say with other people. Messages about the socially acceptable ways to perform gender begin before birth and are accelerated in childhood socialization, through what one is taught by parents and other trusted adults, authoritative religious interpreters, and peers, as well as lessons learned from the media, education, and other systemic forces. Similarly, what is deemed as leadership is a product of dominant narratives about how people view, interpret, and explain the world around them (Owen, 2020). Even answers to the questions, "Who is a leader?" and, "What is leadership?"

are contextualized and crafted by our socialization around identity and power (Dugan, 2017).

Adopt Inclusive Definitions of Leadership, Feminism, and Gender

Socially just educators dispel notions of leadership as only referring to positional power. Rather, leadership is a relational process between and among people who seek to make a positive difference in the world. Activist scholar bell hooks (2000a) defines feminism as "the struggle to end sexist oppression" (p. viii). It does not privilege one gender over others but invites the interrogation of sexist structures in the world around us. Additionally, impactful educators challenge the frequent conflation of sex, gender identity, and gender expression. Gender is far more than one's 'manliness' or 'womanliness'; leadership educators should invite more complex views taking expression, fluidity, and intersectionality into account. Leadership literature that reinforces gender binary approaches hampers gender inclusive feminist praxis.

Move From Feminine to Feminist Leadership

Effective leadership educators shift narratives from feminine to feminist leadership (Shea & Renn, 2017). Labeling leadership as feminine conflates women's gender identity and expression and uses gendered stereotypes to differentiate women's leadership from men's leadership. Historically, "men's leadership" is usually just called leadership. Instead of addressing and dismantling structures that exclude and limit women as well as people who are gender-nonconforming, genderqueer, and transgender, feminine leadership leans into a gender binary and attempts to simply "add women, then stir." Feminist leadership, however, dismantles gendered structures that limit everyone toward a more authentic and inclusive leadership practice. Feminist leadership can be practiced by people of all genders and is supported by leadership educators through intentional pedagogy. To adapt the words of bell hooks (2000a), feminist leadership is for everybody.

Embrace Critical Feminist Theory

Critical feminist theory sits at the intersection of feminist theory and critical theory. While both have a strong change agenda, and include an ideological focus on social and economic inequities, critical feminist theory goes beyond calling attention to the existence, injustice, and negative impacts of sexism (hooks, 2000b) to interrogate structural forces that contribute to systemic subordination, as well as offers specific recommendations for social change (Kalsem & Williams, 2010). As critical feminism begins with gender to better "understand and challenge all forms of contemporary subordination, domination, and oppression" (Mills, 1994, p. 211), the collection of these theories can serve as a framework to reimagine current realities toward more inclusive and liberatory structures and practices.

Apply the CRLL Model

CRLL was developed in response to the proliferation of leadership theories and approaches that do not attend appropriately to identity (Bertrand Jones et al., 2016; Guthrie & Chunoo, 2018). At the core of this model are three dimensions of development which inform the leadership learning process: identity, capacity, and efficacy. CRLL involves addressing five domains of culture that affect leadership learning, including: the historical legacy of inclusion/exclusion, compositional diversity, behavioral dimensions, organizational/structural dimensions, and psychological dimensions.

LINKING CRLL CULTURAL DOMAINS TO FEMINIST LEADERSHIP

The component parts of the CRLL present a myriad of strategies for both individuals and organizations to assess and enhance equity and inclusion for culturally relevant leadership education. Leadership which only focuses on building individual identities, efficacies, and capacities is insufficient. Leaders must also learn to grapple with larger systemic forces, maintained by power and dominant narratives of exclusion, and their effects on individual agency and action. In the same way that critical feminist praxis allows for the examination of oppressive systems toward the creation of reimagined liberatory realities, CRLL requires going beyond individual learning to also identify, interrogate, and disrupt organizational, institutional, and systemic dynamics (Guthrie & Chunoo, 2018; Owen et al., 2017). Table 8.1 offers questions to explore feminist leadership along each of CRLL's five domains. Familiarity with these historical, behavioral, psychological, and structural dimensions of leadership is imperative for educators who seek to develop leadership identity, capac-

Table 8.1. Questions to Explore in the Domains of Culturally Relevant Leadership Learning

CRLL Domain	Critical Questions to Consider
Historical legacy of inclusion/ exclusion	• How does the telling of history through specific lenses give an incomplete view of what leadership is and how it is enacted? How is the leadership of individuals who identify as women often erased from history? • How does a history of exclusion from universities, especially of women of color, shape the mentoring and development of women leaders? • How often is the leadership portrayed by noncisgender men, women, and people who are gender non-nonconforming interpreted as something else, like service or social activism? How do other people's perceptions of one's gender identity potentially discount one's capacity and efficacy to lead?
Compositional diversity	• What are ways to avoid creating a "precarious pedestal" where women are only valued for their gendered traits? How might even positive stereotypes create fertile ground for exclusion by suggesting that women must lead in particular ways? • How might changes in compositional diversity (i.e., women graduating from all levels of college in higher numbers than men) promote more equitable leadership?
Organizational/ structural domain	• What approaches should leadership educators use to teach students how to understand, analyze, and navigate organizations, structures, and systems? • How do one's identities and methods for navigating gendered organizations and structures inform pedagogy? How do they inform students' engagement? • How is sexism identified within and throughout our programs, courses, and curriculum? Once identified, how do we address it and make positive, sustainable changes?
Behavioral domain	• How do systemic expectations of gender perpetuate gender performance (Butler, 1990) in leadership? How do gender microaggressions impact leadership identity, capacity, and efficacy (Yamanaka, 2018)? • What are the intersections and conflicts between gender identity and leader identity? • How do political happenings and current events affect understandings of gender and leadership? What kinds of leadership are occurring within identity-based (gender-based) political movements/activism?
Psychological domain	• What are the effects of psychological safety and generational trauma on leadership? How do leadership educators "create opportunities that foster acceptance of differing opinions and experiences while encouraging trust" (Bertrand Jones et al., 2016, p. 18)? • How do implicit assumptions reflect one's social identities and social location? One's understanding of leaders and leadership? How might people disrupt or address their implicit assumptions, especially when they contribute to social stratification or harm?

ity, and efficacy. These questions are meant to challenge all leadership learners, including facilitators and participants.

LINKING CRLL TO FEMINIST LEADERSHIP

People learn leadership and develop gender identities alongside the interplay and influence of the systems and domains outlined above, among others. All five CRLL domains influence an individual's leadership identity, capacity, and efficacy.

Identity

Identity-based leadership examines the dynamic, influential relationship between social identities and leader identity. CRLL describes an individual's leader identity as an "ever-evolving self-portrait" (Bertrand Jones et al., 2016, p. 13). Leader identities can be personal or prescribed. Personal leader identity comes from an internal belief in one's efficacy to lead without a formal title, while prescribed leader identity comes from a position or power being awarded to an individual (Tillapaugh et al., 2017). Historic messages around what leadership is have communicated to women for centuries that leadership traits are inherently masculine, and leadership capacity comes from positional and/or prescribed leader identity. Johnson (2006) wrote "power looks 'natural' on a man but unusual and even problematic on a woman, marking her as an exception that calls for special scrutiny and some kind of explanation" (p. 91). How power is defined in leadership is even socially gendered, making this systemic belief possible.

Some core reflective questions related to gender and leadership identity include:

- How are gender stereotypes perpetuated through leadership processes and leadership education curriculum? How is a hegemonic view of power harmful to people of all genders?
- What is the difference between personal and prescribed leader identity development (Haber-Curran & Tillapaugh, 2017)?
- How do leadership educators use critical reflection in order to make sense of their own gender identity and the way it shapes their everyday enactment of leadership and facilitation of leadership curriculum?

Capacity

Leadership capacity, in the framework of CRLL, is defined as "the integration of students' knowledge, attitudes, and skills that collectively reflect their overall ability to behave effectively in the leadership process" (Bertrand Jones et al., 2016, p.14). Capacity is the *doing* of leadership within the campus climate shaped by the aforementioned five domains. Previous and recent literature has worked to name the competencies and capacities needed for leadership practice in varied settings, and others have identified the additional capacities required for critical leadership practice (Dugan, 2017; Owen et al., 2017; Seemiller, 2014).

A critical feminist analysis of capacity invites an examination of the forces contributing to systemic subordination, especially those that impact actual abilities and behaviors. The socially constructed nature of gender and leadership indicate expectations about effective leadership behavior are shaped by one's identities, experiences, and socializations. The sexist societal structure even shapes research on leadership; from methods and epistemologies, to the patriarchal, racist, and colonialist roots of empirical research itself. As consumers of knowledge, socially just leadership educators identify how expectations are shaped and commit to decoupling ourselves from these limiting systems.

Applying a critical feminist perspective to the CRLL moves us toward liberation as we consider how to *authentically* integrate the knowledge, attitudes, and skills that make up our leadership practice. In the same ways that we might perform gender in ways that are inconsistent with who we are in order to better navigate the sexist structures through which we move, how might we be performing leadership inauthentically to better navigate oppressive systems? Furthermore, how might we be using our power as educators to encourage students to do the same through our programmatic frameworks, structures, and activities? Socially just leadership educators wrestle with our ability to foster learning environments that shape students' understanding of leadership and development of leadership capacities.

These reflections lead to the following core questions about gender and leadership capacity:

- How can we encourage movement from feminine to feminist leadership in our behaviors and expectations (Shea & Renn, 2017)?
- How might we trouble the definition of leadership capacity, especially the notion of "behaving effectively"? Who determines this, and how has sexism warped our understanding of effective leadership practice?
- How do our own leadership paradigms shape how we see capacity?

Efficacy

Self-efficacy is individuals' beliefs about their capabilities to produce specific performance achievements in a preferred way (Bandura, 1997). Developed from Bandura's concept of self-efficacy, leadership self-efficacy refers to "individuals' belief in the likelihood they will be successful when engaging in leadership" (Dugan et al., 2013, p. 25). Previous studies have found leadership self-efficacy to be vital in developing leadership identity; it is also a significant predictor of socially responsible leadership capacity (Dugan & Komives, 2010; Komives et al., 2005).

Dugan's (2017) research on college students reveals a startling picture of the intertwined nature of leadership efficacy, capacity, motivation, and enactment. He found people may have capacity or ability for leadership, but if they do not also have high efficacy for leadership (the belief that they can be successful in leadership), they are far less likely to act on their capacities. To further complicate matters, his research reveals women score higher than men on seven of eight capacities for socially responsible leadership, yet women score significantly lower than men on efficacy for leadership (Dugan & Komives, 2010). Possible barriers to women's leadership self-efficacy include perfectionism, the need to please, and imposter syndrome (the belief that one will be revealed as less than capable or as a fraud; Owen, 2020). Critical feminist leadership helps align women's capacity for leadership with their efficacy for leadership.

Additionally, while self-efficacy is essential in individual pursuits, people do not live in social isolation, but often work together toward shared goals. CRLL emphasizes individual self-efficacy and collective efficacy to take action through groups and organize with unified effort. Groups share beliefs in collective capabilities to arrange and perform courses of action in order to accomplish desired attainments (Bandura, 1997). The stronger the students' preexisting perceived efficacy, and the more the messages they obtain from others enhancing their beliefs in their capabilities, they are more likely to apply effective leadership practices (Owen et al., 2017). Critical feminist leadership enhances women's collective self-efficacy for leadership.

Reflections on leadership self-efficacy invites the following questions:

- What are strategies to align women's capacity and confidence/efficacy for leadership?
- Since efficacy is a key predictor for women's leadership performance, how do we build systems that increase efficacy rather than diminish it?

- What characteristics of spaces invite women to form and enhance collective leadership self-efficacy? How can leadership education create more of those spaces?

IMPLICATIONS

While there is value in theorizing about gender and leadership, what might fostering critical feminist leadership look like in practice? The following are strategies for moving toward feminist leadership praxis.

Elevate and Amplify Diverse Voices in Leadership Learning

Socially just leadership educators interrogate what is considered as the leadership literature canon and who are considered foundational scholars in leadership learning. One of the implications of an historical legacy of exclusion is that it narrows who is cited and who is published. What other voices might inform a leadership curriculum? What other disciplines and pedagogies may create more inclusive spaces? What other mediums and tools can we use to invite more diverse voices and perspectives into our spaces? There are powerful, yet often ignored, leadership lessons in literature on activism, service, and public scholarship, for example.

Consider the Effects of Campus Climate on Gender and Leadership

How are institutions of higher education gendered spaces? Think about the role of women at your institution. Are pioneering women being honored on campus? If so, how? What vestiges of gendered approaches still exist on campus? What arenas do you find affirming to women's experiences and leadership? To genderqueer and nonbinary individuals? Where do you see gendered messages in the artifacts, espoused values, and underlying assumptions of your campus? What are possible effects of organizational culture on leadership (Owen, 2020)?

Adopt a Feminist Practice of Leadership

Shea and Renn (2017) suggest a shift from feminine to feminist ways of leading as ways to transform organizations while addressing pervasive sex and gender inequality. They describe three interconnected tools of feminist leadership including: using and subverting power structures, complicating difference, and enacting social change. Feminist leaders use and subvert power structures primarily through counteracting powerlessness and fostering empowerment. Second, feminist leaders complicate difference by troubling dualistic notions of both gender (man/woman) and leadership (leader/follower) where they arise. It also means inviting intersectional approaches where one exerts leadership. Feminist leaders understand how people practice different approaches to feminism and seek ways to cross boundaries, finding commonalities among differences. Finally, feminist leaders enact social change. This is done by examining linkages between women's liberation and other social change movements and finding ways to contribute.

Develop a Liberatory Consciousness and Maintain Critical Hope

Love (2013) put forward the idea of a liberatory consciousness. She stated anyone committed to changing systems and institutions to create greater equity and social justice must develop a liberatory consciousness. This kind of thinking enables people to live their lives in oppressive systems and institutions with intentionality and awareness, rather than submit to the forces of socialization. A liberatory consciousness enables people to maintain an awareness of the dynamics of oppression without giving in to despair and hopelessness. People who learn to sustain hope in the face of struggle have discovered the importance of critical hope to leadership (Owen, 2020). This does not refer to naïve hope or negating the difficulties of sustaining the work necessary to overcome injustice.

We wish for leadership educators to go beyond structural attempts at including women, as suggested in the 'add women and stir' approach, and instead create environments to foster feminist leadership and critical hope for a more equitable and just future for all.

REFERENCES

Bandura, A. (1997). *Self-efficacy: The exercise of control.* W. H. Freeman.

Bertrand Jones, T., Guthrie, K. L., & Osteen, L. (2016). Critical domains of culturally relevant leadership learning: A call to transform leadership programs. In K. L. Guthrie, T. Bertrand Jones, & L. Osteen (Eds.), *New Directions for Student Leadership: No. 152. Developing culturally relevant leadership learning* (pp. 9–21). Jossey-Bass.

Butler, J. (1990). *Gender trouble: Feminism and the subversion of identity.* Routledge.

Dugan, J. P. (2017). *Leadership theory: Cultivating critical perspectives.* Jossey-Bass.

Dugan, J. P., Kodama, C., Correia, B., & Associates. (2013). *Multi-institutional study of leadership insight report: Leadership program delivery*. National Clearinghouse for Leadership Programs.

Dugan, J. P., & Komives, S. R. (2010). Influences on college students' capacities for socially responsible leadership. *Journal of College Student Development, 51*(5), 525–549.

Guthrie, K. L. & Chunoo, V. S. (Eds.). (2018). *Changing the narrative: Socially just leadership education*. Information Age.

Haber-Curran, P., & Tillapaugh, D. (2017). Gender and student leadership: A critical examination. *New Directions for Student Leadership, 2017*(154), 11–22.

hooks, b. (2000a). *Feminism is for everybody*. South End Press.

hooks, b. (2000b). *Feminist theory: From margin to center*. South End Press.

Johnson, A. G. (2006). *Privilege, power, and difference* (2nd ed.). McGraw-Hill.

Kalsem, K., & Williams, V. L. (2010). Social justice feminism. *UCLA Women's Law Journal, 18*(1), 131–193.

Komives, S. R., Owen, J. E., Longerbeam, S. D., Mainella, F. C., & Osteen, L. (2005). Developing a leadership identity: A grounded theory. *Journal of College Student Development, 46*(6), 593–611.

Love, B. (2013). Developing a liberatory consciousness. In M. Adams, W. J. Blumenfeld, C. Castaneda, H. Hackman, M. Peters, & X. Zuniga (Eds.), *Readings for diversity and social justice* (3rd ed., pp. 601–606). Routledge.

Mills, P. J. (1994). Feminist critical theory: *Unruly practices: Power, discourse, and gender in contemporary social theory* and *Justice and the politics of difference* [Review of the books]. *Science and Society, 58*(2), 211–217.

Owen, J. E. (2020). *We are the leaders we've been waiting for: Women and leadership development in college*. Stylus.

Owen, J. E., Hassell-Goodman, S., & Yamanaka, A. (2017). Culturally relevant leadership learning: Identity, capacity, and efficacy. *Journal of Leadership Studies, 11*(3), 48–54. htpps://doi.org/10.1002/jls.21545

Seemiller, C. (2014). *The student leadership competencies guidebook*. Jossey-Bass.

Shea, H. D., & Renn, K. A. (2017). Gender and leadership: A call to action. In D. Tillapaugh & P. Haber-Curran (Eds.), *New Directions for Student Leadership: No. 154. Critical perspectives on gender and student leadership* (pp. 83–94). Jossey-Bass.

Tillapaugh, D., Mitchell, D., Jr., & Soria, K. M. (2017). Considering gender and student leadership through the lens of intersectionality. In D. Tillapaugh & P. Haber-Curran (Eds.), *New Directions for Student Leadership: No. 154. Critical perspectives on gender and student leadership* (pp. 23–32). Jossey-Bass.

Yamanaka, A. (2018). *Phenomenological exploration on the experience of microaggression by women faculty of color and its relations to self-efficacy* [Unpublished dissertation]. George Mason University.

CHAPTER 9

"NOTHING ABOUT US WITHOUT US"

Challenging Ableist Leadership Education

Spencer Scruggs and Sally R. Watkins

When thinking of harmonious pairs, disability and leadership do not always come to mind. Historically, disability has been painted as a "defect;" as something to fix or avoid. Rooted in the medical model of disability, this mindset persists through popular media and in educational institutions throughout the world. A consequence of this deficit-oriented model is the preclusion of individuals with disabilities from leadership learning, stemming from the perceived inability of those individuals to meaningfully contribute to our communities. The history of disability rights and disability justice reflects a transition from this model to one of understanding and representation of disability in leadership; one that highlights the vital role that disability identity can play in leadership development. Through the experience of a disability, disability identity influences the development of leadership skills, such as a unique connectedness to one's community, a penchant for affecting change in one's community, and a capacity for resilience in the face of adversity.

Disability identity development can parallel leadership development by cultivating innovative thinking, fostering unique perspective-taking,

Shifting the Mindset: Socially Just Leadership Education
pp. 101–112
Copyright © 2021 by Information Age Publishing
All rights of reproduction in any form reserved.

engendering creative problem solving, and advancing self-advocacy that is innate to the experiences of people with disabilities (Vaccaro et al., 2018). As demonstrated by the disability rights movement and the progression of disability justice, students with disabilities who grow in their understanding of their disability and embrace it as part of their identity capitalize on their educational experiences while becoming leaders in their communities. Deeply exploring how disability intersects with leadership development, we describe the educational experiences of students with disabilities that serve as the foundation of leadership development, particularly focusing on skills and strength-development from both affirming and adverse experiences associated with their education. We then turn to our existing knowledge and understanding of how students with disabilities take these experiences and turn them into the discovery of self and purpose; important for developing a sense of their own leadership philosophy. Finally, we review how to foster and further the opportunities for students with disabilities, taking advantage of in their own journey of leadership development.

EDUCATIONAL SUPPORT FOR STUDENTS WITH DISABILITIES

Many of the formative leadership experiences for students with disabilities stem from their education; particularly those experiences of educational support related to their disability. A plethora of legal and statutory protections exist for students with disabilities, often with very little structure or guidance for those that execute those protections. Among the first were Section 504 regulations in the Rehabilitation Act of 1973; aimed at prohibiting discrimination and exclusion of people with disabilities in programs and services receiving federal funding (Rehabilitation Act, 1973). While Section 504 of the law specifically does not provide funding for implementation of protections, it nonetheless provided the initial framework for equal access and educational opportunities for students with disabilities. With the introduction and expansion of the Individuals with Disabilities Education Act, K–12 schools and resource professionals who work with students with disabilities received further guidance on the implementation of Individual Educational Plans with students with certain disabilities, signaling a greater understanding of the need for more support in educational equity (Education of Individuals with Disabilities Act, 1975).

Section 504 laid the early groundwork for the Americans with Disabilities Act from the early 1990s. The act is a comprehensive prohibition of, and protection from, discrimination solely on the basis of disability in federally funded programs and services, as well as in employment and public accommodation (Americans with Disabilities Act, 1990). This policy greatly expanded educational equity for students with disabilities and bolstered the structures for enforcement of these protections. Subsequent amendments to the Americans with Disabilities Act in 2008 further expanded the definition of "disability," aligning the legal protections with tenets of social justice and socially constructed disability identity (Americans with Disabilities Act, 1990). The most recent reauthorization of the Higher Education Act, which was itself an extension of the 2008 Higher Education Opportunity Act, focused on funding support for students with disabilities in the transition between high school and college, and stricter data collection on students registered with the designated campus authority for accommodations to support better informed choice for students with disabilities (Madaus et al., 2012).

Each of these protective efforts reflect ongoing progress toward disability justice in an educational system that often erects barriers for individuals with disabilities. In K–12 education, students with disabilities often receive extensive protections and academic support under IDEA requiring teachers and school administrators to become familiar with their patterns and processes of learning to eliminate systemic barriers. In their transition to college, students with disabilities may recruit similar assistance through designated accommodations professionals. The importance of these protections, beyond their mere existence, lies in the visibility and autonomy given to students with disabilities with respect to access and ownership of their own educational experiences, especially in leadership learning.

The influence of these protections on the leadership education experiences of students mirrors the efforts of individuals with disabilities to establish those protections in the first place. Much like the civil rights movement, the disability rights movement was led by pioneer activists, such as Judy Heumann and Brad Lomax, who were energized in the fight for their communities and the voices of numerous individuals with disabilities who were tired of being erased (Connelly, 2020; Heumann, 2020). Students with disabilities, Ed Roberts and Tim Nugent, utilized their educational opportunities at University of California at Berkeley and the University of Illinois at Urbana-Champaign to effect change through raising the voices and needs of individuals with disabilities like them (Wu, 2020). Adopting the mantra "nothing about us without us," the disability rights movement has leaned upon previous social justice movements for inspiration in centering members of the disability community in leadership roles within the movement. Taking a cue from the disability rights movement, higher education represents a unique opportunity for students to grow in their own leadership attitudes, knowledge, and behaviors with special attention to how their disability identity influences the ways they lead in their communities.

DISABILITY IDENTITY DEVELOPMENT AND MODELS

Disability as an Identity

Much of higher education's treatment of those with disabilities is grounded by medical and/or functional limitation models. Within the context of higher education, these two models perpetuate perceptions of "disabled individuals as unfit to attend college or work in any capacity" and "disability as dichotomous; that is, there are only two kinds of people in the world—those who have functional limitations and those who do not, emphasizing only "the latter of whom "can be successful" (Evans et al., 2017, p. 60). Despite their popularity, these models are challenged by progressive perspectives, like the social model, which emphasizes environments as impactful to the social construction of disability. This model encourages examining environmental factors that influence how disabilities impact lived experiences (Evans et al., 2017).

While the social model of disability moves away from defining disability as a problem with someone's body, it fails to account for the realities that disability imposes on the lived experiences of individuals with disabilities, which are important to understanding and naming disability as a social construct. The interactionist model of disability (Evans & Broido, 2011) attempts to bridge this gap. Inspired by Lewin's equation, the interactionist model holds that ability status can be seen as intersecting functions of the environment, the individual person, and the impairment (Evans & Broido, 2011).

This model's importance rests in its potential to (re)contextualize how students with disabilities use previous educational experiences with environmental cues and their daily realities to form an identity. For example, students have agency regarding which college or university they intend on attending. Students with disabilities may choose to attend a certain higher education institution based on how their impairments affect them academically and socially. However, they may or may not have environments in their high schools that are supportive of them making the choices that align the most with their impairments; affecting the whole decision process of which college or university to enroll. Through the interactions of these functions, disability truly becomes a social construct; one through which students can develop a sense of self and belonging. How students engage in this process and how these three functions show up on a college campus can be seen through a variety of identity models.

How Students With Disabilities Develop Identity

Identity theorizing naturally moves toward the socially just views of disability present in the Interactionist Model. A variety of factors are important to consider as disability interacts with and itself becomes an identity.

Acceptance. Gibson (2006) focused specifically on the move into acceptance, theorizing acceptance as key to embracing oneself and successfully functioning as an adult with a disability. Most individuals with disabilities begin as a stage of passive awareness of their disability and proceed through a realization stage, characterized by a coming to terms with their disability. After acknowledging the realities of how their disability influences their day-to-day activities and relationships, students with disabilities eventually reach a stage of acceptance, where an integration of oneself with a community and pride in disability identity occurs. This stage model of disability identity formation is an accurate conceptualization of what many students with disabilities may go through during college, shaping their ability to view themselves as potential leaders and effectively engage in the leadership process.

Other models, such as Dunn and Burcaw's (2013) narrative model of disability, highlight acceptance and acknowledgment of disability status as just one part of identity development allowing an individual to thrive and feel comfortable within their own skin. Forber-Pratt and Zape (2017) conceptualized acceptance as a status that may or may not define disability identity for a specific individual. Either way, it is likely to amount to some conceptualization of disability identity when paired with achievements or placements in other statuses. In this way, acceptance could or could not happen for a person with a disability based on a variety of factors. If we look at disability as a social construct, conceptualizing acceptance in this manner is important because it allows us to look at additional factors to equivocate disability identity formation among a group of individuals with disabilities who may experience disability very differently from one another.

Building Community. Students often feel isolated and alone when experiencing struggles and hurdles of the college environment related to their disability. Therefore, building community and strong relationships with peers with disabilities is important to establishing identity (Dunn & Burcaw, 2013; Connor, 2012; Forber-Pratt & Zape, 2017; Vaccaro et al., 2018). The community of students with disabilities dispels the myth of norms set by abled individuals on how to be successful in college. Additionally, community can reduce feelings of loneliness, and provide examples to students that they are not the only ones who feel like they are not understood by faculty, staff, and peers on campus (Dunn & Burcaw, 2013; Forber-Pratt & Zape, 2017).

Activism as Identity-Formation.   A unique part of identity formation among students with disabilities is a call to action as an activist. This desire for activism stems from a desire to help peers who may be in their own disability identity development process. While becoming an activist, students with disabilities accept an active role in building and supporting their community, moving away from assuming that their community is innately present (Forber-Pratt & Zape, 2017). Through actively participating in opportunities such as peer mentoring, participation in student government or disability affinity student groups, or service opportunities working with individuals with disabilities, students often reflect on how activism and active community participation are integral to their sense of self, sharing narratives like:

> I think that it is a part of my identity. It's not something that I think about all of the time, but I do feel that I look at things sometimes from a little bit of a different perspective than the average able-bodied person because of that. It's important to associate yourself with the disabled community for rights and activist purposes and just you know for yourself for support ... it's just such a part of who I am. (Forber-Pratt & Zape, 2017, p. 354)

The call to action many students with disabilities feel alongside their identity development is really the process of developing purpose. Students might engage in purpose development through developing affinity/identity groups on campus, engaging in the education of others on campus, telling their own stories, and caring for other students with disabilities through teaching self-advocacy skills and campus survival skills (i.e., which professors to take, how to both physically and emotionally navigate campus, illuminating safe and welcoming spaces on campus (Kimball et al., 2016; Vaccaro et al., 2018). Because much of their educational and personal trajectory is determined by others, as disability is illuminated as a sociopolitical structure, many students with disabilities begin these steps of purpose development when they get to college. Vaccaro et al. (2018) describes these steps in three different processes:

1. *Imagination:* Students begin to discover what their strengths are and how they can start to use them to change the world around them.

2. *Exploration:* After solidifying what strengths and skills they possess, students with disabilities begin to act upon those. This process often involves students stepping outside of their comfort zone, seeking opportunities on campus, or creating their own opportunities for engagement and learning.

3. *Integration:* Students eventually take the opportunity to prune and hone what they are doing, only retaining goals, commitments, and activities that are the most integral to achieving purpose. This often serves as an important step because it helps establish deep connections to peers, both with and without disabilities, while also solidifying a sense of how their disability both connects them to a community and makes them unique.

Thus, as leadership educators, we must cultivate these opportunities and spaces designed for purpose development for students with disabilities.

RECOMMENDATIONS FOR LEADERSHIP EDUCATORS

The move toward a more socially just approach to leadership development necessitates adjusting and shifting our educational efforts toward inclusive and welcoming opportunities for students with disabilities. Considering how identity formation and leadership development are intricately woven together for college students with disabilities, along with our understanding of both academic and personal success factors in college contributing to identity development, socially just leadership educators work toward students with disabilities. Assuring we have equitable leadership learning opportunities to develop the necessary skills, abilities, and behaviors positively contribute to students with disabilities, the campus communities, and beyond. Developing an informed understanding of the experiences of students prior to and after coming to college offers leadership educators the opportunity to critically assess the ableism in the academic and cocurricular leadership programs specific to their campuses, to consider how students with disability develop identity, and use this awareness to inform program design, challenge assumptions, engage partners, center accessibility, and facilitate leadership learning.

Commitment to Inclusive Design

Students with disabilities cannot engage in opportunities to grow in their leadership skills if these spaces are not created to be accessible and meet their needs. Programmatic spaces and events as well as the classroom must be inviting while signaling a supportive environment and belongingness. Socially just leadership educators critically review their practices to evaluate places where their own ableism might be present. Below are some examples of inclusive design for accessibility.

- Are promotional materials regarding engagement and learning opportunities distributed in an accessible format (i.e., promotional graphics and flyers have alternative text and are readable by a screen reader, flyer availability in a physical and digital format, promotional content includes information on how to request reasonable accommodations, camel backing hashtags)?
- Are visual materials available in an alternative format in advance?
- Have accessible entrances to the venue been clearly marked and shared with members of the audience in advance of an event?
- Have provisions been made for attendees to request communication accommodations (e.g., use of presenter microphones, presence of an ASL interpreter, live captioning options)?
- Do emergency management plans consider how to assist individuals with disabilities in attendance?
- If the engagement and learning opportunity likely includes material or information of sensitive nature, are there plans to provide proper warning to participants regarding the nature of the topics or information being covered?

Important steps like these (or their notable absence) signal the attitudes of the campus community toward participation and belonging of students with disabilities. By planning and designing inclusively for accessibility, we communicate to students with disabilities that we understand their desire to belong, that this space is a safe one in which their narrative is valued and honored, and that the overall campus community is richer and benefits from their participation. While we recognize students with disabilities as self-advocates, to put the responsibility on the individual student without considering the ways identity, power, and environment potentially shape the student's access or lack thereof creating a situation where self-advocacy is stifled or reactive (Karpicz, 2020).

Challenging Assumptions

In promoting growth in leadership among students with disabilities, socially just leadership educators challenge our own assumptions of what that means. The engagement and learning opportunities we provide on campus are not going to be effective or of interest to students with disabilities without this type of consideration. Designing opportunities without consulting with, and providing space for, students with disabilities to share their own narratives, makes dangerous assumptions about what they need to thrive as leaders. Just as students with disabilities may interpret overall achievement with statuses associated with their disability identity, these same students might be at different places of need in becoming leaders. Disability is not a monolithic experience and is often one of many identities that shape the student's collegiate life. Acceptance, or connection to a community, may not look the same to all students with disabilities, therefore; methods of enacting and growing in leadership development may look different too. Manifesting through our socialization in the prevalence of the medical model, leadership educators do more harm when they are not challenging these assumptions because they limit the pathways for leadership learning for students with disabilities. By simply providing spaces where our assumptions are checked and students with disabilities can reflect meaningfully on their curricular and cocurricular engagement, socially just leadership educators facilitate processes where students with disabilities can narrate and own their own leadership education.

Engaging Partners

The socially just leadership education of students with disabilities should mirror the identity exploration they experience during college. Particularly important is building a community of individuals committed to leadership education. Socially just educators often rely on the appropriate professionals on campus, such as those in a disability services office or advisors of an affinity/identity group associated with students with disabilities. As disability is not a monolith, these partners in leadership educators are valuable for providing insight into a variety of populations of students with disabilities, the most effective ways to communicate with students, and any special considerations for students. These professionals frequently serve as the conduits of connections between students with disabilities and the greater campus community. Utilizing disability services professionals in designing engagement and learning opportunities can expand the diversity and representation as well as the focus of leadership education efforts. This collaboration also provides a significant opportunity to help disability services professionals reclassify their work through the lens of leadership education, as much of the day-to-day work of listening to students, helping them grow self-advocacy and self-determination skills, and prioritizing the cultivation of community connections is exactly that: leadership education.

Beyond campus-based partners, leadership development programs often offer opportunities for students to interact and connect with the community beyond the campus via experiential learning through community involvement that includes reflection specific to the engagement.

(McKim & Velez, 2017; Allen & Hartman, 2009; Day, 2001; Eich, 2008; Zimmerman-Oster& Burkhardt, 1999). When cultivating these community-based leadership development programs, the socially just leadership educator assumes responsibility for working with the student and community partner to ensure equitable access and a mutually beneficial experience that affords the student the opportunity to fully participate and realize the unique leadership learning outcomes.

Centering Accessibility

Leadership educators are uniquely positioned to transform the world through the facilitation of engagement and learning opportunities. Socially just leaders who are conscious of the role of identity, privilege, and inequity in the world hold accessibility and disability inclusion as key values that guide their work. Adoption of these values through leadership education happens when educators actively operationalize these values. Accessibility and disability inclusion become natural parts of any discussion leadership educators have with students when we recognize how disability identity intersects with, and is linked to, so many other forms of contextualization and social justice.

The purpose of this chapter was to raise awareness and to challenge the limitations of leadership education for students with disabilities. To truly create equitable leadership learning spaces and programs, leadership educators need to first be informed, then assess the ways in which ableism and other dominate narratives shapes their work, and finally, act on the previously identified suggestions to offer welcoming and supportive programs that offer students the opportunity to gain valuable knowledge, attitudes, and behaviors supportive of their leadership development, diminish the structural and climate barriers that marginalize students with disabilities, and generate the conduits of connectivity so vital to their success.

REFERENCES

Allen, S. J., & Hartman, N. S. (2009). Sources of learning in student leadership development programming. *Journal of Leadership Studies, 3*(3), 6–16. https://doi.org/0.1002/jls.20119.

Americans with Disabilities Act of 1990, 42 U.S.C. § 12101 *et seq.* (1990). https://www.ada.gov/pubs/adastatute08.htm

Connelly, E. A. (2020, July 8). Overlooked no more: Brad Lomax, a bridge between civil rights movements. *The New York Times.* https://www.nytimes.com/2020/07/08/obituaries/brad-lomax-overlooked.html

Connor, D. J. (2012). Helping students with disabilities transition to college: 21 tips for students with LD and/or ADD/ADHD. *Teaching Exceptional Children*, *44*(5), 16–25. https://doi.org/10.1177/004005991204400502

Day, V. D. (2001). Leadership development: A review in context. *Leadership Quarterly*, *11*(4), 581–613. https://doi.org/10.1016/S1048-9843(00)0061-8

Dunn, D. S., & Burcaw, S. (2013). Disability identity: Exploring narrative accounts of disability. *Rehabilitation Psychology*, *58*, 148–157. https://doi.org/10.1037/a0031691

Education of Individuals with Disabilities Act of 1975, 20 U.S.C. § 1400 et seq. (1975). https://uscode.house.gov/view.xhtml?path=/prelim@title20/chapter33&edition=prelim

Eich, D. (2008). A grounded theory of high-quality leadership programs: Perspectives from student leadership programs in higher education. *Journal of Leadership & Organizational Studies*, *15*(2), 176–187. https://doi.org/10.1177/1548051808324099

Evans, N. J., & Broido, E. M. (2011, November). *Social involvement and identity involvement of students with disabilities*. Poster presentation at the Association for the Study of Higher Education, Charlotte, NC.

Evans, N. J., Broido, E. M., Brown, K. R., & Wilke, A. K. (2017). *Disability in higher education: A social justice approach*. Jossey-Bass.

Forber-Pratt, A. J., & Zape, M. P. (2017). Disability identity development model: Voices from the ADA-generation. *Disability and Health Journal*, *10*, 350–355. https://doi.org/10.1016/j.dhjo.2016.12.013

Gibson, J. (2006). Disability and clinical competency: An introduction. *The California Psychologist*, *39*, 6–10.

Heumann, J. (2020, April 28). *"Crip camp" and the disability rights revolution* [Interview]. St. Louis On the Air; St. Louis Public Radio. https://news.stlpublicradio.org/show/st-louis-on-the-air/2020-04-28/crip-camp-star-judith-heumann-explains-how-summer-camp-led-to-a-disability-rights-revolution

Karpicz, J. (2020). "Just my being here is self-advocacy": Exploring the self-advocacy experiences of disabled graduate students of color. *Journal Committed to Social Change on Race and Ethnicity*, *6*(1), 138–163.

Kimball, E. W., Moore, A., Vaccaro, A., Troiano, P. F., & Newman, B. M. (2016). College students with disabilities redefine activism: Self-advocacy, storytelling, and collective action. *Journal of Diversity in Higher Education*, *9*(3), 245–260. https://doi.org/10.1037/dhe0000031

Madaus, J. W., Kowitt, J. S., & Lalor, A. R. (2012). The higher education opportunity act: Impact on students with disabilities. *Rehabilitation Research, Policy, and Education*, *26*(1), 33–41. https://doi.org/10.1891/216866512805000893

McKim, A., & Valez, J. (2017) Informing leadership education by connecting curricular experiences and leadership outcomes. *Journal of Leadership Education*, *16*(1), 81–95. https://doi.org/10.12806/V16/I1/R6

Rehabilitation Act of 1973, 29 U.S.C. § 701 et seq. (1973). https://www2.ed.gov/policy/speced/leg/rehab/rehabilitation-act-of-1973-amended-by-wioa.pdf.

Vaccaro, A., Kimball, E. K., Moore, A., Newmann, B. M., & Troiano, P. F. (2018). Narrating the self: A grounded theory model of emerging purpose for college students with disabilities. *Journal of College Student Development, 59*(1), 37–54. https://dx.doi.org/10.1353/csd.2018.0003

Wu, L. (Host). (2020, July 30). A.D.A. Now! [Audio Podcast Episode], In *Throughline*. NPR. https://www.npr.org/2020/07/27/895896462/a-d-a-now

Zimmerman-Oster, K., & Burkhardt, J. C. (1999). *Leadership in the making: Impact and insights from leadership development programs in U.S. colleges and universities.* W. K. Kellogg Foundation.

CHAPTER 10

FORGING A PROFESSIONAL MILITARY IDENTITY

Leader Education in the U.S. Army Officer Corps

David Gray, Daniel Marshall, and David Dixon

"Yours is the profession of arms ... the will to win ... the sure knowledge that in war there is no substitute for victory, that if you lose, the nation will be destroyed, that the very obsession your public service must be duty, honor, country."

——General Douglas MacArthur,
Center of Military History, *The Profession of Arms* (1990)

In an era of declining faith in institutions, Americans want organizations to invest in values-based leaders who solve complex problems and inspire a higher common purpose. In this regard, the military services regularly garner the American public's trust through their expert leadership, professional competence, loyalty, personal sacrifices, and subordination to civilian authorities as consistent with national values in the U.S. Constitution. The public also respects the military's ability to adapt to diverse circumstances (Newport, 2017; Shane, 2019). Military units have recently

Shifting the Mindset: Socially Just Leadership Education
pp. 113–125

engaged in a broad range of operations, including combat, delivery of humanitarian aid to natural disasters areas, providing medical support to stop the spread of the COVID-19 pandemic, and supporting civilian law enforcement. To maintain this public trust, military officers serve as the standard-bearers of a professional ethos girded in exemplary leadership.

In the U.S. Army, the nation's oldest armed service, officers commit to becoming values-based leaders in the profession of arms. Officers internalize a professional military ethos expressed by the tenets in their official commission and the seven army values—loyalty, duty, respect, selfless service, honor, integrity, and personal courage. The ethos also stresses high competency across the domains of professional military expertise. Military success in modern wars and in wide-ranging peacetime missions rely heavily on officers' intellectual, moral, and physical preparations. This process involves active participation in the army's progressive education system, career experiences, and individual self-study (Department of the Army ADP 6-22, 2012; ADPR 6-22, 2012). An officer's self-concept and professional identity are, therefore, tied to what type of person they want to be, what they must know to lead successfully, and how they should routinely conduct themselves (Hesselbein & Shinseki, 2004).

The efficacy of the army's leader development system evolved over two centuries of service to the nation's common defense. This chapter will examine the evolution of the army's officer education system, its impact on creating a shared professional identity, and its implications for leadership educators in other professions. Values-based leadership centered on a higher common purpose and life-long learning play essential roles in preparing leaders in all career fields for a complicated and uncertain world.

ORIGINS OF ARMY'S PROFESSIONAL MILITARY ETHOS

The officer corps' growth as a profession directly contributed to its unique identity and specialized expertise. Sociologist Andrew Abbott (1998) defined a profession as "exclusive occupational groups that apply somewhat abstract knowledge to particular cases" (p. 8). A profession principally addresses "human problems amenable to expert service" (Abbott, 1988, p. 35). The military profession's particular expertise, according to Samuel Huntington's (1957) seminal *The Soldier and the State*, is "the direction, operation, and control of an organization of whose primary function is application of [state-sanctioned] violence" (p. 3) in pursuit of political objectives. Sir John Hackett has further described the military profession as a "vocation" and life-long calling, similar in "dedication to the priesthood" (Center of Military History, 1990, p. 3). The military profession distinctly involves a personal and collective sense of "unlimited liability"—the willingness to risk one's life—in pursuit of the nation's defense.

An officer's professional identity development is a continuous process involving an understanding of both the army institution and their individual self. These interrelated identities include distinctions between *content* (what we think of ourselves as an officer corps) and *structure* (how do we think of ourselves). An officer's beliefs, values, behaviors, and leadership roles are part of identity content. Identity structure focuses on an individual's understanding of the institution as a profession and their own level of psychological maturity (Forsythe et al., 2005; Keegan, 1982). This chapter focuses primarily on the institutional—individual content portion of officer identity development.

Several critical cultural, intellectual, and legal traditions have shaped the officer corps' professional identity and expertise. First, the American tradition of maintaining a dual-force of citizen soldiers and professionals merges the country's egalitarian culture, the use of community-based militias for local (state) defense and need for highly trained standing forces for sustained conflict. This duality of forces and traditions profoundly influenced the army's command culture/mindset (Millett et al., 2013; Weigley, 1984).

Second, ideas on how to wage and achieve victory in war shaped the professional ethos of successive generations of officers. According to military historian Russell Weigley the army's "way of war" has vacillated between annihilation and attritional strategies (Weigley, 1973). In contrast, Brian Linn identified three distinctive martial philosophies, categorized from guardian, hero, or manager perspectives (Linn, 2007). Sociologist Morris Janowitz's research recognized officers' strategic outlooks as either total victory-seeking "absolutists" or "pragmatists" who weighed the political consequences of force, especially in a nuclear world (Janowitz, 1960).

Finally, adherence to their oath "to protect and defend the Constitution of the United States against all enemies, foreign and domestic" (Title 5 U.S. Code Section 3331) establishes commissioned officers' principal legal and moral commitments. This sacred oath—requiring allegiance to civilian control of the military and the ideals of Constitution, not to specific individuals holding government positions—underscores moral obligations to the American people that have powerfully shaped officer identity.

The officer corps' professional self-concept, therefore, stems from historical context, the abstract knowledge, and multiple identities needed to carry out the profession's expert military practices. Table 10.1 summarizes the four broad domains of expert knowledge relating to a corresponding officer identity.

**Table 10.1.   Army Officer Self Concept:
Facets of Expert Knowledge and Officer Identities**

Army Domains of Expert Knowledge	Description	Army Officer Identity
Military-technical	War-fighting concepts and employment of equipment/units in combat and other future situations	Warrior
Moral-ethical	Legal and moral content of professional ethics	Leader of character
Human development	Education, character, leader development of individual members	Member of profession
Political-cultural	Ability to represent profession in government and multinational settings	Servant of the nation

Note: Adapted from Snider (2005).

To reinforce its professional expertise and service to the nation's citizens, the army instituted over time a progressive military education system. This arrangement reinforced the multiple professional military identities and prepared its combination of citizen soldiers and professional officers to lead more effectively.

PRECOMMISSIONING: PREPARING LEADERS AND WARRIORS

Since the army's founding in 1775, officers relied on a combination of their personal experiences and some training to prepare for leadership duties. During the American Revolutionary War, many of the colonies' militia units elected their officers. More literate officers might have looked at Caesar's *Commentaries* for leadership insights; in most cases, leaders simply learned by doing (Gruber, 1986). As the Continental Army's Commanding General George Washington recognized most of his officers were self-taught amateurs who lacked critical leader and tactical skills, resulting in poor battlefield performance, casualties, and low unit morale (Atkinson, 2019; Weigley, 1984). Later, in *Sentiments on a Peace Establishment*, President Washington called for the creation of a military academy to educate a small body of future professional officers as a partial remedy (Washington,1783). The idea did not become a reality until March 16, 1802, when President Thomas Jefferson founded the U.S. Military Academy at West Point as America's first civil engineering school.

In 1817, Capt. Sylvanus Thayer, a graduate of Dartmouth and the Academy, assumed duties as West Point's superintendent. Thayer implemented a series of reforms making West Point a highly structured "seminary-academy." Known as the Thayer system, the academy's 4-year program heavily prescribed a curriculum blending liberal arts, science, and emphasis on engineering. Thayer broke the corps of cadets into small classes, required cadets to make daily recitations during classes, administered semiannual exams to measure their progress, and produced an academic order of merit list. Thayer later received recognition as the "father of the military academy" and leading colleges of his time adopted key elements of his academic system (Lovell, 1979).

The Thayer system stressed honor and integrity in character-based leader development. A commandant of cadets assisted by first-class (senior) cadets oversaw military training and regulated the corps of cadets' discipline. During the several months-long "beast barracks," plebes (freshman) endured strict regimentation and underwent physical and mental trials to test their character. Every new plebe endured these rites of passage regardless of social standing, race, or creed—equalizing experiences bonding each class together. While critical life events like the "beast barracks" experience contributed to their character growth, cadets also attended weekly chapel services to attend to their spiritual needs and to reinforce personal moral values. Moreover, participation in philosophical debates further contributed to cadet understanding of ethical leadership practices as leaders of character.

Cadets learned military-technical knowledge and leadership techniques through military drill, firing small arms, and taking part in summer tactical training. Only a fraction of the curriculum, however, was devoted to military science. Professor of Civil and Military Engineering and the Art of War Dennis Hart Mahan taught one class dedicated to the lessons of Napoleonic warfare. He later penned the influential text *Outpost* (1847), devoted primarily to military engineering (Millett et al., 2013). The Thayer system promoted the Aristotelian virtues of *valor* expected of future army officers in war (warrior) with the *wisdom* of a rigorous academic education to produce engineers needed for the nation's expansion (servant of the nation; Crackel, 1991).

Following West Point's founding, several states started military model colleges; Vermont's Norwich, Virginia Military Institute (VMI), and The Citadel in South Carolina, to prepare regional citizen-soldier leaders. These schools instituted prescribed academic curriculums, operated within a regimented military environment, and provided rudimentary military training for the future leaders of state militias. During the 20th century, these schools began admitting minority and women candidates as cadets—while retaining much of the military model's structures (Reardon, 1999).

The success of the military academy and military colleges, as well as the need for an expanded officer corps in wartime, caused Congress to expand precommissioning programs to civilian colleges. The Morrill Act 1862 established the land grant college system that provided for military training for college students. As war approached, then raged in Europe 1914–16, U.S. Army Chief of Staff General Leonard Wood initiated military training camps aimed at college students to prepare future military leaders. These camps readied 23,000 volunteers, who received commissions upon America's entry into war. The National Security Act 1916 founded the Reserve Officers Training Corps, or ROTC, program to train and commission college students into the armed services. This successful program subsequently expanded during the 20th Century, ensuring citizen-soldier officers would lead military units for America's increasing global security interests (Millett et al., 2013).

After World War I, the number of military-model secondary and higher education institutions expanded to almost 500; a number that remained strong during the Cold War. The popularity of military-model schools fell considerably after the Vietnam War; nevertheless, the remaining schools continue to attract highly qualified and diverse cadet recruits. As members of the Association of Military Colleges and Schools of the United States, the six senior military colleges; Norwich, VMI, Virginia Tech, Citadel, University of North Georgia, Texas A&M, have special authorities under Title 10, U.S. Code for commissioning their cadets for service as active duty officers or citizen-soldier officers in the reserve components (2020; Reardon, 1999). Graduates of these schools go on to military careers or apply their hard-earned leadership skills to occupations in the civilian world.

Following graduation and commissioning, successive educational and operational assignments socialize junior officers into the profession. All officers attend a basic officer's leader course, followed by specialty training for their designated branch to extend their military-technical and moral-ethical knowledge. Junior officers gain practical experience leading soldiers and honing their military-technical expertise with operational units. Captains attend advanced training and education to learn how to command small units and perform staff work at higher organizational levels (Maneuver Center of Excellence, 2020). These formative years especially reinforce the officer's warrior and leader of character identities.

Command and Staff College: Warriors and Members of a Profession

The scope of military operations during the American Civil War (1861–1865) highlighted deficiencies in the gifted amateur approach to officership. West Pointers had dominated the highest ranks of command.

However, the command of large bodies of troops; the Union Army mobilized over 1 million men, over extended distances across North America required a set of leadership and technical skills beyond those learned at the service academy. Moreover, America's growing industrialism and military developments overseas caused reformers to examine options for comprehensive professional education system for regulars and citizen-soldiers to improve the army's military-technical and human development expertise (Karsten, 1986; Millett et al., 2013).

Stress on scientific management during the progressive era in the 1880–1890s led the army to create a tiered military education system for its small officer corps. Professional military education broadly involved both technical military topics as well as the systematic study of military history, strategy, tactics, and logistics using innovative instructional methods. For example, Lts. Arthur L. Wagner and Eben Swift, two creative officers at the U.S. Army's School of the Line in Fort Leavenworth, Kansas, pioneered the "applicatory method," involving lively student participation in individual and group problem-solving to strategic, tactical, and logistical problems. Students studied leadership during staff rides to battlefields. Organized into small sections, the student officers rode on horseback to selected spots, where they prepared solutions to tactical problems posed by instructors on the ground where actual fighting had occurred (Nenninger, 1978). Graduates of the school, like George C. Marshall, VMI 1901, and Dwight D. Eisenhower, USMA 1915, went on to the highest level of responsibilities and command during World War II (Puryear, 1981).

Today, the U.S. Army Command and Staff College at Leavenworth continues to prepare midlevel officers for professional contributions at all levels of responsibility. Attendance at the resident staff college is highly selective, with most graduates going on to achieve higher rank and command responsibilities. The curriculum covers a gamut of military-technical topics related to unified land operations incorporating governmental, interservice, and multinational cooperation. Coursework stresses critical analysis and thinking, problem-solving, and ethical decision-making across challenging operational scenarios. Officers learn the importance of building personal relationships and using indirect influence to lead large organizations (U.S. Army War College, 2020). Graduates further internalize their professional identity as warriors and members of a profession possessing military-technical, human development, moral-ethical, and political-cultural expertise to handle complex challenges of all types.

Army War College: Servants of the Nation

A third tier of professional education for selected senior officers emerged in the early 20th century. Secretary Elihu Root established the

Army War College in 1901 to prepare senior officers for strategic leadership positions. These students learned higher level command and staff procedures, studied industrial mobilization, war planning, and defense requirements. Officers formed close personal relationships crucial to organizing and leading the mass armies of World Wars I and II (Ball, 1994).

Today, a board of senior field grade and general officers competitively selects each class of War College students from the highest performing officers across the Army. These field grade officers (lieutenant colonels and colonels) attend the course alongside civilian counterparts from government agencies, the National Guard and Reserves, sister service officers, and exchange officers from armies around the world. Students learn about the army as an institution, the global application of land power, and the role it plays in contributing to national security. Organized in small staff groups to promote active learning, officers study military history and theory, national security processes, international and regional studies, strategic thinking and complex problem solving, campaign planning, leadership, and communications (U.S. Army War College, 2020).

A smaller number of students attend one of the joint service colleges, the military schools of other nations, or graduate fellowships. The five colleges under the National Defense University—Joint Forces Staff College in Norfolk, Virginia; National War College, Eisenhower School for National Security, College of Information and Cyberspace, and College of International Security in Washington, D.C.—prepare officers and civilian national security experts to lead joint (interservice), interagency, intergovernmental, multinational, and cyber operations. Finally, highly qualified officers are chosen for fellowships at top universities and think-tanks around the country (Schafer, 1999). Each of these allows officers to broaden their politico-cultural knowledge and interpersonal communications. War College graduates become the army's senior members of the profession, responsible for embodying and leading the officer corps as servants to defend the nation's vital interests.

As it evolved, the army's officer development system mutually reinforced the connection between the expert knowledge and multiple identities undergirding the profession of arms. The system originally emphasized a solid education and military technical subjects, but broadened to address human development, moral-ethical decision-making, and political-cultural expertise as the army's mission and complexity expanded. In the 19th century the army invested heavily in educating its officer corps by selecting its most high qualified members for dedicated attendance at schooling of up to a year. Attendance at these schools became a prerequisite for future promotions. Officers internalized their multiple professional identities through successive schooling and experiential assignments. Army officer professional development, past and present, is a critical mixture of education, skill training, and practical, on-the-job application.

IMPLICATIONS FOR LEADER EDUCATORS

The army's officer education and the profession's developmental systems offer several benefits for the leadership education field. The army's model progressively ingrains the multiple officer identities and professional ethos founded on duty, honor, country through whole person development of mind (education), body (training) and soul (character, ethics, and service). The Virginia Military Institute provides an excellent example of how key aspects of this model work in a higher education environment.

Founded in 1839 as the first public senior military college, Virginia Military Institute remains the leading modern example of a public military model college. The Institute provides a nationally ranked undergraduate education designed to produce citizen-soldier leaders ready to serve the country in peace or wartime. Thoroughly grounded in military traditions, the institute's curriculum emphasizes "whole person" development, captured in the metaphor of a three-legged stool (Figure 10.1). Each of the three legs of the stool represents one of the institute's programs—military, academic, physical—united by the seat representing the cadet honor system.

VMI's progressive leader development system is an integral aspect of the curriculum. During their first six months at VMI, new cadets or "rats" undergo a rigorous Ratline (rites of passage) that assimilates them into the class and regimental systems. Associated rituals, such as the "breakout "ceremony recognizing the rats' new status as full-fledged members of the corps upon successful completion of the Ratline, reinforce individual and collective cadet identities. During their 4-year journey cadets successively pass through developmental stages where they learn, by class year, to: 4th Class (freshmen) lead themselves and to follow; 3rd Class (sophomore) influence others; 2nd Class (juniors) lead within an organization; and 1st Class (seniors) command the corps. Cadets appointed to formal leadership positions within the military structure or as part of the class system practice daily positional peer leadership. The institute's experiential cocurricular programs further enhance cadet leadership opportunities (Virginia Military Institute, 2017). VMI's a multifaceted "leader journey" encourages cadets identity development as citizen-soldier leaders of character prepared to serve the nation.

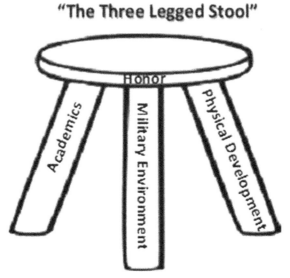

Note. Virginia Military Institute Whole Person Curriculum Model. From "The VMI Leader Journey" by Virginia Military Institute. Copyright 2017.
Reprinted with permission from the Virginia Military Institute Center of Leadership and Ethics.

Figure 10.1.   Whole person development.

Similarly, collegiate leadership education programs can establish a leader development path grounded in their own institution's unique mission and philosophy. Organizations that articulate beliefs, values, and vision attract members who can identify with and embrace those ideals. Colleges and universities could better align coursework and cocurricular activities to provide budding leaders with opportunities to improve their knowledge, abilities, and confidence. Such an acknowledged leader development framework assists individuals towards goal setting, better self-regulation through academic coursework, self-reflection based on the results of various assessment tools, and self-awareness through experiential learning. Integrating faculty and peer feedback reinforces emerging leaders' self-awareness; accelerating capacity and motivation.

Progressive development opportunities aimed at successive levels of leadership responsibility enables organizations to build a bench of seasoned leaders for the future. Combining theory and practice, these opportunities reinforce leader identity and spur motivation to support the organization's common purpose. Incorporating challenging and memorable events, similar to the critical life events described in George's (2015) authentic leadership model, can further shape future identity development. Using successive, standards-based challenges help leaders mature and stimulate adaptive mindsets for overcoming obstacles. Intentionally integrating shared traditions and rituals—awarding a cohort pin or distinctive medal upon program completion, for example—can motivate leaders and provide symbols of their leadership efficacy.

Finally, leader education programs can create a culture of achievement by emphasizing standards-based leader competencies—technical, interpersonal, conceptual—incorporating practical applications. Tiered programs that offer leaders a broader range of competencies to master—especially in the human development, moral ethical, and cross-cultural areas—will hone judgment and abilities to handle increased organizational responsibilities. When each tier focuses on leaders' understanding of leadership processes and on their future competencies—at least two levels of responsibility higher than the current leader's position—they facilitate lateral and vertical succession management within the organization. Moreover, standards-based programs provide measures of leader effectiveness to spur continuous personal and organizational growth. Similar to the army's progressive education system, tiered development programs build leaders' collaborative networks of colleagues who communicate using common frames of reference. Such networks facilitate professional dialogue and individual growth. In sum, a progressive and structured leader development system promotes leader identity development and mastery of the competencies to lead a high-functioning organization.

CONCLUSION

Over the past 245 years, the U.S. Army officer corps has evolved into a profession whose hallmarks are loyalty to the U.S. Constitution's values and ideals, internalization of multiple identities grounded in specialized expertise, and life-long learning in service to the American people. The army's progressive system of leadership education, training, and experiences reinforces abstract knowledge with concrete competencies to accomplish its core missions. Most importantly, the profession's developmental system promotes its defining purpose—selfless service in pursuit of the nation's common defense. Importantly, the army's leader development system provides a well-tested roadmap leader educators may use in shaping their own programs.

ACKNOWLEDGMENT

We are grateful for the insights and suggestions from VMI colleague Captain Catherine Roy used to sharpen the contents of this chapter.

REFERENCES

Abbott, A. (1988). *The system of professions: An essay on the division of expert labor*. University of Chicago Press.

Association of Military Colleges and Schools of the United States. (2020). Our Mission. https://amcsus.org

Atkinson, R. (2019). *The British are coming: The war for America, Lexington to Princeton, 1775–1777*. Henry Holt & Co.

Ball, H. P. (1994). *Of responsible command: A history of the U.S. Army War College*. Alumni Association, USAWC.

Center of Military History. (1990). *Officer's call: The profession of arms*.

Crackel, T. J. (1991). *The illustrated history of West Point*. Harry N. Abrams, Inc.

Department of the Army. (2012, August). Army Doctrinal Publication (ADP) 6-22 *Army Leadership: Influencing people by providing purpose, direction, and motivation*. https://usacac.army.mil/sites/default/files/misc/doctrine/CDG/adp6_22.html

Department of the Army. (2012, August). Army Doctrine Reference Publication ADRP 6-22 *Army Leadership*. (incl. change 1)

Forsythe, G. B., Snook, S., Lewis, P., & Bartone, P. T. (2005). Professional identity development for 21st century army officers. In D. Snider & L. Matthews (Eds), *The future of the Army profession* (2nd ed., pp. 189–209). McGraw & Hill.

George, B. (2015). *Discover your true north: Becoming an authentic leader*. Wiley.

Gruber, I. D. (1986). America's first battle: Long Island 27 August 1775. In C. Heller & W. Stofft (Eds.), *America's first battles 1776–1965* (pp. 1–32). University Press of Kansas.

Hesselbein, F., & Shinseki E. K. (2004). *Be*know*do: Leadership the army way*. Jossey-Bass.

Huntington, S. (1957). *The soldier and the state*. The Belknap Press of Harvard University.

Janowitz, M. (1960). *The professional soldier: A social and political portrait*. The Free Press.

Karsten, P. (1986). Armed progressives: The military reorganizes. In P. Karsten (Eds.), *The military in America from colonial times to the present* (pp. 258–274). The Free Press.

Keegan, R. (1982). *The evolving self: Problem and process in human development*. Harvard University Press.

Linn, B. M. (2007). *The echo of battle: The army's way of war*. Harvard University Press.

Lovell, J. P. (1979). *Neither Athens nor Sparta: The American service academies in transition* (pp. 16–29). Indiana University Press.

Maneuver Center of Excellence. (2021). *The maneuver captain's career course (MCCC)*. https://www.benning.army.mil/Infantry/199th/CATD/MCCC/

Millett, A. R., Maslowski, P., & Feis, W. B. (2013). *For the common defense: A military history of the United States from 1607–2012*. The Free Press.

Nenninger, T. K. (1978). *The Leavenworth Schools and the old army: Education, professionalism, and the Officer Corps of the United States Army, 1881–1918*. Greenwood Press.

Newport, F. (2017, July 17). *U.S. confidence in military reflects perceived competency.* https://news.gallup.com/poll/214511/high-confidence-military-reflects-perceived-competency.aspx.

Puryear, E. F. (1981) *19 stars: A study in military character and leadership* (2nd ed.). Presidio Press.

Reardon, C. (1999). Schools, private military. In J. W. Chambers (Eds.), *The Oxford companion to American military history* (pp. 639–640). Oxford Press.

Schrader, C. (1999). Education, military. In J. W. Chambers (Eds.), *The Oxford companion to American military history* (pp. 243–244). Oxford Press.

Shane, L., III. (2019, July 22). Survey: Public confidence in the military is high, especially in older generations. *Military Times.* https://www.militarytimes.com/news/pentagon-congress/2019/07/22/survey-public-confidence-in-the-military-is-high-especially-among-older-generations/.

Snider, D. M. (2005). The multiple identities of the professional army officer. In D. M. Snider & L. J. Matthews (Eds.), *The future of the army profession* (2nd ed., pp. 142–143). McGraw & Hill.

U.S. Army War College. (2020). *About the US Army War College.* https://www.army-warcollege.edu/overview.cfm

Virginia Military Institute. (2017). *The VMI leader journey: Leading with courage, competence, caring and integrity.*

Washington, G. (1783). *Sentiments on a peace establishment. Founders Online,* National Archives. https://founders.archives.gov/documents/Washington/99-01-02-11202

Weigley, R. F. (1973). *The American way of war: A history of United States military strategy and policy.* Indiana University Press.

Weigley, R. F. (1984). *History of the United States Army* (Enlarged ed.). Indiana University Press.

CHAPTER 11

STUDENT EMPLOYEES

The Fine Line Between Career Readiness and Leadership Learning

Rebecca Pettingell Piers and Amie Runk

In 2019, total U.S. college student debt was an estimated $1.5 trillion (Issa, 2019). As the average cost of education has risen steadily every 5 years from 1980, it is no wonder "student employment is no longer an isolated phenomenon; it is an educational fact of life" (Riggert et al., 2006, p.64). With seemingly ubiquitous debt forcing many students to work while attending college (Planty et al., 2008), and the majority finding jobs off campus (King, 2006), students are often unable to access traditional leadership learning opportunities (Salisbury et al., 2012). If a full-time enrolled student must work to support their education, the hours they can commit to leadership learning through extracurricular activities, including student organizations, student government, or leadership courses can be minimal or nonexistent. Simultaneously, those seeking to employ students after they graduate are spending billions of dollars annually to train employees on leadership (Smedick & Rice, 2018). Therefore, it is important for university communities, and in the private sector's best interest, to support student leadership development in

Shifting the Mindset: Socially Just Leadership Education
pp. 127–138
Copyright © 2021 by Information Age Publishing

college by interrupting systems where employment and development are mutually exclusive.

Although student employment offers many natural leadership learning opportunities, students cannot rely solely on implicit development. Employment on its own is not leadership development. Leadership learning in on and off campus employment is often ancillary rather than deliberate. In this chapter, we discuss the history of student employment and its iterations. Beyond this, we encourage boldly infusing social justice approaches by integrating culturally relevant leadership learning (Bertrand Jones et al., 2016; Guthrie et al., 2017) into on-campus jobs for the betterment of individual students, as well as the institutions employing them.

HISTORICAL VIEWS ON STUDENT EMPLOYMENT

Historically, there have been two contradictory viewpoints represented in research on student employment. The first is of student employment as negatively impacting academic mastery. These studies identify students working more than 20 hours each week as having lower grades than their otherwise comparable peers. These differences are attributed to a variety of reasons, including work as time away from studying (Dundes & Marx, 2007; Kuh et al., 2007; Pike et al., 2008). In a study by Dundes and Marx, students who worked more than 20 hours per week reported having less time than their peers to spend on assignments and study for exams (2006). Kuh et al. (2007) found students working more than 20 hours a week in their first year had lower grade point averages than those who worked fewer than 20. Pike et al. (2008) noted students who worked more than 20 hours had lower grades as compared to their peers. As Salisbury et al. (2012) summarized, the core of this viewpoint focuses on the quantification of the hours worked, which implies time taken away from other activities, including studying and academic work.

However, findings from other research suggests student employment has a positive effect on the college experience. These scholars assert student employment has "the potential to deepen and enrich student learning" (Kuh, 2010). Although Pike et al. (2008) discovered working more than 20 hours had a negative impact on academics, they also uncovered a positive relation between student success and working 20 hours or less on campus, due to "greater levels of participation in active and collaborative learning activities and positive interactions between students and faculty members" (p. 579). Salisbury et al. (2012) found there was a direct positive impact on the development of leadership in first-year students who worked more than 20 hours a week off campus. In Moore and Rago's

(2009) review of National Survey of Student Engagement data on employment and engagement, indicated when students found meaning in their work by making connections between their current job's responsibilities and the transferability of their experience to their future career, they had a higher level of student engagement. As more students demonstrate the financial need to work to support their educational goals, it is critical to align leadership learning with meaningful student employment.

TYPES OF STUDENT EMPLOYMENT

For those employed by a university, the area of student employment most familiar may be traditional on-campus jobs. The top eight student employee hiring areas, as defined in a recent Student Affairs Administrators in Higher Education report on public and private institutions, included student life/student affairs, recreation services or fitness centers, residential life, academic departments, athletics, food service, academic support, and libraries (Burnside et. al, 2019). Some of these common hiring areas may offer more intentionally leadership-focused and empirical-derived development experiences than others. For example, while scholarship can be readily found on student employee leadership learning within recreation services or fitness centers on campus (Hall, 2013; McFadden & Carr, 2015; Tingle et al., 2013), many of the other hiring areas aforementioned are comparatively underrepresented in the extant literature.

On-campus employment funding typically comes from Federal Work-Study, departmental funds, institutional funds, or student activity fees (Burnside et al., 2019). Federal Work-Study shows the clearest relationship between work and financial aid needs, as this federal program funds part-time employment for students, with about 80% of the positions available being on campus (National Association of Student Financial Aid Administrators, 2016). Federal Work-Study has been found to have a self-reported positive effect on the college experience, as well as provide a way for students to integrate into the college environment (Scott-Clayton & Minaya, 2014; St. John et al., 2001). Additionally, one of the requirements of Federal Work-Study is for institutions, when possible, to place students in positions that will relate to their career goals (National Association of Student Financial Aid Administrators, 2016). This is an important linkage since students who make connections between their work and their future are more likely to be engaged (Moore & Rago, 2009).

The other type of employment we know our students are experiencing, but with less available data, is off-campus student employment. Examples of these opportunities span from jobs in the service industry, such as retail and restaurants, to paid internships and freelance work. Students who work off campus tend to spend more hours working and less hours on campus (Lang, 2012). While some research shows students are potentially gaining more leadership capacity in these roles when compared to their peers (Salisbury et al., 2012), time spent off campus leads to less time being able to participate in on-campus activities, elective courses, or on-campus employment, all of which can lead to more traditional leadership learning.

WHY IS STUDENT EMPOLOYMENT A SOCIAL JUSTICE ISSUE?

Primarily, it is important to discuss the financial implications of working. While some students may decide to seek employment to gain experience or as an extracurricular, many of our students have a financial obligation to work to stay enrolled. Between tuition, textbooks, and costs of living, there are students for whom it is necessary to work. We acknowledge the opportunity cost these students experience through loss of free time and energy for studying or seeking additional activities to stay engaged on campus. Focusing on maintaining academic excellence and employment means students choose between studying and working or traditional leadership learning opportunities, including leadership courses or leading a student organization. These same students may have to accept a minimum wage job or capped available hours if they are employed in an on-campus position. Although the potential for leadership learning may be built into these on-campus opportunities, the restrictions on compensation or hours may not ultimately offer substantial assistance. In these instances, an off-campus job offers more of an appeal to students with a greater financial need in order to stay enrolled.

Further consideration of the dichotomy between leadership learning and wage-earning forces us to ask, "Which students tend to suffer most in these scenarios?" All too often, the answer is: members of our community who already face barriers to success. According to University of California Undergraduate Experience Survey data reported by Brint and Cantwell (2010), first-generation and African American students, "spend more hours in paid employment than other students, and are often penalized for doing so with lower grades" (p. 2463). Thus, those underserved students who stand to gain the most from leadership learning opportunities are also those for whom college systems are poorly designed to support.

Next, we consider the power dynamics between supervisors and supervisees. Supervisors have structural authority over their supervisees, with students rarely able to exercise agency over their position. Supervisors often control their student's work schedules, especially in hourly paid positions, as well as wages, and pathways toward promotion into higher wage-earning positions. While on-campus supervisors may consider class schedules or needs outside of their jobs, off-campus supervisors may not make those same concessions. Supervisors also create and facilitate the work environment for the student, which impacts their experience beyond job satisfaction. When supervisors intentionally create employment environments around critical learning and reflection, they close the gap between wage earning and leadership learning.

These ideas permeate creating experiences for students in managerial positions as well. Among students who are outside of positional leader roles (like "manager"), it is usually not a priority for a professional supervisor to incorporate opportunities for leadership into the fabric of their general staff. In Bentrim et al.'s (2013) study on student employment, these disparities triggered the consideration of a "redesign of their student employment positions to include 'beginner' and 'advanced' responsibilities and intended learning objectives" (p. 32). Establishing such objectives and expanding these opportunities within our institutions can enrich meaning making for a larger population of students.

QUESTIONS FOR LEADERSHIP EDUCATORS

Intentionally considering working students' identities and their limited access to enriching leadership learning can help us build systems to provide what they need through positions they already hold. One lens through which to view such institutional structures to build meaningful experiences is with culturally relevant leadership learning (Bertrand Jones et al., 2016; Guthrie et al., 2017). Through this model, we view the identity, capacity, and efficacy of an individual and their effect on the subsequent leadership process. Simultaneously, we look at the impact of the historical legacy of exclusion/inclusion, compositional diversity, behavioral, organizational structure, and psychological dimensions of the environment to determine the best method for creating a socially just, equitable environment for student employees.

You may think of Figure 11.1 as identifying these dimensions as though they were the pieces of a popular trivia board game, with each section emblematic of a knowledge area. You can move forward or backward in the process by having none or all of what you seek to obtain, asking questions and not being correct or simply not answering them at all. However, the individual only succeeds the more categories are fulfilled. Likewise, the process itself is only completed once every represented area's question has been satisfactorily answered. The same can be said of the model in practice. A student employee can be employed without any context for

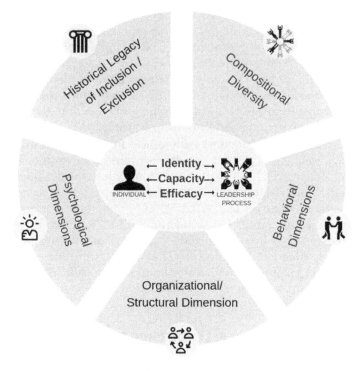

Figure 11.1.   Culturally relevant leadership learning model.

these things being under consideration by themselves, the institution, or the office that employs them. They may sometimes ask these questions about dimensions like historical legacy of inclusion/exclusion or compositional diversity and addressing them can fulfill one need or two for the environment to be more effective. Only by addressing all pieces can the student (and supervisor) understand the role of identity in the workplace, build capacity for doing their work well, and ultimately lead successfully.

Historical Legacy

Historical legacies of inclusion and exclusion involve observing how our practices prohibit people with certain social identities from being a part of our institutions and organizations and interrupting those cycles. For student employment, this can include reviewing staffing practices (including recruitment, hiring, and training) over the years. The broadest questions might stem from whether opportunities exist for Federal Work-Study students to be included in positions that offer traditional leadership opportunities. For housing or orientation, two commonly curriculum-based leadership learning areas, do resident assistants or orientation leaders have an hourly contract limit that curtails access by not allowing Federal Work-Study students to apply? While that may be noted, "It is not simply enough to acknowledge that these patterns of exclusion or inclusion exist(ed); leadership educators must then develop intentional ways to respond to such history" (Bertrand Jones et al., 2016, pp. 16–17). If the 20 hours per week caveat is difficult for offices with heightened hours demands, what are ways an office can change the opportunities they offer to be more equitable?

Compositional Diversity

The previous dimension may co-occur with observing compositional diversity as well. One superficial way to see this is through demographic office make-up and applicant pools. What current representation exists when it comes to students who have less access to traditional leadership opportunities? It also opens the opportunity to assess your team and learn more about the enrichment they get within your space. In the application and interview process for students who have never held a job before being hired, what opportunities are built in to the experience created for them to take an opportunity to lead, once trained?

Psychological Dimensions

For student employment, the psychological dimension can be seen in staff reflections, as well as assessing the environment from the student perspective. Are there methods for conducting reflections with general staff opportunities for feedback, or only among positional leaders? Do students perceive a difference in their experience versus the experiences of positional leaders like student managers and supervisors when it comes to leadership? Is there an opportunity to open up what projects general staff can have ownership over to engage differently? Also, consider the professional staffing within your office. Is there a difference between upper management versus administrative staff in the enrichment and development they can seek? Does a position's workload make it too prohibitive to seek leadership learning opportunities? Are specific positions overlooked in receiving leadership enrichment? Unless we directly ask individuals how they feel or what they perceive, we cannot know their thoughts about the environment.

Behavioral Dimensions

Culturally relevant leadership learning also describes a behavioral dimension, specifically in relation to the diversity of the group. While this can be observed by supervisors in some instances, think about the instances in which no professional staff is present for student interactions. Do certain students experience more trouble when it comes to picking up shifts when there is a defined financial need versus a perceived desire? Do students interact well based on varying social identities or the power dynamic between a positional student leader, as compared to general student staff? Partnering with offices for specific professional development training on campus related to diversity and inclusion can assist your students in building these skills.

Organizational and Structural Dimensions

The organizational and structural dimensions are represented most frequently in higher education through administrative, culture-shaping decisions like budgets, hiring, and promotions. What access is limited based on funding, time, or the structure of these positions? How can the latter be systematically changed to reflect a more cohesive structure intended to engage any student employee in such opportunities for learning?

While the questions previously posed point to some considerations, the best view of your own office can only come from you and your team. Asking broad, open-ended questions of yourself and your staff may focus on how each dimension appears in your office environment and/or parallel to your institution's campus climate. These questions must be looked at honestly, with the intent to make real change, even if they are at times challenging to admit. Who is historically excluded or included within your application, interview, and hiring processes? Do you conduct a needs assessment with your student staff? How do you approach and understand compositional diversity within your area? What do you do to prioritize wellness with psychological & behavioral dimensions? What expectations do you set with staff regarding mental and physical wellness/academics prior to their role on staff? How do you make that clear?

Table 11.1.   Reflection Questions by CRLL Dimension

CRLL Dimension	Reflection Questions
Historical legacy of inclusion/exclusion	• Are there populations of students unable to access certain positions in my office due to the historical make-up of the position?
Compositional diversity	• What current representation exists within your space when it comes to students who have less access to traditional leadership opportunities?
Psychological	• Have you asked student employees how they feel or perceive the office environment and the accessibility of leadership learning in their role?
Behavioral	• How do employees interact based on the varying social identities within the office?
Organizational/structural	• How does your office fund or support diverse learning opportunities, particularly in leadership learning for staff?

ON-CAMPUS EMPLOYERS
AS SOCIALLY JUST LEADERSHIP EDUCATORS

While we have identified some of the challenges students face and highlighted a few options for employers regarding leadership learning, there is still work to be done in deriving and implementing solutions. Whether assessing your own office to implement necessary change with your student employees, or transforming your larger campus or surrounding community, the next steps an individual office or institution takes have the power to shape students' experiences. In doing so, we aim to see how "positive change is self-perpetuating" (Hansen & Hoag, 2018).

In leadership learning activities, it is important to be purposeful when weaving lessons into work. "Lasting, meaningful growth transpires only when leadership lessons are embedded using a sustained approach" (Tingle et al., 2013, p. 11). Therefore, to produce effective leadership learning for student employees, we advise proceeding by educating with intentionality. One model that can be immediately incorporated to intentionally place learning directly into the work position is Iowa Guided Reflection on Work. This model consists of "brief, structured conversations between student employees and their supervisors to help students connect the skills and knowledge they are gaining in the classroom with the work they are doing" (University of Iowa, 2020). These conversations, framed by intentional questions from the supervisor, allows students to reflect on their work in a meaningful way. Iowa Guided Reflection on Work's four questions focus on making connections between work, academics, and the student's career path; however, these conversations could be expanded to include questions that focus on the leadership skills gained in the position.

There are other examples for curriculum building in student affairs employment, particularly related to recreation services. McFadden and Carr (2015) highlighted several institutions' recreation services leadership programs. Among them, Elon University, James Madison University, and Ohio State University are each recognized for their integrative approaches to leadership learning and student employee development. Through an intentional curriculum, a combination of student development and leadership theory are the guiding principles, beyond traditional employee training. If you intend to incorporate intentional leadership learning through the training process with students, it is wise to include that information from the start of their interview process, as "some students may not desire a work environment that is highly engaging with defined learning outcomes. They may be accustomed to performing routine jobs and want to maintain the status quo" (Hansen & Hoag, 2018). When students begin their experience with your office knowing the deliberate learning outcomes and reflection activities will be incorporated, they will not be surprised as they join the team.

Your office may also undertake advocacy as it relates to the creation of Federal Work-Study positions, especially if there are restrictions on your funding resources. In order to do so, we suggest building relationships with human resources and financial aid, as well as understanding how local laws affect these students' opportunities. Next, through building intentional reflections into these roles, the program is enriched and the opportunities for students expand, without having to increase departmental investments when funding sources are limited.

Finally, considering this chapter was written in 2020, we would be remiss to not include a "COVID-19 clause." With the unprecedented move to online learning in the spring of 2020, the nature of student employment was also dramatically impacted. Many positions had been halted or adapted to incorporate new responsibilities, new technology, or otherwise shift in ways heretofore unlike anything we have collectively experienced in higher education. At the time of writing, the reality of the future of student jobs is unknown. Funding cuts, shifting to fewer in-person campus activities and services, and a heavy emphasis on remote work has connected us together in a new, uncharted landscape.

There is, however, an optimistic lesson to be learned by this cultural shift. The systems established within our country and institutions, sometimes thought of as immutable, can be altered more than we may have previously considered. We encourage you to take the opportunity to redesign your positions to be socially just and focused on student leadership learning. In breaking the status quo and challenging "how things have always been done" we leverage our power as supervisors and advisors to create meaningful experiences with focused intentionality.

REFERENCES

Bentrim, E., Sousa-Peoples, K., Kachellek, G., & Powers, W. (2013). Assessing learning outcomes: Student employees in student affairs. *About Campus*, *18*(1), 29–32.

Bertrand Jones, T., Guthrie, K. L., & Osteen, L. (2016). Critical domains of culturally relevant leadership learning: A call to transform leadership programs. In K. L. Guthrie, T. Bertrand Jones, & L. Osteen (Eds.), *New Directions for Student Leadership: No. 152. Developing culturally relevant leadership learning* (pp. 9–21). Jossey-Bass.

Brint, S., & Cantwell, A. M. (2010). Undergraduate time use and academic outcomes: Results from the University of California Undergraduate Experience Survey 2006. *Teachers College Record*, *112*(9), 2441–2470.

Burnside, O., Wesley, A., Wesaw, A., & Parnell, A. (2019). Employing student success. *NASPA Student Affairs Administrators in Higher Education*. https://www.naspa.org/files/dmfile/NASPA_EmploymentStudentSuccess_FINAL_April1_LOWRES_REVISED.pdf

Dundes, L., & Marx, J. (2007). Balancing work and academics in college: Why do students working 10 to 19 hours per week excel? *Journal of College Student Retention: Research, Theory and Practice*, *8*(1), 107–120.

Guthrie, K. L., Bertrand Jones, T., & Osteen, L. (2017). The Teaching, Learning, and Being of Leadership: Exploring Context and Practice of the Culturally Relevant Leadership Learning Model. *Journal of Leadership Studies*, *11*(3), 61–67.

Hall, S. L. (2013). Influence of campus recreation employment on student learning. *Recreational Sports Journal*, *37*(2), 136–146.

Hansen, S. L., & Hoag, B. A. (2018), Promoting learning, career readiness, and leadership in student employment. In K. K. Smith, G. S. Rooney, & G. Spencer (Eds.), *New Directions for Student Leadership: No. 157, Leadership development for career readiness in university settings* (pp. 85–99). Jossey-Bass.

Issa, N. (2019. *U.S. Average Student Loan Debt Statistics in 2019*. Credit.com. https://www.credit.com/personal-finance/average-student-loan-debt/

Lang, K. B. (2012). The similarities and differences between working and non-working students at a mid-sized American public university. *College Student Journal*, *46*(2), 243–255.

King, J. (2006). *Working their way through college: Student employment and its impact on the college experience*. American Council on Education. https://www.acenet.edu/Documents/IssueBrief-2006-Working-their-way-through-College.pdf

Kuh, G. D. (2010). Maybe experience really can be the best teacher. *The Chronicle of Higher Education*. https://www.chronicle.com/article/Maybe-Experience-Really-Can-Be/125433/?sid=cr&utm_medium=en&utm_source=cr

Kuh, G. D., Kinzie, J., Cruce, T., Shoup, R., & Gonyea, R. M. (2007). *Connecting the dots: Multi-faceted analyses of the relationships between student engagement results from the NSSE, and the institutional practices and conditions that foster student success.* Indiana University Center for Postsecondary Research.

McFadden, C. W., & Carr, J. W. (2015). Collegiate recreation student employee as student leader. In D. A. Stenta & C. W. McFadden (Eds.), *New Directions for Student Leadership: No. 147. Student leadership development through recreation and athletics* (pp. 65–76). Jossey-Bass.

Moore, J. V., & Rago, M. (2009). The impact of employment on student engagement: Results from NSSE. In B. Perozzi (Ed.), *Enhancing student learning through college employment* (pp. 87–107). Association of College Unions International.

National Association of Student Financial Aid Administrators. (2016). *NASFAA research on federal work-study: Literature review and policy scan.* https://www.nasfaa.org/uploads/documents/NASFAA_2016_Advocacy_Literature_Review_and_Policy_Scan.pdf

Pike, G., Kuh, G., & Massa-McKinley, R. (2008). First-year students' employment, engagement, and academic achievement: Untangling the relationship between work and grades. *Journal of Student Affairs Research and Practice, 45*(4), 560–582. https://doi.org/10.2202/1949-6605.2011

Planty, M., Hussar, W., Snyder, T., Provasnik, S., Kena, G., Dinkes, R., Kewalramani, A., Kemp, J., & National Center for Education Statistics (Ed.). (2008). *The condition of education 2008* (NCES 2008-031). National Center for Education Statistics.

Riggert, S. C., Boyle, M., Petrosko, J. M., Ash, D., & Rude-Parkins, C. (2006). Student employment and higher education: Empiricism and contradiction. *Review of Educational Research, 76*(1), 63–92.

Salisbury, M. H., Pascarella, E. T., Padgett, R. D., & Blaich, C. (2012). The effects of work on leadership development among first-year college students. *Journal of College Student Development, 53*(2), 300–324.

Scott-Clayton, J., Minaya, V. (2014). Should student employment be subsidized? Conditional counterfactuals and the outcomes of work-study participation (A CAPSEE working paper). *Center for Analysis of Postsecondary Education and Employment.* Center for Analysis of Postsecondary Education and Employment.

Smedick, B., & Rice, E. (2018). An overview of leadership competencies and assessment considerations. In K. K. Smith, G. S. Rooney, & G. Spencer (Eds.), *New Directions for Student Leadership: No. 157. Leadership development for career readiness in university settings* (pp. 55–70). Jossey-Bass.

St. John, E. P., Hu, S., & Weber, J. (2001). State policy and the affordability of public higher education: The influence of state grants on persistence in Indiana. *Research in Higher Education, 42*(4), 401–428.

Tingle, J. K., Cooney, C., Asbury, S. E., & Tate, S. (2013). Developing a student employee leadership program: The importance of evaluating effectiveness. *Recreational Sports Journal, 37*(1), 2–13.

University of Iowa. (2020, July 29). *Iowa GROW.* https://vp.studentlife.uiowa.edu/priorities/grow/

CHAPTER 12

REDEFINING ENGAGEMENT

Including International Students in Socially Just Leadership Education

Benjamin G. Cecil and Pei Hu

International students represent a vital yet often overlooked and misunderstood group within the fabric of our campus communities in the United States. Given the unique challenges international students face, many student affairs professionals are underequipped, timid, or downright unsure of how to engage with members of this population. In this chapter, we define "international student" as a degree-seeking individual present on a U.S.-based campus who holds a nonimmigrant student visa. We chose these factors to highlight leadership education and socially just engagement practices specific to this unique population and to draw parallels and differences between their domestic peers. This chapter provides an overview of today's international student in the United States; highlighting the specific challenges these students face on our campuses, underscoring barriers to academic and cocurricular engagement, and providing strategies to enhance leadership educators' understanding of interculturally competent and socially just engagement practices with international students.

Shifting the Mindset: Socially Just Leadership Education
pp. 139–148
Copyright © 2021 by Information Age Publishing
All rights of reproduction in any form reserved.

DEFINING ENGAGEMENT FOR INTERNATIONAL STUDENTS

The temptation to stereotype this particular group of students is pervasive. To better understand engagement, leadership, and social justice in a cross-cultural context, we must first seek to understand today's international student. According to the 2019 Institute for International Education Open Doors report:

- In 2018–2019, there were 1,095,299 international students enrolled within the United States. This is a growth of 0.05% from 2017–2018.
- The top 10 places of origin of enrolling students in the United States are China, India, South Korea, Saudi Arabia, Canada, Vietnam, Taiwan, Japan, Brazil, and México.
- The top 10 states hosting international students are California, New York, Texas, Massachusetts, Illinois, Pennsylvania, Florida, Ohio, Michigan, and Indiana.
- Of the degree-seeking student population in 2018–2019, nearly 432,000 were undergraduate students and nearly 378,000 were graduate students. The remaining students are nondegree seeking or on optional practical training. Optional practical training allows limited work opportunities for those in the United States on a non-immigrant student visa following graduation.

Importance of Culturally Relevant Engagement in Leadership and Social Justice

International students crave engagement in the U.S. campus experience. Among the most unique and desirable aspects of education in the United States are the flexibility and holistic growth. Engagement opportunities, from leadership programs and experiences to academic involvement or student organizations, are aspects of the campus experience many international students seek. Other educational systems place different values on the cocurricular experience, leading many international students to seek the "American college experience" in the United States. Given the various perspectives of international students, it is important to begin from our assumptions and reconceptualize engagement for an international population.

Student affairs staff often face challenges understanding the specific needs of international students. Culturally relevant engagement requires thoughtful reflection on our own values, beliefs, attitudes, and perspectives. Particularly as they relates to leadership, engagement, and social justice, many of us may find our perspectives to be Western-centric; we understand leadership from the perspective of Western cultural values. Anthropologist Edward Hall (1981) recognized the difference between "high context" and "low context" cultures, noting how we all communicate and understand across a cultural medium is dependent on our own backgrounds. Hall (1981) noted that high-context cultures tend to communicate in implicit ways and rely heavily on the context of the situation, where low context cultures are more explicit. If we only consider engagement from a high-context perspective, what are students who may be more low-context missing? Does engagement perhaps look different, or present unique challenges, for a nonnative English speaker?

Leadership is defined differentially by cultural context. United States higher education tends to favor broader definitions, like Komives et al. (2007) defining leadership as a relational process working to make change. The focus on relationships and capacity building is only one example of the Western influences on U.S. higher education's approach toward leadership. In a 2005 study on leadership identity development, Komives and colleagues acknowledged a shift away from leadership as, "essentially good management behaviors ... in an industrial era where the predominant goals of leadership were production and efficiency" (p. 593). While the U.S. context may be making this shift within higher education, not every culture experiences this in the same way. Societal values and individual cultural values play a large role in defining leadership, beyond only what it means to be a "leader." Concepts of leadership exist beyond hierarchies—a perspective that many international students relate to—and into specific ideas of how students can, or should be, leaders. This often includes dissonance among leadership and gender roles, familial responsibility, and age, among other social location factors.

Socially just student affairs professionals recognize how values orient our understanding of leadership as well as our students' self-perceptions within college. Notably, both individualistic (more low context) and collectivist (more high context) cultures share unique cultural values that extend beyond the individual or family level. Take the idea of orientation to time: The United States values time in very different ways than other cultures—namely, in our constant desire to be "doing" and looking ahead to the future. Engagement, leadership, and access to such experiences within college stem from a U.S.-centric perspective. Moving to a culturally competent and inclusive approach is critical to engage international students into such opportunities.

One of the most complex issues facing leadership education and international student engagement is the shift toward social justice perspectives. Although this perspective has made incredible progress in raising the importance of creating just, fair, and equitable societies through leadership, this perspective can also alienate international students. Much of what is describe as social justice in the United States today finds its roots in historical efforts to marginalize various groups based on identity. With the cultural context of social justice, students lacking cultural capital and understanding of the historical marginalization of such groups remain excluded from these conversations. The term "social justice" may be seen as a taboo inappropriate to discuss in public forums, such as within a university. Although we understand and champion the perspectives of equity and social justice on today's campuses, we also acknowledge how social justice as we have come to know it within our society today reflects a predominately Western perspective.

Common Barriers to International Student Engagement in Leadership

Despite being some of the bravest students on campuses, international students nonetheless face unique challenges from other students. The navigation of multiple, intersecting identities—working to understand and adapt to a new culture while maintaining and finding ways to celebrate one's own native culture—is noble and often undervalued. We note a few obstacles international students may differentially face in engagement and leadership learning:

- **Pressure to perform academically.** Most international undergraduates are full fee- and tuition-paying students. To receive a nonimmigrant student visa, students must show the financial capital available, in liquid funds, to pay for tuition, room, board, and other expenses. This increases pressures to perform academically; not only to maintain high grades, but also ensure their (or their family's) investment yields returns.
- **Engagement processes situated outside of a framework of cultural understanding.** The configuration of student organizations and application-based programs for engagement is another U.S.-centered concept. Programs which are not academically related and carry an application process or fee create cultural and structural barriers for international students.
- **English proficiency.** Most universities in the United States require students to meet score thresholds on the Test of English as a Foreign Language exam. While students may be proficient in English as measured by the exam, they are not necessarily proficient in the associated cultural competency. Popular culture refer-

ences, slang, and regional accents and/or dialects make English communication more challenging than such a test can measure.

- **Visualizing self as "leader."**   Many undergraduate students may lack the cultural capital to visualize themselves as leaders on campus. The focus on academics, lack of understanding as to why cocurricular engagement may be important for their overall success, and not wanting to be viewed as a burden for a lack of understanding of cultural difference all challenge students' leader self-perceptions.

The higher education landscape for all students continues to change in response to COVID-19. Digital engagement remains a relatively new frontier, but one that played a major role on campuses throughout 2020. In the same way engagement strategies and experiences may differ for international students, so will online engagement. Additionally, students who may have chosen to return to their home countries may lack access to common social media platforms used for engagement on a U.S.-based campus, in addition to significant time differences to engage fully with their online courses and activities. These challenges call for an increased understanding of the international student experience when considering engagement and leadership in all formats.

SOCIALLY JUST LEADERSHIP EDUCATION FOR INTERNATIONAL STUDENTS

Higher education institutions in the United States continue to diversify, with increasing numbers of international students coming from all over the world to attend U.S. colleges and universities (Mukminin & McMahon, 2013; Wang et al., 2012). The cultural and economic benefits, which international students bring to colleges and universities in the United States, are clear. Institutions have learned more about student characteristics of international students for recruitment and retention initiatives (Mamiseishvili, 2012). However, our understanding of leadership in this context is still limited, often due to our own cultural perspectives.

Considering student leadership development as a commonly stated outcome of undergraduate education (Association of American Colleges and Universities, 2012; Guthrie et al., 2013), higher education's success is deeply intertwined with its understanding of leadership education for international students on U.S. campuses. A growing number of scholars and leadership educators have explored college student leadership identity and capacity development (Day et al., 2009; Dugan & Komives, 2007; Komives et al., 2005; Komives et al., 2006). Some scholars sharpen their focus on the intersection of leadership and diversity; this intersection is valuable as U.S. higher education experiences constant transformation within the context of globalization and diversification. Leadership programs increasingly open doors to engagement for students from diverse populations identifying within the racial or ethnic minority, LGBTQ+ students, and students with disabilities, to name a few. However, not enough have focused on international student leadership development. Higher education offers little regarding how leadership education and programs cultivate leadership identity and capacity within members of international student populations.

A Missing Piece—
International Student Engagement in the Literature

The existing literature discussing leadership as it pertains to international students is scant, at best. Does this show that leadership development for international students is not an important topic worthy of further research? Reviewing the educational goals of higher education and institutional mission statements of multiple institutions in the United States, we posit leadership development for international students shares the same importance as their domestic peers. There are many unanswered questions for leadership educators, particularly those with a social justice orientation, to answer by opening narratives and challenging stereotypes around leadership education for international students, thereby removing barriers to their engagement.

One reason for the lack of scholarship around international student leadership development may stem from assuming 'international' as international students' most salient identity. Such stereotyping creates subconscious challenges for leadership educators who may not know how to engage members of this population across cultures. Another reason may be how different cultures define, value, and understand concepts of leadership. As Dorfman et al. (1997) noted, "while the phenomenon of leadership is widely considered to be universal across cultures, the way in which it is operationalized is usually viewed as culturally specific" (p. 233). Cultural values influence how international students perceive themselves as leaders. Socially just leadership educators understand diverse cultural values shared by international students, as these values influence their views of the campus experience. When leadership educators understand international students' perceptions of leadership from cultural values-based lenses, they are better suited to create environments for international students to explore leadership identity. A reconciliation of these values proves challenging for international students who may or may not return to their home countries following graduation. The perception of being "not American enough" in the United States and subsequently 'too Americanized' in their respective home culture has implications related to acculturative stressors. As such, values play a large role in a student's educational journey on campus, understanding how those values may be in harmony or may conflict with the in-college experience and postcollege environment.

The relational leadership model (RLM; Komives et al., 2007) allows student affairs professionals to approach international student leadership development from a socially just lens by developing process-oriented leadership education for international students. Komives et al.'s definition of leadership within the RLM shows how definitions we use excludes members of international populations. As Komives et al. (2007) mentioned, the RLM is not a tool used to describe how leadership functions in all groups and organizations, but an aspirational model to support "healthy, ethical, effective groups" (p. 75). The five primary components in the RLM are purpose, inclusive, ethical, empowering, and process. For example, if the purpose of the international student office is to engage international students with leadership development programs, we need to consider how the international student office could achieve this goal while benefiting international students involved in the process. At the individual level, students also benefit from knowing themselves (culture values, leadership perspectives, etc.) before they engage in leadership opportunities. Developing leadership education programs using the RLM fosters interculturally competent environments for international students and encourages all students to work across cultures, influencing change and achieving common goals.

RECOMMENDATIONS FOR PRACTICE

This chapter highlighted several barriers international students face related to engagement on modern U.S. college campuses. We encourage student affairs professionals to be aware of these perspectives when learning with international students. However, it is important to reframe these challenges from the deficit narrative and gain a deeper sense of empathy and desire to create socially just learning. When colleges and universities view international students beyond the revenue they bring to campus, they more fully realize the promise of producing global leaders for the next century and beyond. To those ends, we offer the following recommendations for socially just leadership learning with international students:

- **Reflecting on cultural values deeply embedded into our own perspectives.** The most difficult first step on the journey toward socially just leadership learning among members of international populations is to reflect on our own culture, cultural values, and culture-bound definitions of leadership. It is important to ask ourselves how we came to believe what we believe, how we define leadership, and the life experiences informing such beliefs. We each hold identities and biases, but how we experience those identities depends on the cultural lenses we use to view the world. It is critically important to train ourselves as leadership educators to refrain from negatively judging cultural phenomena we interpret as different. Different is not inherent good or bad—it is simply what we are unaccustomed to. We may readily understand these differences, but we can nonetheless accept and value the cultural perspectives our students bring to campus.

- **Embed leadership opportunities within academic contexts.** Working with academic units to situate leadership opportunities within academic activities will be increasingly important in the coming years. This requires critical assessment of how academic units can be involved with leadership learning opportunities and the creation of specific opportunities to connect such experiences directly to students' academic pursuits.

- **Reorient leadership opportunities toward equity.** Socially just leadership education moves beyond Western perspectives and considers leadership as a global phenomenon. This means teaching students the importance of difference, how to understand others, and working through differences when our own values may come into conflict with what we perceive to be unequitable or unjust in other cultures. This work is not the sole responsibility of the professionals in the international student services office. Cultural inclusivity demands an institutional commitment to global perspectives and a prioritization within the ethos of student affairs and services units.

- **Reframe student training and development to be interculturally competent.** How do you train your student leaders to be more interculturally competent? Are your students able to communicate effectively with their peers from different cultural or language backgrounds? Are your programs set up to include opportunities to understand leadership from a variety of cultural perspectives?

- **Make recruitment and selection processes culturally responsive.** How are you working to make processes like interviews more culturally sensitive? Not all cultures view eye contact as a sign of confidence and strength—for some, it is a sign of disrespect. How do you define professionalism or professional dress? What if shaking hands with someone of a different gender is inappropriate? Would you understand this cultural difference, or view it as a student's inability to connect with others? When considering these perspectives from a strictly American lens, it puts international students at a disadvantage and increases potential for exclusion when interviews or processes for selection lie in elements of cultural capital of which students may not have access.

- **International student education in graduate preparation programs.** Graduate preparation programs must embed global engagement and inclusive leadership perspectives into curricula, exposing budding student affairs professionals to global ideas early in their careers. Creating a global mindset through study abroad and opportunities to explore student development theory beyond a noninternational student audience contributes not only to the professional development of young practitioners but also to diversity and inclusion efforts.

CONCLUSION

We hope our chapter shifts your mindset around socially just leadership education with members of international populations. The precipice for effective engagement and leadership education for international populations starts with effectively understanding the cultural values orientation we bring to our work. From here, develop deeper understandings of difference without judgment; moving away from deficit-based approaches to those that relish how we teach and learn through difference. Moving beyond a truly Amero-centric approach to leadership education serves educational outcomes, as contemporary society demands graduates who are competent with leadership skills and proficient in skills in intercultural communication, and the ability to work across cultural contexts. Although we may find it challenging to return to the introspection and reflection required to understand our own cultural perspectives and values, the humbling experience of doing so may challenge what we believe to be true within leadership education, theory, and student development. This challenge requires a great deal of bravery in its own right to rethink and critically assess how we understand leadership. The return, however, creates more inclusive campus environments and leadership education opportunities that actually include all students—regardless of where they may call home.

REFERENCES

Association of American Colleges and Universities. (2012). *A crucible moment: College learning & democracy's future*.

Day, D. V., Harrison, M. M., & Halpin, S. M. (2009). *An integrative approach to leader development: Connecting adult development, identity, and expertise*. Routledge.

Dorfman, P. W., Howell, J. P., S., Lee, J. K., Tate, U., & Bautista, A. (1997). Leadership in Western and Asian countries: Commonalities and differences in effective leadership processes. *Leadership Quarterly, 8*(3), 233–274.

Dugan, J. P., & Komives, S. R. (2007). *Developing leadership capacity in college students: Findings from a national study*. National Clearinghouse for Leadership Programs.

Guthrie, K. L., Bertrand Jones, T., Osteen, L., & Hu, S. (2013). *Cultivating leader identity and capacity in students from diverse backgrounds: ASHE Higher Education Report, 39*(4). Wiley.

Hall, E. T. (1981). *Beyond culture*. Random House.

Institute of International Education. (2019). *Open Doors Report 2019*. https://www.iie.org/Why-IIE/Announcements/2019/11/Number-of-International-Students-in-the-United-States-Hits-All-Time-High

Komives, S. R., Longerbeam, S. D., Owen, J. E., Mainella, F. C., & Osteen, L. (2006). A leadership identity development model: Application from a grounded theory. *Journal of College Student Development, 47*(4), 401–418.

Komives, S. R., Lucas, N., & McMahon, T. R. (2007). *Exploring leadership: For college students who want to make a difference* (2nd ed.). Jossey-Bass.

Komives, S. R., Owen, J. E., Longerbeam, S. D., Mainella, F. C., & Osteen, L. (2005). Developing a leadership identity: A grounded theory. *Journal of College Student Development, 46*(6), 593–611.

Mamiseishvili, K. (2012). International student persistence in U.S. postsecondary institutions. *Higher Education, 64*(1), 1–17.

Mukminin, A., & McMahon, B. J. (2013). International graduate students' cross-cultural academic engagement: Stories of Indonesian doctoral students on an American campus. *The Qualitative Report, 18*(69), 1–19.

Wang, K. T., Heppner, P. P., Fu, C. C., Zhao, R., Li, F., & Chuang, C. C. (2012). Profiles of acculturative adjustment patterns among Chinese international students. *Journal of Counseling Psychology, 59*(3), 424–436.

CHAPTER 13

BEYOND COMPETITION

Developing Student-Athletes
Through Socially Just Leadership Education

Kathryn C. King and Catherine A. Badger

The role of intercollegiate athletics in American higher education, and its effect on students who participate in certain highly emphasized sports, have been subjects of a long-standing debate (Hood et al., 1992). This debate stems from concerns "athlete" is emphasized over "student" in the university setting. The term student-athlete denotes individuals who are asked to manage and succeed at the tasks that make up two different realms of life: athletics and academics (Woodruff & Schallert, 2008). Student-athletes have extreme demands placed on them to perform on the athletic field; demands which may risk academic and individual development, causing scholastic achievement and motivation to suffer. For these reasons, questions persist regarding the growth and development of student-athletes beyond competition (Howard-Hamilton & Sina, 2001). One natural connection point for growth and development between roles is the leadership development of athletes. Leadership is a fundamental aspect of sports, particularly within team sport environments (Cotterill & Fransen, 2015). Additionally, leadership development allows students to gain skills that transfer far beyond their years as a student-athlete (Weaver

Shifting the Mindset: Socially Just Leadership Education
pp. 149–160
Copyright © 2021 by Information Age Publishing

& Simet, 2015). This chapter identifies ways to engage student athletes' leadership development through the use of social justice education.

LEADERSHIP DEVELOPMENT

Leadership is socially constructed through interpersonal relationships and dependent on the surrounding context of teammates, coaches, and other student-athletes (Cotterill & Fransen, 2015; Dugan, 2017; Guthrie & Jenkins, 2018). A large part of student athletes' identity is rooted in their athletic self (Hill et al., 2001). The contexts of academic and athletic pursuits join together two different sets of motivations and perceptions to create a major part of the experiences of the student-athlete at the institution (Woodruff & Schallert, 2007). Playing an intercollegiate sport adds an unexpectedly complex layer to student life (Watt & Moore, 2001), which creates complications in the college environment. Student-athletes as a group have problems adapting to, and succeeding in, a university system that fails to recognize their unique developmental challenges (Engstrom et al., 1995).

Leadership Identity Development Model

A review of the literature associated with student-athletes and leadership development confirmed there is little to no athlete-specific research in this area. Findings focused on the athlete-only population are often underreported as access to study athletes is often limited. Many athletic departments are wary of exposing athletes to experiences beyond sport and academic pursuits. There is great concern for the time demands placed on student-athletes and those who are considered the gatekeepers to study athletes are often closed to considering new opportunities. Lastly, the National Collegiate Athletic Association has required surveys athletes must take on a rotating basis. Even though a student-athlete specific model is not referenced in this chapter, a model that separates this population from their peers is not needed. As such, this chapter is informed by the leadership identity development (LID) model (Komives et al., 2005; Komives et al., 2006).

The six stages highlighted in the LID model provide a phased approach to the leader development process. Stage development occurs with the assistance of time, influence of others and a willingness to engage in identity development (Komives et al., 2005). Student athletes have traditionally already transitioned through the first and second stages of the LID model, *awareness* and *exploration/engagement* respectively, as members of athletic teams assist in the identification of external leaders during their involvement in youth sport. Stage 3, *leader identified*, begins during high school as leadership is often attached to a specific individual within their team or organization (Komives et al., 2005). Commonly referred to as a captain, the other members of the team follow this individual, frequently viewing them as a role model. Prior to beginning college, a student athlete may progress to *leadership differentiated*, Stage 4, and bring an understanding that the responsibility of leadership does not rest with a lone individual as captain but includes all members of the team, or may arrive in Stage 3 with the potential to progress. The recognition that the process of leadership requires the entire group, and one does not need a formal position to be involved in the process, is a key component in continuing to progress through LID stages (Komives et al., 2005; Komives et al., 2006).

Often seen among upperclassmen, junior and senior student-athletes, Stage 5 of *generativity* highlights the sense of recognizing one's individual style of leadership and the desire to assist others in progressing through their stages of leadership (Hall, 2015; Komives et al., 2005). On athletic teams, mentorship between older and younger teammates can develop organically, or with the specific direction by a coach. Leadership is shared within teams where the coaches, captains, and informal leaders work together and share different leadership roles (Cotterill & Fransen, 2015). The final LID stage, *integration/synthesis*, may or may not occur during the tenure of a collegiate student athlete. An awareness that leadership development continues through one's lifespan requires a confidence in their leader identity that may require time after college to fully develop (Hall, 2015).

Student-Athlete Identity

Student-athletes learn to adapt athletically to a new environment and a new level of challenge as well as to the other changes facing their peers, e.g., expanded social, emotional, and academic experiences (Hester, 1990). Student athletes' identity is also strongly rooted in their athletic self (Hill et al., 2001). Unlike other college students, student-athletes face an additional set of complex demands, stresses, and challenges that arise from their involvement in a competitive sport (Broughton & Neyer, 2001). Sedlacek (2004) argued student athletes meet the definition of a nontraditional population in college because of the unique experiences and the great deal of time student athletes spend together. Athletes, as a nontraditional group, are burdened with many demands resulting from the existing structure of intercollegiate athletics that pose challenges to their academic success and the overall quality of their college experience (Comeaux & Harrison, 2011).

Many who are not aware of the typical athlete schedule may develop negative biases toward the student-athlete (Weaver & Simet, 2015). There are common misconceptions about student-athletes' dedication to academic work and the larger campus community (Comeaux, 2011; Weaver & Simet, 2015). Student-athletes may experience prejudice and discrimination, much as students from other nontraditional cultures or groups (Sedlacek, 2004). Professors and staff who discount the possibility of good work coming from athletes perpetuate the belief that is difficult for those students to be successful. High-quality academic performance of student-athletes is often questioned in university environments (Watt & Moore, 2001). Student-athletes must cope with public scrutiny and extensive time demands on top of regular coursework, which is not the typical experience of the average college student (Carodine et al., 2001).

As with many population-specific definitions, athletes can be discriminated against by solely having the title assigned and in different situations. Athletes are often stereotyped and believed to have a singular purpose on college campuses. Watt and Moore (2001) found when the athlete identity is emphasized, it leads to the perpetuation of stereotypes in which student-athletes are portrayed as academically unequal, unintelligent, and socially impotent. This is particularly true when the athlete is from higher revenue generating sports, and have serious professional opportunities. Decisions about their motivation and ability are greatly assumed to be against the academic mission. DeBard and Eberly (2014) found student affairs practitioners desire to include those traditionally socially ostracized in higher education. How we engage these students to be part of the whole campus depends greatly on the socially just beliefs held by administrators on campus about the athlete's desire to be a holistically engaged student. When professional development with staff who will and want to engage with athletes avoid excessively highlighting athlete identity, and allow the student have an identity tied to the institution independent of their athletic association, they contribute to a culture of respect toward student athletes.

Intersection of Athletes and Social Justice

During the 2020 spring championship segment in athletics, competition seasons were cut short and a crisis in athletics began. The COVID-19 pandemic required massive changes for higher education as a whole; athletic departments across the country struggled for identity and connectivity without sport. At the same time, calls against systematic racism and organized protest after the death of George Floyd, and other incidents of police violence against Black people, occurred and college athletes are at the front line leading the conversations about racial injustice and using their power to initiate change at their institutions (Anderson, 2020). In a time of crisis in college athletics, many Division I athletic programs announced new positions related to diversity and inclusion on their senior staff recognizing the need to promote the initiative. These positions are described as well integrated into the campus community and work in concert with student affairs professionals to support the institution's infrastructure across all departments. These new roles and the voice of the athlete being heard, demonstrate the importance of socially just education and leadership development among athletes. Student-athlete activism is leading the charge for voter registration (Thamel, 2020), changing the state flag of Mississippi to remove the Confederate symbols (Anderson, 2020), and shaping the national conversation through the use of social media (Tracy, 2020). With the backdrop of a global pandemic, student-athletes are activating their power to create change. Socially just practitioners equip themselves to assist in the leadership development of these students by understanding how they impact the social justice landscape.

PRACTICAL IMPLICATIONS

The athletic staff who work with student-athletes start with the recruiting process during high school. These relationships allow for trust-building before students arrive on campus. In turn, students perceive added value to the programming the athletic staff offers when they enroll. Student affairs professionals with a desire to engage the student-athlete population develop relationships over time, similarly to athletic staff members, and provide safe spaces for dialogue surrounding leadership development. Socially just practitioners are mindful of word choice to avoid athlete versus nonathlete scenarios, thereby creating socially just conversations. They also acknowledge the language used by athletes and athletic department staff in these spaces. It is common to refer to the programming offered to all students as "on campus" and the places that students need to go outside of the athletic complex as on campus too. This distinction occurs on many large, Division I, campus constructs. While it is not automatically problematic, phrasing influences feelings of separateness among students, as well as the internal versus external nature of programming. There are ways to approach this intersection and to engage the professionals in both areas of campus to think about overlapping priorities and initiatives. Involving a social justice lens represents a different way of thinking; not specifically what to think (DeBard & Eberly, 2014). Providing the opportunity for reflection on their own actions, as well as on the actions taken by others, expands personal leadership identity definitions and development.

Despite popular misconceptions, there is no reason to believe that all athletes naturally gain leadership skills through sport. Although the recognition of leadership may occur, it is important to intentionally develop these skills. Leader identity, and leadership orientations, evolve over time. In the early stages of leadership identity, adults were more influential as role models (Komives et al., 2005). This example is representative of the focus we have on our students with the leadership teachings coming from the student-athlete development professionals and academic athletic professionals.

Athletic Support Professionals and Campus Connection

Student-athletes benefit from opportunities to develop a broad foundation of perspectives, knowledge, and experiences to make appropriate career choices and successful transitions (Hill et al., 2001). Even in the case of an academically gifted student, the combination of academic and athletic requirements can cause incredible strain (Carodine et al., 2001). For these reasons, all Division I schools are required by the National Collegiate Athletic Association to provide academic support and counseling services to enrolled student-athletes (Friedman, 2004). These services are provided to all student-athletes regardless of sport, scholarship status, or prior academic achievements. While specific athletic areas can parallel the support available to all students on campus, specific support professionals tend to work with athletes on a daily basis, providing an opportunity for enriched relationships. When student affairs professionals who work to engage the athletic department staff are involved in the planning of athlete specific programming, they help create an overlap which encourages athlete engagement and involvement with the institution at large. Socially just student affairs professionals start with academics or student-athlete development areas because of the shared desire to integrate athletes more fully with the campus at large. Coaches, while instrumental to athlete decision making and support, may be underinformed on social justice initiatives in the same frame. In a broad sense, coaches may tend to think about the connection to athletic success with a secondary focus on development. This understanding is not meant to devalue how coaches engage with students, but to acknowledge the reality of collegiate athletics.

When we think about leadership development of student-athletes, we recognize the ability of athletic departments to work with students over time. Much of the collegiate focus is on one class, one semester, or one retreat. Within the realm of the athletic department, it is possible to have a student for up to 5 years and see dramatic growth over that time. Despite attrition due to transfer, general professional sport opportunities, and roster management, the unusual nature of having students from the summer before their freshman year through graduation, (or even graduate school) is a significant advantage in learning leadership. Consequently, we continually update and adjust programming to meet the needs of the students. Since relationships are established early, fewer superficial experiences occur. Therefore, taking advantage of highlighting in conversation, opportunities for leadership within the team setting is a possibility; thus setting the stage for movement from Stage 4 to Stage 5 of the LID model. Regularly challenging student-athletes to move beyond predesignated leaders requires expansion in thought process and patience to follow the evolution over time. This longitudinal approach to leadership development deeply impacts the continually evolving athlete's identity.

Connecting student-athletes with the experiences of the general campus student population is important to prevent students from becoming isolated and missing the tremendous opportunities available for all students. The design of leadership learning must vary since athletes' available time is so limited. Student-athletes encounter new ideas, values, and norms as they navigate their college careers, but the degree to which this integration occurs varies (Comeaux & Harrison, 2011). Student-athletes may feel isolated from the other students as they spend so much time and energy participating in athletics with their athletic peers (Simons et al., 1999). A disconnection to campus can result from participating in athletics, which can cause a negative experience for the student-athlete (Carodine et al., 2001).

Peer Mentors

Many athletics programs incorporate adult mentors and leaders to support student athletes (Weaver & Simet, 2015). Hall (2015) highlighted the importance of experienced students as mentors to new students. Many institutions use the summer to provide programming geared specifically for transitioning student-athletes to college expectations; academically and athletically. Leadership opportunities exist for returning student-athletes to mentor new students who are about to embark on their collegiate journey. For incoming students, these mentors are leaders to emulate. Providing role models during the impressionable transition time helps new student-athletes move through leadership development processes as soon as the following year. Those serving as mentors benefit from embracing their own leadership identity and empowering their mentees.

When selecting peer mentors, we advise searching beyond those students who have the highest grades or are the best athlete in the program. Interview and select athletes who have had the opportunity to grow and reflect meaningfully on their development while at the institution. We find these students are uniquely suited to connect to the experiences of freshmen and understand times of failure are ahead. These students are all coming into the university as top recruits from their high schools, and from a long-standing emphasis on their athletic ability. Once the student arrives at the college, their athletic identity is immediately highlighted through the transition to college workouts and new teammates. Summer bridge programming gives students opportunities to connect across sports, while simultaneously learning from seasoned student-athletes who successfully navigated similar circumstances.

In an effort to meet student-athletes where they are in the LID model, and assist in development to and through Stage 4, a first year programming course is an often utilized opportunity. Creating their own "brand" as a student athlete representing as an individual, as a member of their team and their institution provides a comfortable atmosphere to assess their impact on the bigger picture. Additionally, coach involvement has a significant impact on the leadership trajectory of student-athletes. A lack of focus on leadership development among their charges may slow movement from Stage 3 or 4 upon arrival, or to 5 or 6 upon departure.

Athlete Leadership Programming

The relationships built with athletics support staff foster students' sense of belonging, especially among those who are having trouble viewing themselves as undergraduates. By highlighting the experiences of athletes through focused leadership development programming, with a foundation from social justice education, we provide avenues for successful transition in the college environment and beyond. The basic tenants of social justice education include dialogue, critical thinking, reflection, and understanding the experience of others (Guthrie & Chunoo, 2018). The framework intercollegiate athletics provides, with application of leadership programs, fosters dialogue, reflection, and practice to occur. Focusing on the connections between leadership programming in athletics and the ideals of social justice education benefits everyone involved.

It is important to think about the type of athlete who is participating in the leadership programming. Wolniak et al. (2001) provided a context for having the different type of sport athlete as a part of the planning process. They found participating in revenue-generating sports may entail involvement in a peer subculture, which differentially impacts student learning and cognitive development during college when compared to participation in nonrevenue sports. As such, a universally applicable model for the leadership development of all athletes may not be possible. However, some social identity-based leadership development interventions for student-athletes exist. We choose to highlight one such program as an example to inspire others.

Leaders Yearning for Excellence (LYFE): *Beyond the Spear;* a development program for academic and personal growth among Black male student-athletes, connects Florida State University student-athletes with members of both the campus and surrounding communities. Since the program's inception in 2015, the LYFE team has planned and executed over 40 events aimed at accomplishing objectives derived from culturally relevant pedagogy (Mungin et al., 2018). This program provides leadership and life skills to support members of a student athlete demographic who traditionally come to universities underprepared. Based on trends in existing data, individuals in this group benefit greatly from additional levels of support and mentorship not garnered in the classroom. Through the use of targeted, efficient trainings we pinpoint ways to engage the time-limited student-athlete. The program also provides mentorship through our administrative team. LYFE programming combines guest speakers, competitive activities, and team building that fosters leadership development in a manner that involves social justice education (Mungin et al., 2018). Socially just programming supports and encourages critical reflection in learning (Boss et al., 2018). The mentorship provided by the administrative team is specifically designed to involve a social justice focus, which maximizes its impact.

Socially just leadership educators understand the impact of the institution, athletic department, and the sport program on students' social justice development. As athletes work together, real change can be seen nationwide. Through the efforts of several athletes, and with guidance from student affairs professionals and support staff in athletics, the National Collegiate Athletic Association (2020) officially designated election day 2020 as a competition- and practice-free day for all student-athletes. Comeaux and Harrison (2011) discussed how athletic demands placed on student-athletes, and the types of engagement activities provided for them, influence learning and personal development in relation to academic success and college experience. They acknowledged the role of student affairs professionals in athlete development. Student affairs leaders who use authentically responsive strategies maximize their effectiveness with student-athletes across difference (Comeaux & Harrison, 2011).

CONCLUSION

Understanding the impact of the athlete identity on the development of these students as future leaders helps inform programming with members of this population. Athletes are often isolated and need nuanced support to be integrated into the campus community. Through the work of dedicated individuals in athletics departments and various student affairs offices, these students can be reached at multiple points in their career. In addition to the daily routine of college life, student-athletes have many sport-related activities that take up a substantial amount of time (Watt & Moore, 2001). As outlined in this chapter, much of the efforts focused on athlete leadership development can be framed from a social justice context. Athletes are often categorized and pigeon-holed into a place that is negative and against the mission of the institution of higher education; however, quite the opposite is often true. These students are well rounded, embody the ideals of holistic development, and often become productive citizens ready to take on the world. Socially just leadership education for student athletes moves them beyond competition and into lives oriented around making the world a fairer, just, equitable place for everyone.

REFERENCES

Anderson, G. (2020, July 2). *Athletes push for and achieve social justice goals.* https://www.insidehighered.com/news/2020/07/02/athletes-push-and-achieve-social-justice-goals.

Boss, G. J., Linder, C., Martin, J. A., Dean, S. R., & Fitzer, J. R. (2018). Conscientious practice: Post-master's student affairs professionals' perspectives on engaging social justice. *Journal of Student Affairs Research and Practice*, 55(4), 373–385. https://doi.org/10.1080/19496591.2018.1470004

Broughton, E., & Neyer, M. (2002, November 15). *Advising and counseling student athletes.* https://onlinelibrary.wiley.com/doi/abs/10.1002/ss.4.

Carodine, K., Almond, K.F., & Gratto, K.K. (2001). College student athlete success both in and out of the classroom. *New Directions for Students Services, 93*(2), 19–33.

Comeaux, E. (2011). A study of attitudes toward college student-athletes: Implications for faculty-athletics engagement. *The Journal of Negro Education, 80*(4), 521–532.

Comeaux, E., & Harrison, C. K. (2011). A conceptual model of academic success for student–athletes. *Educational Researcher*, *40*(5), 235–245. https://doi.org/10.3102/0013189x11415260

Cotterill, S. T., & Fransen, K. (2016). Athlete leadership in sport teams: Current understanding and future directions. *International Review of Sport and Exercise Psychology*, *9*(1), 116–133. https://doi.org/10.1080/1750984x.2015.1124443

DeBard, R., & Eberly, C. G. (2014). Diversity for all: Opening perspectives on campus. *About Campus*, *19*(3), 9–16. https://doi.org/10.1002/abc.21157

Dugan, J. P. (2017). *Leadership theory: Cultivating critical perspectives*. John Wiley & Sons.

Engstrom, C. M., Sedlacek, W. E., & McEwen, M. K. (1995). Faculty attitudes toward male revenue and nonrevenue student-athletes. *Journal of College Student Development*, *36*(3), 217–227.

Friedman, E. R. (2004). *Does winning on the court equal losing in the classroom? The influence of team climate on the academic performance of Division I men's basketball players* [Unpublished doctoral dissertation]. Michigan State University, East Lansing, MI.

Guthrie, K. L., & Chunoo, V. S. (2018). *Changing the narrative: Socially just leadership education*. Information Age.

Guthrie, K. L., & Jenkins, D. M. (2018). *The role of leadership educators: Transforming learning*. Information Age.

Hall, S. L. (2015). Linking the leadership identity development model to collegiate recreation and athletics. In D. A. Stenta & C. W. McFadden (Eds.), *New Directions for Student Leadership: No. 147. Student leadership development through recreation and athletics* (pp. 32–41). Jossey-Bass.

Hester, C. L. (1990). *The effect of an athlete mentor program on student-athletes: Making the transition from high school to college* [Unpublished master's thesis], Michigan State University, East Lansing, MI.

Hill, K., Burch-Ragan, K. M., & Yates, D. Y. (2001). Current and future issues and trends facing student athletes and athletic programs. In M. F. Howard-Hamilton & S. K. Watt (Eds.), *New Directions for Student Services: No. 93. Student services for athletes* (pp. 65–80). Jossey-Bass.

Hood, A. B., Craig, A. F., & Ferguson, B. W. (1992). The impact of athletics, part-time employment and other activities on academic achievement. *Journal of College Student Development*, *33*(5), 447–453.

Howard-Hamilton, M. F., & Sina, J.A. (2001). How college affects student-athletes. In M. F. Howard-Hamilton & S. K. Watt (Eds.), *New Directions for Student Services: No. 93, Student services for athletes* (pp. 35–45). Jossey-Bass.

Komives, S. R., Owen, J. E., Longerbeam, S. D., Mainella, F. C., & Osteen, L. (2005). Developing a leadership identity: A grounded theory. *Journal of College Student Development*, *46*(6), 593–611. https://doi.org/10.1353/csd.2005.0061

Komives, S. R., Longerbeam, S. D., Owen, J. E., Mainella, F. C., & Osteen, L. (2006). A leadership identity development model: Applications from a grounded theory. *Journal of College Student Development*, *47*(4), 401–418. https://doi.org/10.1353/csd.2006.0048

Mungin, S. D., Evans, C., Henderson, A., Coles, D., Francis, J., & Catanach, K. A. (2018, June). *LYFE beyond the spear*. Paper presented at the annual meeting of the N4A, Washington, DC.

National Collegiate Athletic Association. (2020, July 6). *NCAA Board of Governors statement on social activism*. https://www.ncaa.org/about/resources/media-center/news/ncaa-board-governors-statement-social-activism

Sedlacek, W. E. (2004). *Beyond the big test: Noncognitive assessment in higher education*. Jossey-Bass.

Simons, H. D., Van Rheened, D., & Covington, M. V. (1999). Academic motivation and the student athlete. *Journal of College Student Development, 40*(2), 151–162.

Thamel, P. (2020, June 5). *College athletes on voter-registration spree: 'We have a chance to change the world'*. https://sports.yahoo.com/college-athletes-on-voter-registration-spree-we-have-a-chance-to-change-the-world-010953352.html

Tracy, J. (2020, June 10). *"I just can't be silent anymore": The rise of student-athlete activism*. https://www.axios.com/student-athlete-activism-protests-college-sports-3cdcb5a3-8afd-406a-b523-19138a6c651f.html

Watt, S. K., & Moore, J. L., III. (2001). Who are student-athletes? In M. F. Howard-Hamilton & S. K. Watt (Eds.), *New Directions for Student Services: No. 93, Student services for athletes* (pp. 7–18). Jossey-Bass.

Weaver, A., & Simet, K. (2015). Intercollegiate athlete as student leader. In D. A. Stenta & C. W. McFadden (Eds.), *New Directions for Student Leadership: No. 147. Student leadership development through recreation and athletics* (pp. 53–63). Jossey-Bass.

Wolniak, G. C., Pierson, C. T., & Pascarella, E. T. (2001). Effects of intercollegiate athletic participation on male orientations toward learning. *Journal of College Student Development, 42*(6), 604–624.

Woodruff, T., & Schallert, D. (2008). Studying to play, playing to study: Nine college student-athletes' motivational sense of self. *Contemporary Educational Psychology, 33*(1), 34–57.

PART II

SOCIALLY JUST LEADERSHIP EDUCATION CONTEXTS

CHAPTER 14

APPLYING THE LENS OF INTERSECTIONALITY TO LEADERSHIP LEARNING

Susan R. Jones and Adrian L. Bitton

The complexities of leadership education in contemporary times call for sophisticated ways to develop socially just leaders. Intersectionality provides a framework for shifting the mindset on the influence of identity in leadership learning. That is, intersectionality requires leadership educators to examine their practices through lenses of marginalization, inequalities, and higher education power structures; including those contexts where leadership education is emphasized. Applications of intersectionality in higher education scholarship and practice have grown immensely in the last years; however, this has come with misuse and misappropriation of the term (Harris & Patton, 2018). Often, the term intersectionality is invoked to study *identity* and identity-related experiences. However, the potential of intersectionality is more accurately described by Collins (2019):

> Using intersectionality as a heuristic not only has facilitated the rethinking of existing knowledge—violence and similar social problems, work and similar social institutions, as well as identity and similar social constructs—it has

Shifting the Mindset: Socially Just Leadership Education
pp. 163–173

also brought new systems of power into view … such as sexuality, ethnicity, age, ability, and nation as similar categories of analysis. (p. 37)

Thus, the connection between identity and intersectionality emphasizes interlocking and mutually reinforcing social locations or categories of analysis.

In this chapter we present one model, the intersectional model of multiple dimensions of identity (I-MMDI)—developed to reflect the core tenets and assumptions of intersectionality to an understanding of multiple social identities (Dill & Zambrana, 2009; Jones & Abes, 2013). We begin by suggesting that ideas reflected in the I-MMDI complement the shifts in leadership education toward more critical perspectives (Dugan, 2017). We then make specific connections between the I-MMDI and leadership education, and conclude by exploring how intersectionality may be used by leadership educators to create and facilitate socially just leadership learning.

LEADERSHIP EDUCATION CONTEXT

Recent leadership education scholarship calls for a move toward critical perspectives (Bertrand Jones et al., 2016; Dugan, 2017). With growing recognition of the limitations of leader-centric, hierarchical, trait-based, and positional conceptualizations of leadership, newer theories and models promote leadership as participatory, relational, transformational, and concerned with the common good (Dugan & Osteen, 2017). Despite stated goals of promoting social change and social justice, these recent conceptualizations of leadership do not necessarily interrogate structures of inequality and power dynamics pervasive in higher education. In fact, as Dugan and Osteen (2017) emphasized, "The sociohistoric and systematic oppression that characterizes U.S. society interacts with unchallenged ideal leader prototypes contributing to a marginalizing effect and potentially distancing people from the concept of leadership altogether. This only serves to reinforce unequal power structures" (p. 410). It is exactly the presence of unequal power structures that intersectionality is designed to interrogate and that critical perspectives on leadership emphasize.

Critical perspectives on leadership education bring attention to cultural and social constructions of leadership, individuals' social identities and social locations, and power dynamics to the forefront of analysis and practice. These dynamics then influence all aspects of leadership, including how leaders are educated and how they learn about leadership. In addition, critical perspectives on leadership education are congruent with the core tenets of intersectionality and provide possibilities for incorporating intersectionality into leadership education. As Collins (2015) noted, "practitioners are often frontline actors for solving social problems that are clearly linked to complex social inequalities, a social location that predisposes them to respond to intersectionality as critical praxis" (p. 15). We now turn to presenting one model that leadership educators can use to engage in the critical praxis required for socially just leadership education.

INTERSECTIONAL MODEL
OF MULTIPLE DIMENSIONS OF IDENTITY

The model of multiple dimensions of identity (MMDI; Jones & McEwen, 2000) was redrawn to apply critical perspectives to multiple social identities. Although the model addresses intersecting social identities, and the influence of context, it was not created with the core constructs of intersectionality; particularly an insistence on analysis of power and interrogation of structures of inequality. In the I-MMDI, the elements of the MMDI remain intact (e.g., intersecting social identities, core, salience, meaning-making filter, and contextual influences). We now introduce and describe how these interventions were applied to create the I-MMDI.

A growing number of scholars are offering definitions of intersectionality and applications for its use in higher education. While definitional consensus is not the goal (Collins, 2019), some overlapping commitments and core assumptions exist among these varying conceptualizations of intersectionality. In creating the I-MMDI, we adopted the four theoretical interventions developed by Dill and Zambrana (2009) which included: centering the experiences of People of Color; complicating identity; unveiling power in interconnected structures of inequality; and promoting social justice and social change. These interventions were used as a guide for the drawing of the I-MMDI, which we present now.

In the I-MMDI, macro- and microanalyses of multiple identities was provided with the MMDI (individual microanalysis), nested within a larger macro system which represents larger structures of inequality where individuals exist (e.g., racism, sexism, ableism, heterosexism, genderism). The macrosystem—or context—is elevated in importance given the power analysis underlying the foundation of an intersectional lens. The core of the model—conceived in the MMDI as a personal identity or characteristics that an individual holds as core to who they are, is present but reimagined to center the experiences of People of Color in analysis. This foregrounding of identity categories as systems of power embraces the question for individuals of what it means to live authentically when larger structures of inequality are considered.

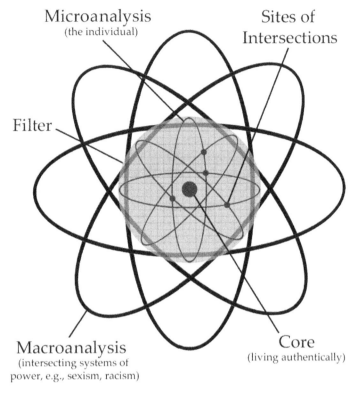

Source: Adapted from Jones & Abes (2013).

Figure 14.1.   Intersectional model of multiple dimensions of identity.

The meaning of social identities as seen in the MMDI shifts to social locations, or the relationship between social identity and institutional systems controlling access to resources and privileges (Kendall & Wijeyesinghe, 2017). Understanding identity salience in the I-MMDI also shifts given the power analysis intersectionality requires. That is, rather than considered as an individual's perceptions of which identities are salient in what contexts, an intersectional view of salience suggests the omnipresence of larger systems that influence an individual whether or not they are aware of this influence (Wijeyesinghe, 2019); and emphasizes the agency individuals do have in considering who they want to be (Collins & Bilge, 2016).

Finally, the meaning-making filter is drawn to reflect the relationships among the core, social identities, larger contextual structures, and meaning making. In particular, the meaning-making filter in the I-MMDI is portrayed as a layer between the micro- and macrosystems to illustrate how meaning making influences experience at both levels (Jones & Abes, 2013). As summarized by Jones and Abes (2013) the I-MMDI

> emphasizes systems of oppression, permits the centering of the experiences of students of color, complicates identity, and makes power dynamics explicit, components that when taken together hold the potential for promoting a more socially just society. (p. 162)

CONNECTING THE I-MMDI TO LEADERSHIP LEARNING

A more socially just society is only made possible by the people committed to advancing it. In using the I-MMDI as an analytical framework, leadership educators apply a holistic approach to leadership learning by critically examining the relationships between identities, power, and leadership. In this section we discuss the elements of the I-MMDI relative to leadership learning and the potential for creating new and meaningful pathways for developing socially just student leaders.

Context

People frequently use the MMDI to reflect upon their own intersecting identities, however; identities are always mediated by context. Therefore, the I-MMDI requires individual identities to be considered within a broader societal context. In doing so, interlocking systems of power are revealed allowing analysis of context on both the micro- (individual) and macro- (structural) levels. These systems often reinforce dominant narratives of leadership by mapping privileged social identities onto leadership, shaping our expectations of who a leader is (in terms of identities) and how they should lead (behaviors and qualities). For example, within higher education, White students, often get labeled as leaders, whereas students of color, who exhibit similar behaviors, are more likely to be labeled as activists or troublemakers (Linder et al., 2020). The I-MMDI illuminates how context and structural power inform every aspect of leadership learning within higher education.

Identity Salience and Sites of Intersection

An intersectional lens emphasizes identity salience as based upon social location and a person's identities in relation to power, privilege, and oppression. The location where social identities intersect with dominant narratives of leadership and other systems of inequalities (the -isms) is known as a site of intersection. It is in sites of intersection where leadership development disproportionally privileges certain identities over others. For example, social class may become a particularly salient social identity for working social class students when a list of leaders compiled by students in a cocurricular leadership program include celebrities and wealthy business executives. Cocurricular leadership programs, retreats, leadership classes, student organizations, and all of higher education more broadly, can all be sites of these intersections.

The Core

Noting how identity salience is inextricably linked to larger systems of power, privilege, and oppression, the I-MMDI encourages analyzes at the core at macro- and microlevels. First, centering the leadership experiences and counternarratives of minoritized people requires analyses beyond the individual level to the structural level of leadership learning in a higher education context. Secondly, how a person defines authenticity for themselves and authentic leadership is mitigated by a person's own sense of self as a leader, the perception of others involved in the leadership process, and how a person suppresses or highlights certain aspects of their identity in a leadership situation. Authentic leadership is reflected by the congruence between a person's values and actions despite shifting leadership contexts. However, this conception of authenticity may fail to consider what it takes to disrupt the dominant narrative of leadership and that authenticity may look different when a person's social identities are not the ones mapped onto leadership.

Multiple Identities

Although a growing recognition exists of the multidimensionality and intersectionality of identities held by student leaders, much of leadership education has focused on singular aspects of identity and their relationship to leadership (e.g., cocurricular women in leadership programs, leadership studies classes on African American leadership). However, socially just leadership education is learned through the lens of intersectionality to examine how privileged and oppressed identities influence relationships to leadership and leader identity. For example, Asian American women are often stereotyped as quiet and submissive, whereas loud and angry are often stereotypes attributed to African American/Black women (Eagly & Carli, 2007). Intersections of identities can either reinforce or work against the dominant narratives of leadership. These larger intersectional structures influence how and if students think of themselves and/or others as leaders and what access they have to leadership opportunities.

A Leadership Meaning-Making Filter

The meaning-making filter emphasizes the relationships nested among the broader context, a person's intersecting social identities, and their meaning-making capacity (Jones & Abes, 2013). We propose a leadership lens can be applied to the meaning-making filter; and this filter is shaped by systems of privilege and oppression, including the dominant narrative of leadership. The expansion and contraction of the leadership meaning-making filter reflects evolving conceptualizations of leadership. Moreover, it is situated between the micro- and macrolevels of context, thereby allowing power to flow in both directions. Just as the dominant narrative of leadership exerts pressure on the individual, individuals also have agency to resist contextual forces to advance more socially just societies, whereby leadership experiences and conversations take on new meaning. This explains why people exposed to the same context/institutional culture (e.g., higher education institution, cocurricular leadership program, class), have different conceptualizations and experiences with leadership. In the next section we explore how educators build students' leadership meaning-making filter to resist dominant narratives of leadership and develop more socially just orientations.

INFUSING AN INTERSECTIONAL LENS INTO LEADERSHIP EDUCATION

The I-MMDI, anchored in the tenets and interventions of intersectionality, guides inclusive leadership learning for developing socially just orientations. In this section, we provide suggestions for translating theory into practice and pose questions for educators to consider.

Unveiling Power in Interconnected Structures of Inequality

Power, privilege, and oppression are inherent in leadership practices. Yet, analyses and discussions of power are largely absent from many leadership development programs (Barnes et al., 2018). The connotation of power, emphasizing control and manipulation, violates the aspirational vision for leadership, and redirects focus on individual leadership development (which in many cases is still devoid of context). However, leadership and leadership learning are never power neutral. Students who understand historical and present-day manifestations of power within society are better suited to develop a socially just orientation toward leadership. By examining the effective organizing strategies and principles of past and present social movements and integrating power conscious frameworks, students learn new skills such as power mapping, power analysis, and how to build power with others. Socially just leadership educators who unveil power in interconnected structures consider:

- What structures of inequality are evident within my leadership programs and/or classes?
- Who facilitates leadership learning on my campus? Does power reside in one office or a leadership "expert," or do multiple functional areas support students' leadership?
- How can I empower student leaders to understand structures of inequality and work towards socially just leadership practice?

Centering Minoritized Students

In order to address structures of inequality, socially just leadership educators center students with minoritized identities in leadership learning. In doing so, higher education and student affairs professionals are called to examine the institutional history of leadership, the leadership culture, as well as current policies and programs related to leadership education (Jones & Abes, 2013). Oftentimes, leadership programs are named after people or symbols associated with the institution, which can be problematic. For example, a leadership program named after a Christian religious figure might result in lower participation of Jewish or Muslim students. Students of color might receive conflicting messages about leadership if a leadership program is held in a room decorated with portraits of past university presidents who are all White cisgender men. Leadership educators who center minoritized students contemplate:

- How can I promote collaborations between leadership offices and cultural and identity-based programs to center minoritized students' leadership learning and experiences?
- What types of leadership do my leadership programs and/or classes privilege (e.g., Western; White; upper class)? By centering minori-

tized identities, what other forms of leadership would students be exposed to (e.g., collectivist; indigenous; feminist)?

- What opportunities are there to incorporate intersectionality through the use of examples, assigned readings, and facilitated discussions in leadership learning?

Complicating Identity

The I-MMDI requires leadership education programs to go beyond recognizing and appreciating difference or acknowledging multiple identities. Rather, socially just leadership educators take on the responsibility of designing leadership programs and facilitating leadership learning that honors the complexities of intersectional identities nestled within systems of power, privilege, and oppression. For example, an intersectionality-based curriculum for a weekend-long retreat focused on socially just leadership encourages participants and facilitators to recognize how power, privilege, and oppression shaped their experiences with leadership, as well as in larger society. They could explore both their privileged and minoritized identities in relation to the dominant narrative of leadership; and connect and share how they want allies, accomplices, and coconspirators to show up for them as well as learn how they can do the same from others. Educators who complicate identity in leadership learning inquire about:

- Who is considered a leader on my campus?
- What privileges are associated with being a leader on campus?
- Who has access to leadership development resources?
- How might I discuss topics such as social location and intersectionality with students?

Promoting Social Justice and Social Change

Chunoo et al. (2019) called for leadership educators to think beyond their role of facilitating leadership learning, and to consider how leadership educators and social justice educators are one in the same. Therefore, promoting social justice and social change through leadership education considers the intersectional identities of students engaged in leadership learning, and those of educators facilitating leadership learning. A recent study by Jenkins (2013) of over 300 leadership educators revealed an overwhelming majority self-identified as White (83.8%) and as women (54.8%). These statistics prompt leadership educators to acknowledge how the field of leadership education remains a privileged space. Socially just leadership educators disrupt these realities, invite diverse perspectives, and challenge themselves and each other to expand boundaries toward the promotion of social change. This is the only way to prepare the next generation of leaders to tackle the complex and intersectional social issues of human rights, climate change, and economic justice that society faces. Promoting social justice and change requires wrangling with questions addressing:

- How am I continuing to educate and commit myself to issues of social justice?
- Whose perspectives are missing?
- How am I disrupting the dominant narrative of leadership?

CONCLUSION

A commitment to socially just leadership education requires grappling with power and structures of inequality. Intersectionality provides leadership educators with a sophisticated lens to view leading and promote socially just leadership practices. In this chapter, we described the I-MMDI as one model that highlights important areas of consideration (centering the experiences of people of color, complicating identity, unveiling power, and promoting social change) for developing student leaders, designing leadership programs, and teaching leadership classes. Applying intersectionality to leadership learning holds great potential for creating opportunities for all students to see themselves as leaders, and to promote real social change on campuses.

REFERENCES

Barnes, A. C., Olson, T. H., & Reynolds, D. J. (2018). Teaching power as an inconvenient but imperative dimension of critical leadership development. In J. P. Dugan (Ed.), *New Directions for Student Leadership: No. 159. Integrating critical perspectives into leadership development* (pp. 77–90). Jossey-Bass.

Bertrand Jones, T., Guthrie, K. L., & Osteen, L. (2016). Critical domains of culturally relevant leadership learning: A call to transform leadership programs. In K. L. Guthrie, T. Bertrand Jones, & L. Osteen (Eds.), *New Directions for Student Leadership: No. 152. Developing culturally relevant leadership learning* (pp. 9–21). Jossey-Bass.

Chunoo, V. S., Beatty, C. C., & Gruver, M. D. (2019). Leadership educator as social justice educator. In K. L. Priest & D. M. Jenkins (Eds.), *New Directions for*

Student Leadership: No. 164. Becoming and being a leadership educator (pp. 39–53). Jossey-Bass.

Collins, P. H. (2015). Intersectionality's definitional dilemmas. *Annual Review of Sociology, 41*(1), 1–20.

Collins, P. H. (2019). *Intersectionality as critical social theory.* Duke University Press.

Collins, P. H., & Bilge, S. (2016). *Intersectionality.* Polity Press.

Dill, B. T., & Zambrana, R. E. (2009). *Emerging intersections: Race, class, and gender in theory, policy, and practice.* Rutgers University Press.

Dugan, J. P. (2017). *Leadership theory: Cultivating critical perspectives.* Jossey-Bass.

Dugan, J. P., & Osteen, L. (2017). Leadership. In J. H. Schuh, S. R. Jones, & V. Torres (Eds.). *Student services: A handbook for the profession* (6th ed., pp. 408-422). Jossey-Bass.

Eagly, A. H., & Carli, L. L. (2007). *Through the labyrinth: The truth about how women become leaders.* Harvard Business School Press.

Harris, J. C., & Patton, L. D. (2018). Un/doing intersectionality through higher education research. *The Journal of Higher Education, 90*(3), 347–372.

Jenkins, D. M. (2013). Exploring instructional strategies in student leadership development programming. *Journal of Leadership Studies, 6*(4), 48–62.

Jones, S. R., & Abes, E. S. (2013). *Identity development of college students: Advancing frameworks for multiple dimensions of identity.* Jossey-Bass.

Jones, S. R., & McEwen, M. K. (2000). A conceptual model of multiple dimensions of identity. *Journal of College Student Development, 41*(4), 405–413.

Kendall, F. E., & Wijeyesinghe, C. L. (2017). Advancing social justice work at the intersections of multiple privileged identities. In C. L. Wijeyesinghe (Ed.), *New Directions for Student Services: No. 157. Enacting intersectionality in student affairs* (pp. 91–100). Jossey-Bass.

Linder, C., Quaye, S. J., Lange, A. C., Evans, M. E., & Stewart, T. J. (2020). *Identity-based student activism: Power and oppression on college campuses.* Routledge.

Wijeyesinghe, C. L. (2019). Intersectionality and student development: Centering power in the process. In E.S. Abes, S. R. Jones, & D.-L. Stewart (Eds.), *Rethinking college student development theory using critical frameworks* (pp. 26–34). Stylus.

CHAPTER 15

NEVER NEUTRAL

Challenging the Presumed Centrality of Ethics in Socially Just Leadership Education

Jasmine D. Collins and Shane L. Whittington

The clarion call for social justice leadership in the United States has never been more apparent than in the summer of 2020. Protests for racial justice erupted in all fifty states while affirmations that "Black Lives Matter" echoed abroad. Institutions of higher education have long espoused a mission of developing the next generation of leaders to transform communities and improve lives, but in response to the racial justice flashpoints ignited by the murders of George Floyd, Ahmaud Arbery, Breonna Taylor, and others, colleges and universities are poised to do more. They are primed to translate rhetorical commitments to diversity and inclusion into organizational changes, "to eradicate systems of discrimination and injustice both in public life and within the academy" (Thomas et al., p. 4). Leadership education is a central component of achieving this sustained commitment. Leadership programs rooted in social justice particularly, are fertile ground for preparing emerging leaders to address contemporary societal challenges.

Shifting the Mindset: Socially Just Leadership Education
pp. 175–189
Copyright © 2021 by Information Age Publishing

Guthrie and Chunoo (2018) expressed social justice pedagogy is not only "based in moral and ethical development, but rather arousing critical thinking, student reflection, and experiential responses to a better understanding of what social justice actually means" (p. 4). This statement provided an important reflection point, as we have both had opportunities to ponder the *presumed centrality* of moral and ethical development to social justice teaching and learning through our work as socially just leadership educators. Shane reflected,

> I have been engaged in social justice work since my years as an undergraduate student. In this time, I have come to recognize that social justice work requires a certain combination of awareness, knowledge, and skill. For instance, awareness of self; knowledge of the history of social justice trailblazers and their movements as well as the institutional limitations and opportunities under which social justice leaders must operate; and skill in being able to openly engage with controversial topics. At no point; however, from my undergraduate years to now, have I been asked to consider the *ethical* awareness, knowledge and skills required for socially just leadership. I believe that this is because it is inherently assumed that persons who are fighting for equitable solutions to social injustices are ethical by nature, or at least by training.

In Shane's experience, and through his familiarity with leadership education and social justice literature, processes of moral and ethical development are largely taken for granted as natural byproducts of social justice. Perhaps this is due to social justice's roots in justice, fairness, equality, liberation and transformation; each of which are typically viewed as noble.

Jasmine teaches an undergraduate course which combines the study of both leadership ethics and social justice. She reflects on the challenges she has faced in designing such a course,

> Four years ago, I taught a course called Leadership Ethics and Multiculturalism as part of an undergraduate leadership studies curriculum. The learning objectives of the course included the ability to "associate the ethical decisions of leaders with the practice of multicultural competence in today's society" and to "describe the influence of power in leadership on moral and ethical behavior." In practice, the course felt more like 8 weeks of leadership ethics followed by 8 weeks of diversity and social justice curriculum. Each time I teach this course, now called Leadership Ethics and Society: Addressing Contemporary Challenges, I get a little bit closer to a balance that feels right, but the struggle to integrate two seemingly disparate bodies of work into one syllabus remains.

Beyond the challenge of merging disciplines, Jasmine contends with considerations of breadth versus depth of content, as well as pinpointing the appropriate level of difficulty, knowing students may come to the course with varying levels of preexisting knowledge and vastly different motivations to engage often-uncomfortable conversations that arise in a class where participants critically reflect on their power, privilege, identity and social responsibility.

Despite the experiences we have had in grappling with the connections between leadership ethics and social justice, we believe the integration of ethics into socially just leadership education is paramount to the development of change agents for social justice. Thus, our chapter engages two fundamental questions: (1) What is the relationship between leadership ethics (as a field of study), leadership for social justice (as a community practice) and socially just leadership education (as a pedagogical approach)? and; (2) How might foundational principles of leadership ethics be interwoven with social justice leadership to inform socially just leadership education?

The chapter occurs in two parts: a conceptual exploration of connections between leadership ethics and social justice, and practical suggestions for centering ethical development within socially just leadership pedagogy. Together they answer our fundamental queries.

LEADERSHIP ETHICS AND SOCIAL JUSTICE ETHICS AND MORALS

Organizational ethicist and professor emeritus of leadership studies, Craig E. Johnson, asserted *ethics is the heart of leadership*. "When we assume the benefits of leadership, we also assume ethical burdens. As leaders, we must act in such a way as to benefit rather than damage others, to cast light instead of shadow" (Johnson, 2020, p. xxi). Some of these burdens include the duty to behave in consistent and temperate ways, to take responsibility for misdeeds, to protect the privacy of sensitive information, to honorably navigate conflicts of interest, and to responsibly steward the power and privileges of leadership. The *science of ethics* investigates these and other challenges, engaging the systematic study of how and why behavior is considered right or wrong, good, or bad (Johnson, 2020; Shapiro & Stefkovich, 2016).

Ethical principles are closely related to morals, which provide the *specific standard* of right and wrong conduct. These moral standards are generally accepted and sanctioned by a given society or organizational context, and can be discerned through proverbs, fables, texts, or adages instilled at an early age (Ethics Unwrapped, n.d.). Some examples include, "slow and steady wins the race" or, "thou shalt not steal." Philosopher Bernard Gert (2004) contended 10 universal moral principles dictate acceptable human behavior and must be accounted for when broken in an effort to protect ourselves and one another (Johnson, 2020). Such laws include: do not kill; do not cause pain; do not disable; do not deprive of freedom; do not deprive of pleasure; do not deceive; keep your promises; do not cheat; obey the law and do your duty. However, it is more common for philosophers, anthropologists, sociologists, and others who study ethics to adopt understandings of ethical pluralism and moral relativism (Johnson, 2020).

Values

Ethical pluralism acknowledges multiple ethical perspectives and decision-making frameworks, while moral relativism recognizes there is no such thing as universal morality because morals are rooted in values. Societal/cultural, organizational, and personal values guide decision making, set priorities, and distinguish right from wrong.

Universal Values.   Kluckhohn and Strodtbeck's (1961) values orientation theory posits all human societies face a common set of problems; therefore, there exists a finite set of foundational questions with which all societies must contend. These questions center on the universal values of time (how do we focus on time—past, present, future); nature (what is the ideal relationship between man and the natural environment?); social relationships (how should individuals and groups be organized to relate to one another?); human nature (what is man's true nature—evil, good, mix, fixed, mutable?), and motivation for human activity (what is the proper mode of human activity—being, becoming, achieving?). The answers to these questions shape human behavior in a given societal context and also serve as the basis for what is considered normal and deviant, right and wrong (Hills, 2002; Kluckhohn & Strodtbeck, 1961).

Societal/Cultural Values.   Social psychologist Geert Hofstede (1984) identified four dimensions through which members of a culture are "programmed" to act on a spectrum from high to low. These programmed value patterns include power distance, individualism versus collectivism, masculinity versus femininity, and uncertainty avoidance. Hofstede's (1980) work on programmed value patterns provided the foundation for the Global Leadership and Organizational Behavior Effectiveness study (Hofstede, 2001; House et al., 2004) which examined the relationship between cultural values such as performance orientation, assertiveness, in-group collectivism and power distance and effective leadership behaviors.

Personal Values.   Personal values are core beliefs and principles which remain central to an individual's self-concept over time. Some examples of core values include harmony, respect, authenticity, family, fame, peace, wealth, and love, among others. Clarity of personal values drives commitment to action and helps an individual determine right and wrong. Adherence to personal values often supersedes commitment to organizational values (Kouzes & Posner, 2006).

Astin and Astin (2000) distinguished leadership from management insofar as management is concerned with preservation of the status quo, while leadership is a process fundamentally concerned with fostering change. The ends to which leadership is directed reflect the core values of the leader and those engaged in the leadership process (Komives & Wagner, 2017). Socially just leadership presumes an adherence to humanitarian values that prioritize deep-seeded, sustainable, social change for the betterment of those most underserved.

Justice as a Value.   The value of justice focuses on rights and law. In the democratic tradition, justice is concerned with how governments are differentially dedicated to upholding fundamental principles which govern society (Shapiro & Stefkovich, 2016). Although status inequalities exist within democratic societies, philosopher John Rawls (1971) argued a democratic society can be deemed just based on the extent to which:

1.   all persons maintain equal civil rights and liberties (such as voting and owning property);
2.   social and economic inequalities rely on talent and ability, not opportunity; and,
3.   goods and services are distributed in favor of the least advantaged members of society, understanding these resources are inherently unequally distributed in society.

From Rawls' *Justice as Fairness* perspective, democratic societies should prioritize the needs of the poor, immigrants, minorities, and other marginalized groups (Johnson, 2020).

Social Justice and the Ethic of Critique. The value of justice is concerned with the degree to which governments are dedicated to upholding the principles which are said to govern society, but, "writers and activists are not convinced by the analytic and rational approach of the justice paradigm" (Shapiro & Stefkovich, 2016. p. 13). Therefore, an ethic of critique is necessary to engage in leadership for social justice. Shapiro and Stefkovich (2016) elaborated,

> Some scholars find tension between the ethic of justice, rights and laws and the concept of democracy. In response they raise difficult questions by cri-

tiquing both the laws themselves and the process used to determine if the laws are just (p. 13).

Critical legal theory, as referenced above, represents one dimension of critical social theory—the conceptual analysis of how power functions in a society, how this flow of power contributes to social stratification, and ways that society might be restructured to toward more just ends (Dugan, 2017). Critical race theory, more accurately described as a collection of theories, is another branch of critical social theory. Critical race theory accounts for the role of structural racism in shaping societal inequalities in an effort to eliminate structural racism and its intersections with other forms of subordination based on gender, class, sexual orientation, language, religion, and national origin (McCoy & Rodricks, 2015; Solórzano & Yosso, 2002).

Dismantling oppressive social structures reflects the central aim of social justice, which Bell (2018) defined as process involving social actors who have a sense of their own agency as well as a sentiment of social responsibility, toward and with others, to ensure the "full and equal participation of all groups in a society that is mutually shaped to meet their needs," and, "includes a vision of society in which distribution of resources is equitable and all members are physically and psychologically safe and secure" (Bell, 2018, p. 34). Social justice also centers "equitable social processes, including recognition of and respect for marginalized or subjugated cultures and groups" (Bell, 2018, p. 34). Socially just leadership attends to the visibility, recognition and equitable participation of marginalized individuals, groups, and communities.

LEADERSHIP FOR SOCIAL JUSTICE: SURFACING ETHICAL COMPONENTS

Social justice is rooted in equity, fairness, critique, liberation and, of course, justice. Socially just leaders initiate and sustain change efforts to eliminate structural subordination based on social identity and other forms of systemic oppression, to ensure full and equal participation of all groups in a democratic society, which is inherently unequal. From this perspective, leaders who enact laws, policies, and practices to intentionally and systematically disenfranchise and/or cause physical, psychological, or economic harm to individuals, groups, and communities on the basis of social identity, are unethical leaders. But what about those who engage the fight *for* social justice? If these leaders and their followers are not using their power to disenfranchise or to cause harm on the basis of race, class, gender, socioeconomic status, sexuality, ability, and the like, does this mean they are ethical leaders by default?

Johnson (2020) defined unethical leaders as those who hoard privileges, abuse power, mismanage information, behave inconsistently, mishandle their loyalties and obligations, and fail to take responsibility for their actions and the actions of their subordinates. Kellerman (2005) identified a typology of unethical leadership as callous, corrupt, insular, and evil behaviors enacted by leaders and followers who ignore and/or discount the needs of others, prioritize personal interests over the good of the organization and/or public, disregard the needs of those not within their in-group, and use tactics such as fear and harm to obtain their desired results.

CENTERING ETHICS
IN SOCIALLY JUST LEADERSHIP EDUCATION

Centering ethics within socially just leadership education is critically important because the study of ethical leadership is largely concerned with the ways leaders and followers use and abuse power, and the concept of social justice is fundamentally concerned remedying the social stratification that is caused by deep-seeded structures of power in a democratic society. The following section provides tips, suggestions, tools, and strategies for socially just leadership educators looking to infuse ethical considerations into their pedagogical approaches.

Focus on Developing Moral Imagination

Leadership learners begin to develop skills necessary to lead for social justice when they recognize the presence and impact of oppressive societal structures and become willing to adopt an ethic of critique to deconstruct and reimagine more equitable solutions. These skills are closely related to the ethical leadership concept known as *the moral imagination*. According to Godwin (2015), a moral imagination "encompasses the capability of not only being aware of the moral implications of one's actions in a situation, but also reframing a situation and creating moral alternatives to the situation at hand" (p. 258). Johnson (2020) discerned three key components of moral imagination, including: (a) sensitivity to ethical dimensions of situations; (b) perspective-taking (considering other people's point of view), and (c) creating new solutions.

Help Students Understand Why Ethical Failures Happen

Helping leadership learners develop into ethically minded leaders for social justice requires understanding factors which contribute to unethical leadership. Kellerman (2005) and Johnson (2020) identified a toxic *web* or *triangle* of leaders, followers, and context. Individual leaders may engage in unethical behavior due to a lack of ethical efficacy—the confidence to recognize moral dimensions of a situation, make an ethical decision, and follow through on it due to lack of experience using ethical decision-making frameworks to guide their actions. Leaders may also fall victim to their own biases and untested assumptions about themselves and/or others. Followers may go along with unethical behaviors to fulfill their own need to belong, because they fear consequences associated with speaking up, or because they truly believe in the leader's mission. Contextual pressures, such as the need to stand out or to look "woke" on social media may also drive unethical social justice behaviors.

Introduce an Evaluative Framework

The study of ethics is concerned with how and why behavior is considered right or wrong, good or bad. The determination of what is considered good and bad varies based on the ethical perspective(s) being applied. Utilitarianism, for example, seeks to do the greatest good for the greatest number of people. Following a specified approach, a leader examines the decision at hand, considers who will be affected and how, and decides on the best course of action by summing the good and bad consequences, and going with the option that maximizes good (Johnson, 2020). As another example, Altruism uses the metric of concern for others as the determination of whether behavior is ethical. If a leader can embody compassion, selflessness and an ethic of care, their actions are regarded as ethical (Johnson, 2020).

Since ethical principles are derived from morals, which themselves are rooted in values, an evaluative framework that centers values is appropriate. Thus, we introduce the concept of the *values braid* as a conceptual tool for assisting leadership learners in the process of evaluating the ethicality of leader and follower behavior. Leadership is a socially constructed process that is ultimately concerned with fostering change. The direction and intended result of such change is determined by the values of the leader and larger context. One way to determine if leadership behavior is ethical or not is to evaluate the conduct against a predetermined set of values. The notion of "ethical leadership" implies leaders have a personal duty or responsibility to carry out the functions of their roles in ways that do not cause harm to others and that leaders (and their followers) should be held accountable when such ethical standards are not met.

The framework of the values braid (Figure 15.1) illustrates how morals, values, behaviors, responsibility, and accountability are interwoven to form a cumulative notion of what it means to lead ethically, given a particular value orientation.

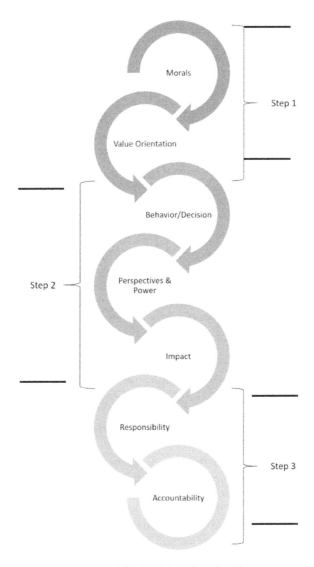

Figure 15.1. Ethical leadership values braid.

This framework, used alongside a social justice orientation, might encourage students to consider ethical dilemmas more deeply, like the return to college football amidst the 2020 global pandemic. We will use this example in the sections that follow to illustrate this approach.

Step 1. The fundamental question is whether it is morally justifiable to bring college athletes back to the field, knowing their lives are at stake. When layering a socially just value orientation, our next question is whether it is ethical to resume play knowing: (a) Black athletes make up the largest demographic in the Power Five conferences which are primarily governed by White Coaches and Athletic Directors (Axson, 2020; National Collegiate Athletic Association, 2019); (b) Blacks and Latinos are nearly five times as likely to be hospitalized with COVID-19 than non-Hispanic Whites, even though they are only 13 percent of the U.S. population (Axson, 2020) and (c) college athletes do not receive a wage, yet the NCAA generates roughly $1 billion annually (Axson, 2020).

Step 2. Our next thread to consider is the leader behavior or decision to be made in conjunction with the perspectives of those involved in making the decision, and the positions of power they occupy. Positions of power may refer to occupations within a given organizational context and/or the *social location* an individual or group occupies, given the hierarchies established by social systems of oppression (Kirk & Okazawa-Rey, 2018). In considering the return to football, we advise leadership educators directing students to think about *who* is in the position to make this decision, *who* will be impacted by the decision, and *how* each stakeholder or constituent group might be impacted (for better or for worse) given their respective locations.

Step 3. Leadership learners evaluate *who should be held responsible* for the impact of the final decision, and what measures of accountability should be taken related to adverse intended and/or unintended effects. In the tragic event of death of a team member, for instance, who is responsible for this loss of life, and what should the ramifications be?

Use Campus Context as a Learning Laboratory

Leadership learners benefit greatly from opportunities to use their local educational environments as sites of ethical investigation. For instance, Jasmine uses the University of Illinois Racial Microaggressions Report (Harwood et al. 2015) in her Leadership Ethics and Society class to help students identify and classify the various types of racial microaggressions persons of color experience in their daily lives, and to place these acts of discrimination within a familiar context—rendering visible that which may be quite difficult to pinpoint otherwise.

Shane teaches his students about the truth, racial healing, and transformation (TRHT) framework (W. K. Kellogg Foundation, 2016) which can be used to examine campus entities who wish to bring campus speakers addressing *hot button* topics. The framework parses through both the general ethical nature and the specific context of the school and societal environment when deciding on such a speaker. The framework, (W. K. Kellogg, Foundation 2016) uses five areas to address history, social context, current political environments, the individual, and community cultural perspectives. Each point of the framework includes questions to contextualize the situation and prepare entities for informed decision-making.

The first area of the truth, racial healing, and transformation framework is *narrative change*. Ask students to consider the role that media will play. What physical structures will best accommodate traffic? Does the college/university currently have curricula that will inform engagement prior to and after the event as a means to facilitate understanding and community building? The second is *racial healing and relationship building*. Ask students in what ways will this event build relationships and trust by lifting the veil of past racial pain and/or intentional healing? The third component is *separation*. Ask students to assess whether this event will further perpetuate the colonization, segregation and poverty in their local neighborhoods? The penultimate component is *economy*. Prompt students to consider how economic barriers and opportunities impact individuals connected to their campus community and the degree to which the event might directly or indirectly promote further inequality. The last component is *law*. Ask students to analyze the impact of laws and policies on community members belonging to particular identity groups as a direct or indirect result of this event and/or the content and messages associated with this event. Encourage the students to brainstorm alternative solutions if the proposed event yield concerns regarding equity, fairness, justice and/or harm, as indicated by the answers to the questions above.

Model Socially Just Pedagogy and Professional Engagement

Leadership educators are tasked with continuously scaffolding our knowledge to strengthen the quality and relevance of content we present to students. Although it is important to focus our attention on *what* we are teaching, it is also crucial to not lose sight of *how*. By balancing *checking in* and *checking up*, leadership educators are better positioned to educate *about* leadership ethics and social justice, and to model the way.

***Check In*.**   We invite educators to check in with their surroundings and learning environments. Observe, measure, and document how the environment reinforces and/or undermines socially just and ethical instruction. Questions for leadership educators include:

- Is your physical space fit for ethical instruction?
- Do students share information about environments that work for them?
- Can individuals safely practice internal reflection, reinterpretation, or open expression?
- What protects all individuals?
- How much thought is given to how students might be adversely impacted by the nature of content that is discussed in the class?
- For classes that lack adequate racial representation, what are the safeguards against tokenization and marginalization?
- What events and practices are happening in society that set the context and directly impact the environment? How are you responding to these events?

We also advocate educators checking in on academic structures:

- Who sits on hiring committees and what are their ethical goals?
- Where are the outlets to redesign programs and curriculum in a more ethical way?
- Are syllabi built on a socially just framework of acknowledging people?
- Are there training and professional development for ongoing ethical considerations?
- What are the touch points for all employees, guests, and students to interact with ethical definitions, practices, and language from orientation to graduation and beyond?
- What measures are currently in place to ensure ethical and socially just structures are in place and who approves and can make changes? What kinds of reporting structures are in place when an ethical violation occurs either in person or online and how are these policies and procedures enforced?
- Is there clarity about who reviews reports and investigates occurrences? How are programs and departments collaborating and working across difference?
- Where are the spaces for healing and accountability?
- Who is tasked with creating and maintaining these spaces?

Check Up. We challenge leadership educators to ask themselves and others:

- How do I model what is ethical and what is not when interacting with students, colleagues and supervisors?
- Where do I go to sharpen my skills and deepen knowledge of leadership ethics and social justice?
- Who are my mentors? How do they embody the principles of fairness, justice, equity, compassion and critique?
- Can I recognize the difference between opinions and informed knowledge?
- How often do I rely on personal anecdotal evidence when teaching?

On a professional level, consider:

- How do we verify that an educator fully understands their ethical obligations in an educational environment, especially when teaching for socially just leadership learning and development?
- What kinds of ethical standards, structures and procedures might we need to adopt as a profession?
- How can we grow our capacity to educate, train, mentor, energize, inspire and otherwise develop the next generation of socially just leadership educators?

CONCLUSION

This chapter sprouted from a series of contemplations: Socially just leadership education—what has ethics got to do with it? How are these principles related? Isn't social justice work inherently ethical? How do we teach emerging social justice leaders to lead in ways that are ethically minded? What's at stake if we don't? Through the investigation of these questions, we have journeyed through theoretical foundations, pedagogical challenges, instructional strategies, and guiding questions to move the profession of leadership education forward. The year 2020 proved to be a monumental catalyst for social justice leadership on a national scale, and the conceptions provided within this chapter will undoubtedly serve as a springboard to propel our discipline forward as we prepare our students and ourselves for the long road ahead.

REFERENCES

Astin, A. W., & Astin, H. S. (2000). *Leadership reconsidered: Engaging higher education in social change*. W. K. Kellogg Foundation.

Axson, S. (2020, August 27). College football means big money. Black athletes stand at the intersection of risk and profit. *NBC News*. https://www.nbc-news.com/news/nbcblk/college-sports-mean-big-money-black-athletes-stand-intersection-risk-n1238450.

Bell, L. A. (2018). Theoretical foundations for social justice education. In M. Adams, W. J. Blumenfeld, D. C. J. Catalano, K. S. DeJong, H. W. Hackman, L. E. Hopkins, B. J. Love, M. L. Peters, D. Shlasko, & X. Zuniga (Eds.). *Readings for diversity and social justice* (4th ed., pp. 21–35). Routledge.

Collins, J. D. (2020). Untangling the destructive leadership web: The case of Team Foxcatcher. In K. L. Guthrie & D. M. Jenkins (Eds.), *Transforming learning: Instructional and assessment strategies for leadership education* (pp. 22–23). Information Age.

Dugan, J. P. (2017). *Leadership theory: Cultivating critical perspectives*. Jossey-Bass.

Ethics Unwrapped. (n.d.). *Morals*. McCombs School of Business. The University of Texas at Austin. Retrieved September, 3, 2020 from https://ethicsun-wrapped.utexas.edu/glossary/morals

Gert, B. (2004). *Common morality: Deciding what to do*. Oxford University Press.

Godwin, L. N. (2015). Examining the impact of moral imagination on organizational decision-making. *Business & Society, 54*(2), 254–278. https://doi.org/10.1177/0007650312443641

Guthrie, K. L., & Chunoo, V. S. (2018). *Changing the narrative: Socially just leadership education*. Information Age.

Guthrie, K. L., & Jenkins, D. M. (2018). *The role of leadership educators: Transforming learning*. Information Age.

Harwood, S. A., Choi, S., Orozsco, M. Browne-Huntt, M. & Mendenhall, R. (2015). *Racial microaggressions at the University of Illinois at Urbana-Champaign: Voices of students of color in the classroom*. University of Illinois at Urbana-Champaign. https://www.racialmicroaggressions.illinois.edu/files/2015/03/RMA-Classroom-Report.pdf

Hills, M. D. (2002). Kluckhohn and Strodtbeck's values orientation theory. *Online Readings in Psychology and Culture, 4*(4). https://doi.org/10.9707/2307-0919.1040

Hofstede, G. (1980). *Culture's consequences: International differences in work-related values*. SAGE.

Hofstede, G. (2001). *Culture's consequences: Comparing values, behaviors, institutions, and organizations across nations* (2nd ed.). SAGE.

House, R. J., Hanges, P. J., Javidan, M., Dorfman, P. W., & Gupta V. (Eds.). (2004). *Culture, leadership, and organizations: The GLOBE study of 62 societies*. SAGE.

Johnson, C. E. (2020). *Meeting the ethical challenges of leadership: Casting light or shadow* (7th ed.). SAGE.

Kellerman, B. (2005). How bad leadership happens. *Leader to Leader, 35*, 41–46.

Kirk, G., & Okazawa-Rey. (2018). Identities and social locations: Who am I? Who are my people? In M. Adams, W. J. Blumenfeld, D. C. J. Catalano, K. S. DeJong, H. W. Hackman, L. E. Hopkins, B. J. Love, M. L. Peters, D. Shlasko, & X. Zuniga (Eds.). *Readings for diversity and social justice* (4th ed., pp. 10–16). Routledge.

Kluckhohn, F. R., & Strodtbeck, F. L. (1961). *Variations in value orientations*. Row, Peterson.

Komives, S. R., & Wagner, W. (2017). *Leadership for a better world: Understanding the social change model of leadership development* (2nd ed.). Jossey-Bass.

Kouzes, J. M. & Posner, B. Z. (2006). *The leadership challenge* (Vol. 3). John Wiley & Sons.

McCoy, D. L., & Rodricks, D. J. (2015). *Critical race theory in higher education: 20 years of theoretical and research innovations: ASHE Higher Education Report, Vol. 41, No 3*. John Wiley & Sons.

National Collegiate Athletic Association. (2019). *NCAA demographics database: Executive summary 2018–2019*. http://www.ncaa.org/about/resources/research/ncaa-demographics-database

Shapiro, J. P., & Stefkovich, J. A. (2016). E*thical leadership and decision making in education: Applying theoretical perspectives to complex dilemmas* (4th ed). Routledge.

Solórzano, D. G., & Yosso, T. J. (2002). Critical race methodology: Counter-storytelling as an analytical framework for education research. *Qualitative inquiry, 8*(1), 23–44.

Thomas, N., Gismondi, A., & Upchurch, K. (2020). *Election imperatives 2020: A time of physical distancing and social action*. Johnathan M. Tisch College of Civic Life Institute for Democracy & Higher Education, Tufts University.

W. K. Kellogg Foundation. (2016). *Racial Equity Resource Guide*. https://heal-ourcommunities.org/

CHAPTER 16

LEADER ACTIVISTS

Connecting Leadership Learning and Student Resistance

Michaela A. Shenberger and Kathy L. Guthrie

American higher education seeks to help students explore their individual identities, and become productive members of society. These institutions consider core values such as "civic mindedness, social responsibility, political engagement, and social change" (Martin et al., 2019, p. 9) as intended outcomes. These values can be explored and expressed through activism; in fact, Martin et al. (2019) stressed student activism should be viewed as developmental with many benefits for students' education, including their leadership development. This chapter provides direction in weaving student activism into the fabric of leadership development, as well as pushes higher education toward student activism as a vital function of socially just leadership.

DEFINING STUDENT ACTIVISM

Leadership is socially constructed (Guthrie et al., 2013), and so is activism. This social construction occurs over time as our understanding of

Shifting the Mindset: Socially Just Leadership Education
pp. 191–203

these complex ideas are created alongside others. This creation is influential because of the cultural influence they have. Therefore, the meaning and effectiveness of activism is collectively built and constantly evolving. Students participating in activism mirror larger societal understandings of what is qualified as activism, while also customizing elements and expressions of activism based on their immediate environment; for example, a campus culture. The shifting nature of what is recognized and perpetuated as student activism is crucial when engaging with students, as what we say and how we react to activism has a lasting impact on the students walking with us.

An example of how definitions of and approach to activism have shifted comes from comparing the 1965 Bloody Sunday march, and more recently, the protests associated with Black Lives Matter movement. Although resistance itself has not changed, the accessibility of information brought by modern-day social media was inconceivable during the 1960s. The brutality of Bloody Sunday was front page news and broadcasted into countless American homes; but in 2020, live streams of police brutality can be witnessed on millions of smart phones around the world. Beyond the shift in scope of outreach, many instances can be seen from multiple angles, with observers immediately reaching for their phones to capture any and everything they can. Essentially, the tools of activism continue to evolve; therefore, our definitions of student activism must also accommodate all involved.

With the continual evolution of activity in mind, we offer a few definitions reflective of our own personal understandings of what constitutes student activism. Despite these suggestions, we challenge you to follow Mendes and Chang's (2019) guidance in "[expanding] your definition of activism. Ask students both informally and through programming about their definitions of [activism]. Model and highlight diverse manifestations of agency by pointing them out and encouraging student to be active in ways that they deem meaningful and authentic" (p. 75), as our views of activism may differ from yours and your students'.

In one of the most cited student activism resources, Rhoads (1998) asserted student activism is "a form of participatory democracy" (p. 623); we stand by Rhoads' definition because it provides students, educators, and institutions with a flexible foundation to build their own understanding of how student activism takes shape on their campus. A participatory democracy occurs when all individuals involved have power and ability to influence political decisions that affect their lives. For clarification, the United States of America is not a participatory democracy; it is a representative democracy where elected officials act as proxies for their communities and advocate for their electorate's concerns. Despite this difference in approaches, a representative democracy can still contain elements of a participatory democracy by valuing the development of individuals' skills in advocating for their rights and beliefs (Pateman, 1970), and protecting the rights of citizens to participate in activism when deemed necessary by those same citizens. Institutions of higher education typically have a representative means for students to advocate for themselves and others (e.g., Student Government Associations); however, there are situations where direct participation is required. Although it is not typically our duty to determine the worth of cause(s) students advocate for or against, it is our responsibility to frame advocacy itself as leadership learning.

We encourage you to consider including Stewart and Williams' (2019) resistance matrix and Linder et al.'s (2019) emphasis on the labor of student activists as other activism frameworks to consider. Inclusion of these powerful words provided us an enhanced foundational understanding of student activism: "We use *activism* to describe students' efforts to interrupt power and dominance to create more just campuses" (Linder et al., 2019, p. 39); additionally we recognize "*activist* as a term cannot be universally applied to every person who engages in resistance work," (Linder et al., 2019, p. 39), and we recognize the work done by individuals who "[make] a choice to reject and avoid succumbing to a system of dominance … [our students may] start where they were and simply resist, sometimes by sharing their experiences to disrupt. These actions are a form of resistance as daily action" (Stewart & Williams, 2019, p. 214). Taken together, the foundational definition of student activism we are using is: *Student activism is an expression of participatory democracy when students work to interrupt the current status quo of their campuses with the goal of shifting toward being socially just.* Student activism both includes, and goes beyond, the visible and active participation of students in activism work, to include the more subtle disruptions and interrupts of the current system; specifically recognizing those whose existence in spaces designed to inflect harm or damage on to them, as well as those who both refuse to reject the status quo in their day-to-day operations and decision-making.

From this foundational understanding of activism, we believe it is critical to engage with students, colleagues, and campus communities to expand our understanding of activism within each unique interaction and situation as leadership development.

PREVALENCE OF STUDENT ACTIVISM

We believe it is important to understand the prevalence of students expecting and wanting to participate in activism in college. Understanding information related to student activism assists leadership educators in two major ways: first, by preparing us to engage with students dedicated to resistance work; and second, by acting as a foundation for language around decision-making at all levels of our organizations. *The American Freshman: National Norms*, published by the Higher Education Research Institute, reported almost 97% of incoming students either witnessed first-hand, or participated in, activism in the fall 2015 incoming cohort (Eagan et al., 2015). Students represented by this report are likely to have graduated by the publication of this chapter; however, we note this cohort of students came to higher education prior to more recent social movements such as Black Lives Matter, #MeToo, and March for Our Lives. If five years ago, almost 97% of our incoming first-year students were meaningfully exposed to activism prior to joining our communities, increases in the volume of students ready, willing, and able for collegiate activism by percentage is likely even greater today.

IDENTIFYING STUDENT ACTIVISM AND RESISTANCE WORK

Student activists are often identified as those physically and loudly present at rallies, riots, and other events; which unfortunately aligns with outdated notions of leaders as extroverts. Although the field of leadership studies seeks to counter this misattribution, higher education has made little progress understanding the value of student activists who do not display these stereotypical characteristics. When students emerge as activists and/or leaders, they tend to be groomed as such. However, if this is our only means of cultivating activist and leaders, we risk devaluing and alienating students who do not embody the student activist mold, their work, their leadership, and even their very existence (Anthony, 2018). With this in mind, we offer two examples of how students manage activism, resistance, and leadership. These prototypes are not the only ways our students act, but we believe exposure to, and reflection upon these patterns are helpful in unlearning our expectations, to make space for our own growth.

The Overlooked

Overlooked student activists and leaders are those who do not resemble the stereotypes we carry of students in such roles. As Stewart and Williams (2019) stated, students may be practicing activism simply by "[making] a choice to reject and avoid succumbing to a system of dominance ... [our students] start where they were and simply resist, sometimes by sharing their experiences to disrupt. These actions are a form of resistance as daily action" (p. 214). Despite this resistance work, too often we overlook their contributions to social movements; preferring instead to seek students who practice visible and public fearlessness. This false equivalency does a disservice to our students, their development, and their causes.

The overlooked include students who live in the shadow of the habitual recognition and valuing of public resistance work, such as protests, sit-ins, and social media initiatives. It is not the students themselves who have chosen to live in this shadow, but rather our construction of recognition systems that force them there. To counter this, Mendes and Chang (2019) chipped away at the structure itself by working with students who were undocumented and afraid. Within their work, Mendes and Chang (2019) compared the expectation and elevation of undocumented student activists who publicly disclosed their statuses and were praised, to two women who could not participate in this way. By centering these women and their experiences, Mendes and Chang rebuilt systems to recognize existence as activism, while calling on us as educators and researchers to do the same. They advised us to "validate silent activism by not privileging the most vocal or physically present students but rather by weighing differing manifestations of activism equitably" (p. 75). This is not a call to push these silent leaders into the light; we are called instead to, "invite participation without the pressures of outing themselves or adopting a kind of performativity that misaligns with [students'] sense of safety and self" (p. 75).

The Silenced

In addition to casting a shadow on the overlooked, students on our campus may be actively silenced by our institutional policies, practices, and by our own personal beliefs as educators, as "college campuses are regularly accused of restriction the constitutional rights of outspoken conservatives and maintaining a hostile environment toward deviant worldviews" (Gowen et al., 2019, p. 43). We recognize the difficultly, personally and professionally, to support causes poorly aligned with our beliefs. This silencing can be conscious and subconscious in nature; we could actively work against a movement within our professional role or make decisions based on biases we are unaware of possessing. Acts of silencing can include prioritizing the approval of one event over another or interrupting a student during a discussion. "When leadership educators struggle to find the value in student activism, critical self-reflections on the dynamics of power, privilege, and oppression may be necessary. Activism often emerges from members of marginalized groups not being heard or validated by those in power. Whether they agree or disagree with the cause at hand, socially just leadership educators emphasize students' voices" (Anthony, 2018, p. 47). Ultimately, socially just leadership educators are those who listen, engage, and amplify students' voices.

BRIDGING ACTIVISM AND LEADERSHIP

The potential harm in making qualifications and judgment-calls regarding what is activism has been reiterated throughout this chapter. Acknowledging how this ambiguity can be frustrating, we once again empower you to embrace the shifting sand of understanding and recognize the potential it holds while focusing on your understanding of leadership. The sheer volume of leadership theories, definitions, and models alone can be overwhelming. Overlaying tenets of activism and resistance may complicate matters more but yields considerable social justice potential. Our students may differentially identify as a leader, or an activist, but not usually both. Socially just leadership educators recognize the intersectional and parallel nature of leadership and activism to guide our students through this complexity.

To assist in this difficult feat, we present one of the many ways prominent scholars have tried to capture this connection; Martin et al.'s (2019) notion of a *leader activist*. The term leader activist was created "to highlight leadership qualities and capacity that student activists have the potential to cultivate through their experiences and education" (Martin et al., 2019, p. 5). These ideas describe the undeniable connection between activism and leadership, which socially just leadership educators share and reinforce within our areas of influence. Beyond acknowledging the connection between leadership and activism, we believe this connection and understanding is cocreated among students who authentically engage in various forms and combinations of activism and leadership processes.

Self-Education

We encourage you to continue educating yourself on foundational and emerging conceptualizations of leadership and activism. While potentially tiring and overwhelming, high-quality scholarship provides, "congealed experience, which, in a concentrated form, can bring years of accumulated knowledge to bear on a particular [topic] and help prevent strategic mishaps" (Austin, 2009). We believe sourcing appropriate literature prior to developing curricula and programming is essential to meaningful experiences in the cocreation of knowledge and understanding around leadership and activism. In addition to the plethora of resources available in the higher education and leadership education fields; including many of the sources we used to create this chapter, we strongly advise diversifying your reading list to include authors from minoritized social groups (people of color, women, LGBTQIA+ community members, and disabled/differently-abled, among others), various areas of study (e.g., sociology, science, technology, engineering, and mathematics, business, etc.), as well as mediums (books, articles, dissertations, blogs, social media); all of which are essential to developing and maintaining robust approaches to activism and leadership.

We caution against relying on unrevised previously facilitated materials, and/or overreliance on programs and curriculum we experienced as students; especially when related to activism and leadership. Socially just leadership educators continually contend with the impact of an ever-changing local, national, and global landscape. As such, we are best served when our expectations, content, and approach are updated to reflect the modern context. As our collective understanding of activism and leadership shift and change, "the question becomes whether or not we have acknowledged, supported, and valued such change" (Mendes & Chang, 2019, p. 66).

Include Students Perspective

Although the extant literature is wide and deep, campus context and culture need to be considered when considering how activism development and leadership learning occurs. Students tend to be in tune with the context and culture of their communities; therefore, they should be partners in co-creating leadership and activism programs and education. Socially just leadership educators recognize the expertise and lived experiences of students, and develop praxes around engaging with students in their context. This recognition of expertise and experience empowers students to engage in egalitarian partnerships. Balancing power is fraught with challenges, and may ultimately be unattainable, but there are ways to try nonetheless:

- frame partnerships as optional;
- clearly express your intention and expectations for the partnership;
- provide opportunities for participants to engage anonymously (to enhance their ability to express themselves and provide feedback safely);
- craft opportunities for autonomy and creativity;

- implement a "snowball" recruitment approach, rather than a "cold call" approach; and
- empower and encourage (counter)stories of student activism within the partnership space.

Interactions characterized by these factors highlight the reality that, "a one-size-fits-all approach to creating social change does not exist" (Anthony, 2018, p. 50). Informed educators leverage varied approaches to leadership learning opportunities for their students.

Recognizing Educators' Power and Responsibility

Well before many of our undergraduates were born, bell hooks (1994) wrote "the classroom remains the most radical space of possibility in the academy" (p. 12). Within classrooms, educators bear the power, privilege, and responsibility of living hooks's words. Prior to engaging student activism and leadership development, personal education, reflection, and development, when started early and revisited frequently, facilitates growth and change. Beyond this dedication to growth and flexibility, socially just leadership educators recognize and grapple with the reality that the power and authority they hold cannot fully be dismantled; and as a result, we are complicit in our oppressive systems. This realization is crucial in authentically engaging with students. However, regardless of the title and power we hold as educators, it is our responsibility to ensure our students are not the only ones growing from our shared experiences.

ACTIVISM AND LEADERSHIP DEVELOPMENT PROGRAMS

Once we have built our own connections, intersections, and parallels between student activism and student leadership, we are primed to assist our students in creating their own understanding of activism and leadership. It is critical to identify all students who are engaged in activism and resistance as leaders. Simple and collective shifts in language are the cornerstones of societal shifts, though their impact may not be felt immediately, the ripples will remain in how our students view themselves and how our peers consider the work of student activism.

Suggestions to Creating a Conducive and Supportive Community

Approaches to creating a community with the ability to exist outside of the predetermined shared space in which the educator resides (e.g., within a classroom, or during a scheduled meeting) differs greatly depending on the characteristics the community holds (e.g., community purpose, size of the group, identities represented, etc.). The following suggestions are intended for recurring instances rather than a singular encounter (e.g., a course, a regularly meeting club or organization, a multi-session workshop.).

Connecting Beyond Shared Experience

Although icebreakers are popular when first interacting with a fledgling community, socially just educators must move beyond attempting quickly trying to learn names. There are several ways we suggest using to guide students into making more sustainable connections:

- Make using names a fundamental part of every discussion and interaction between members of the community. Set a standard from the first interaction where first names are used as much as possible. For example, when a student indicates via a pronoun or a physical movement, they are referring to a peer, clarify who the student is referring to by saying something along the lines of "[insert name of student] are you referring to [other student]?" Nametags are also helpful to build confidence.
- Encourage regular peer-to-peer check-ins, especially during shared times of stress. Ask students to check on how one of their peers is doing. This can be a regular practice where students push past the tendency to reply with one-word answers when asked how they are.
- Challenge students to break out of their pattern of sitting in the same spot during every interaction. Ask students if and why they tend to sit in the same seat, even when assigned seats are not required in their classes; most times a sense of comfort is part of the reason. Building a few minutes at the beginning of every class for the first week or so and start each class by reminding folks to make sure they are sitting with someone new is a good practice.
  - Recognize your student's ability and willingness to change their physical space in each class as some students need consistency; instead, provide alternative ways for students to meet peers through in-class activities.

Shared Decision-Making

A community cannot be crafted solely by an educator; therefore, students need to be involved in the construction of their experiences. There is a sense of comfort when a predetermined plan is in place; however, when developing students' leadership skills, empowering them to join decision-making processes provides practice opportunities for leadership and activism skill in safe environments. We suggest:

- Community guideline development should be handled mainly by students, but the experience should be prompted and supported by the educator. While you may present some example foundational elements, such as using names or regularly checking on each other, students should work together to create mutual understanding regarding interactions within the community. Also, empower students to work together to set expectations for not only each other, but for you, too. Frequently, "respect" and "honesty" are mentioned during these exercises. Encourage deeper descriptions. Does everyone hold the same understanding of these words? How would these principles show up in a specific community space? Regularly revisit these guidelines, encourage flexibility, and empower students to shift as they see fit. The guidelines and standards set at the beginning may not serve the community by the end.

- If possible, hold space for the student community to make decisions regarding curriculum and direction of the program. The determination of what content is valuable and how shared time is spent can be viewed through the lens of power dynamics (Choudry, 2015). When possible, we suggest creating environments where students have agency in their experience. By engaging them in the cocreation and selection of knowledge, you model activism in your position by changing the system for enhanced learning. Potential areas to consider include: determining how assignments will be graded and weighted throughout the semester; decisions regarding revisiting topics and the speed at which the community progresses; building opportunities for peer-to-peer education and facilitation; as well as selecting what resources will be referenced and utilized (readings, podcasts, videos, etc.).

Establish the Baseline

Each individual has a unique lived experience, which results in different knowledge and varying opportunities in applying their understanding. With all this variability, it is important to establish a common starting point for all involved. Before establishing the common starting point, it is helpful to gauge where the community is; both individually and collectively. Information gathering approaches, such as questionnaires, can clarify your understanding of students' knowledge base; however, we suggest more interactive approaches. When trying to establish comprehension and prior knowledge at an individual level, exercises involving reflection and the expression of personal narratives are incredibly insightful. Two-minute essays can provide brief glimpses while longer reflective activities provide students with the time and space to create more depth. Writing and conversational prompts might include:

- When and how are you a leader/activist?
- Who is someone you look up to and why?
- If you could snap your fingers and instantly have something change within our campus community, what would you snap for?

When focusing on a collective understanding of your community from a knowledge stand-point, collaboration and interaction within the community is vital. Although large group discussions and activities are telling, providing a scaling activity empowers quieter members to engage differently, especially if this assessment is happening early in the timeline. A scaling activity allows students to collect their thoughts and consider their responses individually, before collaborating and sharing with a partner or small group. Then, students work together to share thoughts and ideas with the community. Writing and conversational prompts might include:

- Compare and contrast the similarities and differences between an activist and a leader.
- Are all activists also leaders? Why or why not?
- Does anyone hold an activist identity? Why or why not?
- How would you (as an individual/pair/community) enact a successful activism movement on our campus?

In addition to prompts, more creative activities might serve the community well, such as 'Build the Perfect Campus Leader', where students work together to create a visual representation of what believe is a perfect campus leader, elements such as personality characteristics, identities, items on their resume, as well as various skills may be represented. After the perfect leader is created, the community should have a discussion regarding:

- How they came to their conclusions on what should be included in this representation?
- Do they see themselves reflected in this 'perfect campus leader'?

- Did anyone think about themselves when working through this activity?
- How realistic is this representation?

Collectively Acknowledge the Starting Point

Once you have established the baseline, let your students know where you located a potential starting place for the community. We suggest approaching this as a conversation, rather than a unilateral decision. We encourage you to open the conversation for feedback and check-in with students' sense of comfort. Once a consensus has been reached regarding the starting point, provide students with a way to refresh their knowledge, such as providing helpful readings and explanation videos on an online platform, or creating a primer containing essential information.

Find Experts for Institutional Context and Culture

It does not always fall on you to hold all the expertise within the curriculum or program. We encourage including faculty and staff whose academic or professional expertise aligns with your goals, as well as students and alumni who have leadership and activism experience within the area of interest for students. Including others into students' education serves several purposes, including: interdisciplinary connection between various subjects; inclusion of diverse perspectives and modes of engagement; exposure to tangible experiences; expertise regarding policies and practices; the ability to ask questions and receive answers to a plethora of individuals; and, personal/professional network growth beyond their current community.

LEADERSHIP EDUCATORS ARE ACTIVISM EDUCATORS

In the last academic year alone, we have experienced dramatic social justice movements; massive protests; a global pandemic; a shift to distance learning at an unprecedented scale; countless political upheavals, and humanitarian crises at local, national, and international levels. During this same time, we have welcomed new students onto our campuses, into our classrooms, and experienced our students transitioning to alumni with the turn of a tassel. Higher education has persisted, and we expect it will continue for the foreseeable future. With that perseverance comes a great responsibility—we must cultivate and empower student activist and leaders to face an increasingly uncertain future. With each new student cohort comes a new perspectives and approaches to both leadership and activism. Our duty as educators is to recognize and value these advances, as the tools of yesterday are not be adequate to meet tomorrow's demands.

REFERENCES

Anthony, M. (2018). Intersecting activism and social justice in leadership education. In K. L. Guthrie & V. S. Chunoo (Eds.), *Changing the narrative: Socially just leadership education* (pp. 41–46). Information Age.

Austin, D. (2009). Education and liberation. *McGill Journal of Education, 44*(1), 107–117. https://mje.mcgill.ca/article/view/3026/3050

Choudry, A. (2015). *Learning activism: The intellectual life of contemporary social movements.* University of Toronto Press.

Eagan, K., Stolzenberg, E. B., Bates, A. K., Aragon, M. C., Suchard, M. R., & Rios-Aguilar, C. (2015). *The American freshman: National norms fall 2015.* Higher Education Research Institute. https://www.heri.ucla.edu

Gowen, G. H., Hemer, K. M., & Reason, R. D. (2019). Understanding American conservatism and its role in higher education. In D. L. Morgan & C. H. F. Davis, III (Eds.), *Student activism, politics, and campus climate in higher education* (pp. 43–59). Routledge.

Guthrie, K. L., Bertrand Jones, T., Osteen, L., & Hu, S. (2013). *Cultivating leader identity and capacity in students from diverse backgrounds.* Jossey-Bass.

hooks, b. (1994). *Teaching to transgress: Education as the practice of freedom.* Routledge.

Linder, C., Quaye, S. J., Lange, A. C., Roberts, R. E., Lacy, M. C., & Okello, W. K. (2019). "A student should have the privilege of just being a student": Student activism as labor. *The Review of Higher Education, 42,* 37–62. https://doi.org/10.1353/rhe.2019.0044

Martin, G. L., Williams, B. M., Green, B., & Smith, M. J. (2019). Reframing activism as leadership. In G. L. Martin, C. Linder, & B. M. Williams (Eds.), *Leadership learning through activism* (Vol. 161, pp. 9–24). Jossey-Bass. https://doi.org/10.1002/yd.20316

Mendes, J., & Chang, A. (2019). Undocumented and afraid: Expanding the definition of student activism. In D. L. Morgan & C. H. F. Davis, III (Eds.), *Student activism, politics, and campus climate in higher education* (pp. 60–76). Routledge.

Pateman, C. (1970). *Participation and democratic theory.* Cambridge University Press.

Rhoads, R. A. (1998). Student protest and multicultural reform: Making sense of campus unrest in the 1990s. *The Journal of Higher Education, 69*(6), 621–646.

Stewart, T. J., & Williams, B. M. (2019). Nuanced activism: A matrix of resistance. In A. Dache, S. J. Quaye, C. Linder, & K. M. McGuire (Eds.), *Rise up!: Activism as education* (pp. 201–224). Michigan State University Press.

CHAPTER 17

SOCIALLY JUST LEADERSHIP EDUCATION IN ACTION

Applying the Culturally Relevant Leadership Learning Model

Vivechkanand S. Chunoo and Gregory E. French

Socially just leadership education can be enacted through learning models rooted in cultural relevance. Helpfully, the culturally relevant leadership learning model (CRLL; Bertrand Jones et al., 2016; Guthrie et al., 2017) provides a roadmap for social change and social justice leaders. However, little empirical data exists regarding the validity of this model or how its associated outcomes might be assessed. Our chapter describes the operationalization of essential CRLL elements to make leadership education (and therefore, leading) accessible to greater numbers and different kinds of people. More egalitarian leadership learning experiences present opportunities to maximize the impact of a CRLL approach on socially just leadership education.

Inspired by scholarship on campus climate (Solorzano et al., 2000; Yosso et al., 2009) and culturally relevant pedagogy (Ladson-Billings,

Shifting the Mindset: Socially Just Leadership Education
pp. 205–217

1995, 2014), CRLL builds on individual leader identity and leadership capacity toward engagement across social differences. The model includes pathways to improve knowledge of self and others, as well as contextual and systemic awareness (Guthrie et al., 2017). The CRLL model frames leadership learning environments along domains of intra- and interpersonal dynamics, as well as through five dimensions centering on history, diversity, psychology, behavior, and structure. Despite calls to use this model toward stewardship and collective action (Bordas, 2016) as well in the service of activism and advocacy (Anthony, 2018), few empirically based practices have been offered to support these aims. We attempt address the gap between theoretical and conceptual formulations of CRLL and its practical application in socially just leadership education praxis.

We take a two-part approach to operationalizing CRLL: first addressing CRLL's central domains, then focusing on the five dimensions of culturally relevant leadership learning. We describe how essential elements of the CRLL model can be practically implemented and suggest additional considerations when applying various aspects of this approach. These recommendations include Dugan's (2017) suggestions of motivation and enactment in leading, as well as intersections of social identities with leader identity, the psychosocial aspects of leading, and the formal and informal ways the model are enacted in our everyday lives.

CENTRAL DOMAINS
OF CULTURALLY RELEVANT LEADERSHIP LEARNING

Identity, capacity, and efficacy link individual leaders to the processes of leadership. Additionally, other meaningful dynamics, like motivation and enactment (as described in Dugan, 2017), are important to leadership expression. To operationalize the components of CRLL, we briefly review each of the originally stated central dynamics as well as explain our thinking around some vital additions. First, "Identity is our ever-evolving self-portrait" (Bertrand Jones et al., 2016, p. 13). Personally held identities include roles played in society, communities, and homes, as well as personality traits and leader identity itself. Within leadership processes, individuals contend with personally held self-portraits and the perceptions others hold of them; their ascribed identities. Thus, within the domain of identity, culturally relevant leaders balance private and public personae to be individually successful and to enable the success of others.

Capacity is our abilities to lead effectively (Bertrand Jones et al., 2016). We frame individually held capacity as "capability," while describing capacity for leading processes as "competence." As individuals develop the skills associated with leading others (competence), they also refine their self-management abilities (capability). These dynamic processes reinforce each other, enhancing capacity for culturally relevant leadership.

Efficacy is a belief in our own effectiveness (Bandura, 1977, 1997). We situate individually held efficacy as "confidence," or the belief that one can do something regardless of historical successes. We also locate the process side of efficacy as "agency"; the expectation leaders have of their own success as well as the success of others in leadership environments. Leadership processes impacted by agency can include activism and advocacy toward deep social improvement. Culturally relevant leaders improve their efficacy by performing individual actions to benefit themselves and others, improving confidence as better social change agents.

Motivation is an individual's intensity of effort or persistence in leading (Chan & Drasgow, 2001; Dugan, 2017). This persistence can be internally driven (intrinsic) or externally driven (extrinsic; Deci & Ryan, 2009). We adhere to this positioning, identifying individually held motivation to be a leader as "intrinsic leader motivation" and persistence to participate in leadership processes as "extrinsic leadership motivation." While many leaders have affinities for one motivational type over the other, culturally relevant leaders recognize the impact of both and attempt to strike a parity between them for themselves and others.

Finally, enactment is the "functional practice of leadership" (Dugan, 2017, p. 14). We see the human capital of leading in two ways: self-work and cooperation. As an individual applies energy toward themselves as a leader, they are enacting self-work. However, as human effort is applied to leading alongside others, individuals are expressing cooperation. Culturally relevant leaders understand how self-work improves their ability to collaborate and how to apply interpersonal learning obtained through cooperation in their personal- and leader- development.

Our conceptualization (Figure 17.1) includes additional factors to supplement these domains. Reflection, meaning-making, and values impact how these dynamics are enacted in leading (Volpe White et al., 2019). Reflection includes acts of intentional consideration to outcomes and stimuli leading to change. Values are personally held beliefs and guiding principles. Meaning-making is the process of understanding and expressing significance in a given situation or experience. These concepts do not necessarily function linearly, but are nonetheless part of a continuous and regularly revisited cycle. These considerations provide nuance in operationalizing CRLL in useful ways to promote lasting achievement through personal interpretation and context.

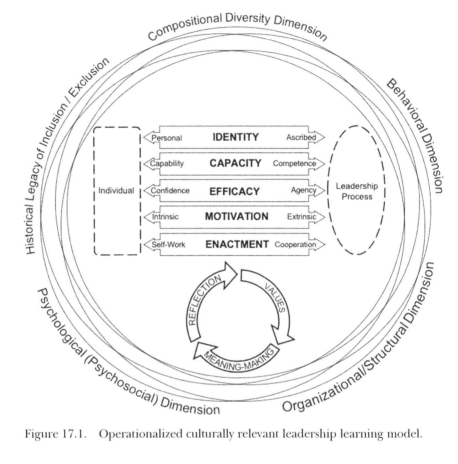

Figure 17.1. Operationalized culturally relevant leadership learning model.

FIVE DIMENSIONS
OF CULTURALLY RELEVANT LEADERSHIP LEARNING

We Cannot Change the Past, but We Can Alter the Future

The historical legacy of inclusion and exclusion contextualizes social justice leadership and its purpose in shaping the future. As an explanation of how things have come to be, the historical legacy of inclusion and exclusion highlights systemic advantages and disadvantages in leadership learning; explicitly naming who it was built to benefit and those for whom it still constrains. In many ways, a college or university's founding and its mission, as well as its values and principles influence how its traditions, symbols, rituals, policies, and practices take shape (Chunoo & Osteen,

2016). Socially just leadership educators recognize how oppressive systems in one cohort perpetuate disadvantages of the next cohort. Socially just leadership educators advocate for awareness of these systems and drive progress through their praxes.

One specific step socially just leadership educators can take involves seeking blind spots they may have been unaware of in the past. For example, if a university is located on indigenous land, a territory acknowledgment is a means of showing mindfulness and consciousness for the privileges that students, faculty, and community members may benefit from today because of that land. This can be printed in the syllabus and included in the first course meeting to spread understanding of the historical legacy of the foundation upon which our courses are (literally) built. An awareness of these issues drive progress toward accurately representing our individual and collective values through the messages we send. We can evolve the story we tell students, and each other, to invoke positive change in the future.

Understanding the past influences how we build an inclusive future. Socially just leadership educators encourage students to ask questions, such as: "Where and how is leadership situated in our institution?" and "How does power flow on campus and how can we influence it?" Socially just leadership educators approach these perspectives with a mindfulness that recognizes how students' diverse backgrounds impact their own historical legacies. These steps foster progress in students and institutions by: (1) reducing the likelihood of repeating marginalizing action, (2) acknowledging the impact of past activities, regardless of intention, on members of specific student populations, and (3) leveraging current and future conditions toward improved sensitivity, responsiveness, and inclusion.

Applying CRLL drives leadership educators to examine who benefits from historical narratives (i.e., past privileges) and identify who suffers because of them. Symbolic features history may exist throughout campus; therefore, it is important remove discriminatory symbols and language from our courses and programs. These seemingly small changes can echo across the campus community. Every day, we make tomorrow's history. Socially just leadership educators proactively build a culture of recognition characterized by the idea of not moving on (we cannot change the past) but moving forward (we *can* change the future).

It's Not Just Getting on the Bus; it's Also Where You Sit

Compositional diversity includes student population demographics and the overall representation in organizational and institutional contexts. That said, the physical representation does not always translate equality. This framework evaluates movement beyond just representation, but inclusion with a voice. Our goal is to increase cultural diversity to develop a wider range of perspectives to share their experience, which in turn creates inclusiveness and opens dialogue. Socially just leaders strive to help students find their place while challenging the status quo; encouraging an open-minded mentality comfortable admitting, "I never thought of it that way." This, in effect, shows the ways in which dialogue and compositional representation can have an impact on the viewpoints, values, and voices of students to expand perspectives and increase recognition of our unique and valuable differences.

Beyond the theoretical, socially just leadership educators implement opportunities for engagement and experience. Students who are invested in experiential learning take opportunities to questioning their own leadership styles and intentions. This can be done through leadership workshops, leadership coaches, and mentorship programs. These types of engagement facilitate dialogue and creates opportunities for listening and exposure to new ideas and ways of being. Formal leadership workshops create social interaction, start conversations, call for reflection, and facilitate follow-up action. Socially just leadership educators use this as a way to confront feelings, emotions, and vulnerability – "These differences not only influence who engages in addressing what issues but also shape how those students in particular work in the communities most affected by these issues" (Bertrand Jones et al., 2016, p. 17). Ultimately, socially just leadership educators play the role of facilitating and interpreting these actions, through a model of engagement, action, and reaction.

As this lens is examined, there are opportunities for personal change and agency to occur, but with change can come challenge. Conflict manifests when beliefs are challenged, but this can be a healthy form of engagement and questioning. When approached respectfully, conflict (internal and/or external) can encourage deep change and break down proverbial walls that may be present. Individuals should be safe, but the ideas and beliefs that students hold can be challenged. Through vulnerability, exposure can create more authentic dialogue and eventual change beyond superficial surface-level conversations. This is an opportunity for all students, across personal identities, to better understand each other, and create a mutual respect.

Liberating Others as You Free Yourself

The psychological dimension contextualizes how students navigate intrapersonal feelings and interpersonal interactions. We frame this dimension as "psychosocial" to highlight its ability to explain individual feelings in group contexts. Identifying and understanding these perspectives, beliefs, and positions is important for students of all backgrounds due to the emphasis on interpersonal interaction in leading. Effective social justice educators understand how students perceive societal constructs and barriers which isolate or exclude others. For example, students from marginalized racial backgrounds may feel a lack of representation when attending historically White colleges and universities (Mahoney, 2017), especially when institutional leaders, faculty members, or administrators do not actively foster an environment of inclusion or support. Social justice leadership educators are aware of the distinctions between intent and impact to support an understanding of perception and awareness to help students navigate dissonance between perceptions, attitudes, and beliefs.

Important layers of the psychological dimension include its visible and invisible concurrent presence, and the potentiality of being constructed or deconstructed along various dimensions of privilege. The psychological dimension seeks to better understand these systematic conflicts, as "leadership educators are called to assess the learning environment for marginalized students and create opportunities that foster acceptance of differing opinions and experiences while encouraging trust" (Bertrand Jones et al., 2016, p. 18). In a paradoxical sense, colleges and universities often perpetuate the systems of oppression or privilege they seek to disrupt (Edwards, 2007). For these reasons, socially just leadership educators proactively engage students *and* institutions of higher education in engaged reflection to improve the perceptions which shape our environment. Individual reflection is a necessary first step in liberating others as we first free ourselves toward a growth-oriented mindset (Dweck, 2017). Further empowering others creates opportunities for proactive and action-oriented relationships across institutions. Leadership educators who facilitate opportunities through skill-development conversation and workshops for students foster grit, resiliency, and integrity (Duckworth, 2016).

Social justice leadership educators examine *both* oppression *and* privilege to unpack "invisible knapsacks" we each carry (McIntosh, 1989). Students have inherent privileges from their race, religion, class, or other social identities. Deeply rooted advantages can often be identified more readily by those who do not possess them. Through meaningful dialogue and substantive perspective-taking experiences, socially just leadership educators mitigate the effects of vicious cycles and create virtuous cycles; supporting engagement of diverse students.

Your Voice Matters If You Use It

The behavioral dimension of the CRLL model centers on preparing students to interact across social differences as well as within culturally similar groups. These interactions can be especially challenging when students disagree on whether social differences even exist. The work then falls on socially just leadership educators to highlight inequitable social power structures and raise awareness regarding how these imbalances result in differential outcomes. One way of working along the behavioral dimension involves social capital mapping. In this exercise, students draw individual maps of their social networks, highlighting communities where they claim membership, and underscoring the relevant resources these connections represent. Once done individually, students compare social capital maps in increasingly larger groups (e.g., pairs, trios, an entire course or program) to clarify the caucuses (groups of similar students) and coalitions (groups of unlike students) available. These maps explicitly portray implicit similarities, differences, and opportunities for resource sharing. Socially just leadership educators meaningfully engage these caucuses and coalitions toward intergroup dialogue and strengthen students' capacities to communicate collaboratively with similar and dissimilar peers.

Additionally, the behavioral dimension encourages students to, "be reflective of their own experiences and those of others who may not mirror their own" (Bertrand Jones et al., 2016, p. 18). This does not mean students must agree with the worldviews of others, however; deep consideration of different life experiences promote increased capacity for perspective-taking. A method of motivating this reflection is creating a "Leadership Gallery" where students compose artistic responses to the question: "What is Leadership?" Individual answers might be drawings, paintings, sculptures, collages, video, audio, or other multimedia creations. When openly displayed together, students review each other's depictions and consider original artist's response to the question (content), and how they leveraged their medium (process) as authentic expressions of self. Observing diverse responses, portrayed in creative ways, assists students in confronting their own ideas about leading as well as in gaining appreciation for others' notions.

Social justice actions taken after college are predicated on the quality and frequency of culturally relevant behaviors students enact in college. Socially just leadership educators scaffold opportunities for engagement in unfamiliar and uncomfortable social situations. Students benefit from relatively low-stakes practice environments where they cooperate with like and unlike peers. Confronting students with issues of social power imbalances, contrasting perspectives, and diverse world views helps to make meaningful progress along CRLL's behavioral dimension. Additionally, coupling these activities with substantive reflection moves isolated behavioral skills into patterns of socially just actions.

The Spoken and Unspoken Rules
About How We Do What We Do

The organizational and structural dimension of CRLL draws focus to the explicit and implicit forces that govern the routine functioning of leadership learning organizations. These influences include: overall program structure; individual course curriculum; budget construction and partitioning; admission and transfer requirements and practices; recruitment and hiring strategies; professional review, tenure, and promotion criteria; as well as reward and recognition opportunities. Each of these institutional levers can change our trajectories toward social justice in leadership learning. However, we recognize leadership educators themselves are bound by the influences that differentially impact their students and their learning contexts. We empower leadership educators of all social locations to identify their areas of greatest impact (among those listed earlier as well as others) and encourage them to push against the forces of the status quo.

Attempting to change organizational culture and/or long-standing structures and practices can be some of the most seemingly intractable issues leadership educators can pursue; in part because the tactics and strategies necessary to influence formal policies can be quite different from the labor necessary to disrupt the invisible curriculum of the workforce. Often, we inherit workplace norms from predecessors and face immense pressure to conform despite disagreeing with what happens around us. In these instances, socially just educators remember that culture is an emergent property of group and team work; we are the agents of culture and cultural norms shift based on our ability and willingness to comply or resist. Finding others who share our beliefs (caucuses) around organizational culture issues, as well as enlisting help from others with differing beliefs (coalitions) who intend similar outcomes, is vital to culture change efforts. These caucuses and coalitions promote institutional awareness around how unique experiences and individual values are expressed through (and sometimes, despite) organizational culture.

Furthermore, CRLL's organizational and structural dimension gives inclusivity-minded educators thinking and acting tools to dismantle, or at least confront, implicit and explicit threats to social justice in leadership learning contexts. Formal rules and policies with social justice implications (which is to say, all of them) can and should be revisited regularly, scrutinized deeply, and rewritten actively to accommodate changes among social, cultural, and political forces. When organizational habits and taken-for-granted assumptions are forced into the light of public accountability, social injustice cannot thrive. Additionally, deeply embedded patterns we perpetuate that are not policy-driven, or contextually-bound, contribute to the institutional momentum which hinders socially just leadership learning experiences. Wrangling with these institutional forces represents risk on behalf of leadership educators; however, the cost of not confronting these issues is lost potential for a fairer and more equitable world.

TAKING A STAND: CRITICAL QUESTIONS AND CALL TO ACTION

At the heart of the culturally relevant leadership learning model (Bertrand Jones et al., 2016; Guthrie et al., 2017), is a continual reminder to advocate for social justice leadership and an urgency to take action. Alongside awareness, there are increased opportunities to better understand these frameworks and how they can be operationalized through a CRLL lens. Throughout this chapter, our objective was to define the different ways these frameworks are practiced and implemented by individuals to better support the overall advancement of leadership education to support more socially just and culturally relevant practices. Our goal was to understand what might constrain leadership opportunities and impede the growth of individuals in leadership development. Our approach was rooted in a call to action—to shift the mindset of leadership education toward social justice and equity.

We suggested beginning by contending with issues of history and historical context as means to craft a fairer future. We advocated understanding ourselves from psychosocial and behavioral aspects, while encouraging deep examinations of compositional and structural dynamics impacting how leadership practices are valued and portrayed. Alongside a practical reading of the CRLL model, its central domains were further expanded to show how each domain might be perceived or experienced. Our operationalized model includes an intersected visualizations of the five dimensions (Figure 17.1) accompanied by two new central domains; motivation and enactment, building on the existing domains of identity, capacity, and efficacy. These domains were expanded to illustrate the potential range of experiences students encounter. It also helps socially just leadership educators relate to individual viewpoints and consider how these perspectives translate to leadership processes. These layers and positions were used to conceptualize the value in understanding the CRLL model and how it move theory to action.

Our ideas are intended to offer practical solutions to current day issues. By using these concepts, and moving toward a better understanding and awareness, we challenge readers to confront their own feelings on these issues. With this in mind, we present five critical questions to conclude our chapter and promote reflection. These questions not only help individuals take a stand, but also exemplify the values of socially just leadership education in practice:

1.   How does your *understanding of your past* inform the future you want to see?

2.   How might you *privilege share* with others to help them achieve the social location they need to succeed?

3.   How can you *challenge the status quo* to allow yourself and others new ways of knowing, being, and doing leadership?

4.   How can you *amplify the voices* of people who have historically been quieted (or silenced) to *break past patterns* and *influence an environment of equity*?

5.   How do we *manage overt and covert influences and pressures* that keep things as they are instead of as they should or could be?

Ultimately, our goal behind a practical CRLL model is to address the explicit call to action and demonstrate engagement in practice. It is important to remember that the domains and dimensions of the CRLL model are dynamic and always changing. Individuals and groups will react and respond to each of these ideas differently based on past experiences and personal disposition. Social justice leadership educators also understand the importance of authenticity in delivery and ensure these suggestions are not implemented in a performative or superficial manner. Otherwise, there is a risk of tokenizing and patronizing certain students or groups, which affects how they reflect, express values, and find meaning alongside social justice leadership educators. When approached authentically, there are genuine opportunities to create real meaning and lasting impact on the lives of students. By nature, this work is risky because it challenges existing beliefs and present circumstances, calling individuals to do the same on a personal level. It is possible that these concepts will create more questions than answers, but this also reveals the true urgency and deep need for this work to be prioritized and enacted. Our goal is to ensure the intentions of this model can have an equally meaningful impact in the lives of students with an effort to proactively influence the future direction of leadership education.

REFERENCES

Anthony, M., Jr. (2018). Intersecting activism and social justice in leadership education. In K. L. Guthrie & V. S. Chunoo (Eds.) *Changing the narrative: Socially just leadership education* (pp. 41–56). Information Age.

Bandura, A. (1977). Self-efficacy: Toward a unifying theory of behavioral change. *Psychological Review, 84*(2), 191–215.

Bandura, A. (1997). The anatomy of stages of change. *American Journal of Health Promotion, 12*(1), 8–10.

Bertrand Jones, T., Guthrie, K. L., & Osteen, L. (2016). Critical domains of culturally relevant leadership learning: A call to transform leadership programs. In K. L. Guthrie, T. Bertrand Jones, & L. Osteen (Eds.), *New Directions for Student Leadership: No. 152. Developing culturally relevant leadership learning* (pp. 9–21). Jossey-Bass.

Bordas, J. (2016). Leadership lessons from communities of color: Stewardship and collective action. In K. L. Guthrie, T. Bertrand Jones & L. Osteen (Eds.), *New Directions for Student Leadership, No. 152. Developing culturally relevant leadership learning* (pp. 61–74). Jossey-Bass.

Chan, K. Y., & Drasgow, F. (2001). Toward a theory of individual differences and leadership: Understanding the motivation to lead. *Journal of Applied Psychology, 86*(3), 481–498.

Chunoo, V. S., & Osteen, L. (2016). Purpose, mission, and context: The call for educating future leaders. In K. L. Guthrie & L. Osteen (Eds.), *New Directions for Higher Education, No. 174. Reclaiming higher education's purpose in leadership development* (pp. 9–20). Jossey-Bass.

Deci, E. L., & Ryan, R. M. (2009). Intrinsic motivation. In I. B. Irving & W. E. Craighead (Eds.), *The Corsini encyclopedia of psychology* (pp. 1–2). John Wiley & Sons.

Duckworth, A. (2016). *Grit: The power of passion and perseverance*. Vermillion.

Dugan, J. P. (2017). *Leadership theory: Cultivating critical perspectives*. John Wiley & Sons.

Dweck, C. (2017). *Mindset: The new psychology of success*. Robinson.

Edwards, K. E. (2007). Aspiring social justice ally identity development: A conceptual model. *Journal of Student Affairs Research and Practice, 43*(4). https://doi.org/10.2202/1949-6605.1722

Guthrie, K. L., Bertrand Jones, T., & Osteen, L. (2017). The teaching, learning, and being of leadership: Exploring context and practice of the culturally relevant leadership learning model. *Journal of Leadership Studies, 11*(3), 61–67.

Ladson-Billings, G. (1995). Toward a theory of culturally relevant pedagogy. *American Educational Research Journal, 32*(3), 465–491.

Ladson-Billings, G. (2014). Culturally relevant pedagogy 2.0: Aka the remix. *Harvard Educational Review, 84*(1), 74–84.

Mahoney, A. D. (2017). Being at the heart of the matter: Culturally relevant leadership learning, emotions, and storytelling. *Journal of Leadership Studies, 11*(3), 55–60. https://doi.org/10.1002/jls.21546

McIntosh, P. (1989, July/August). White privilege: Unpacking the invisible knapsack. *Peace and Freedom Magazine*, 10–12.

Solorzano, D., Ceja, M., & Yosso, T. (2000). Critical race theory, racial microaggressions, and campus racial climate: The experiences of African American college students. *Journal of Negro Education*, *69*(1), 60–73.

Volpe White, J. M., Guthrie, K. L., & Torres, M. (2019). *Thinking to transform: Reflection in leadership learning*. Information Age.

Yosso, T., Smith, W., Ceja, M., & Solórzano, D. (2009). Critical race theory, racial microaggressions, and campus racial climate for Latina/o undergraduates. *Harvard Educational Review*, *79*(4), 659–691.

CHAPTER 18

COMMUNITY-UNIVERSITY PARTNERSHIPS AS SOCIALLY JUST LEADERSHIP EDUCATION

Julie B. LeBlanc and Kathy L. Guthrie

Higher education in the United States has wrestled with its embodiment of the public good for quite some time. Although higher education's historic origins support a commitment to educate students to benefit the public good (Boyer, 1990; Volpe White & Guthrie, 2017), scholars still contest its fulfillment of this charter (Kezar, 2004). Community engagement is one way higher education works toward its public good purpose. Within the context of leadership education, developing leaders is part of higher education's public good purpose (Chunoo & Osteen, 2016; Guthrie & Jenkins, 2018).

Community engagement's formula is effective if not simple in theory: colleges and universities send students into the community for hands-on experiences and reflection, and students are transformed as leaders and thoughtful citizens, while communities benefit from students' involvement. Yet, in the quest for equity, community engagement research and practice must encompass holistic partnerships between colleges and community partners. As such, socially just leadership educators rethink traditional frameworks of community engagement and advance emerging

Shifting the Mindset: Socially Just Leadership Education
pp. 219–228
Copyright © 2021 by Information Age Publishing
All rights of reproduction in any form reserved.

research which positions critical community engagement as a more equitable and systems-oriented approach (Volpe White, 2018).

Conventional wisdom about community engagement emphasizes students' development and situates "the community as the domain of the problem and the college as the domain of the solution" (Yapa, 1996, p. 19). While recent literature positions community engagement as critical pedagogy, we lack a theory to capture *how* to facilitate community engagement in this way. Emerging research suggests its importance, but there is still a gap between research and practice (Mitchell, 2015). Given roughly three million college students engage in community service annually (Corporation for National and Community Service, 2015), developing and implementing community engagement initiatives to address systemic causes of community needs is of the utmost importance for the field of higher education.

Community engagement has been labeled as the "'Whitest of the White' enclave of postsecondary education" (Butin, 2006, p. 482). Although we acknowledge, scrutinize, and resist the hegemonic norms, policies, and practices evident in traditional community engagement, the purpose of this chapter is not to deconstruct Whiteness in community engagement programs and initiatives (for more insight into this, see Telles, 2019). Rather, our intent is to paint a broader picture about approaching and designing community-university partnerships as a critical focus for socially just leadership educators.

TRADITIONAL COMMUNITY ENGAGEMENT

Definitions and frameworks regarding traditional community engagement vary among institutions (Mitchell, 2008). Further, higher education uses a variety of terms to identify the topic, including *community engagement, civic engagement, volunteerism, service, service-learning,* and *community service,* just to name a few. This variance of terms contributes to the topic's ill-defined nature and has hindered scholars and practitioners from establishing a singular framework. Mitchell (2008) warned of the perils of higher education's stagnation in the traditional service-learning paradigm: "in this way, the needs of service-learning students often take precedence over community issues and concerns, and the service work performed is less than transformative" (p. 54). We offer Jacoby's (1996) definition of service-learning as a starting point for the traditional approach: "a form of experiential learning in which students engage in activities that address human and community needs together with structured opportunities intentionally designed to promote student learning and development" (p. 5).

Jacoby's (1996) definition of service-learning is problematic for several reasons. First, it focuses on service-learning as an activity with an emphasis on student learning, given the fact that *learning* is mentioned on two separate occasions. It is clearly written from a higher education lens, which perpetuates the elitism and inequitable power dynamics of service-learning. This definition also begs the question: *who* is identifying the human and community needs? Are they jointly established based on mutually beneficial partnerships between higher education institutions and the community; or more likely, are they established solely by the higher education institution's good intentions? Although Jacoby's definition offers a starting point, it falls short in leveraging service-learning as an equitable partnership between higher education institutions and the communities in which they exist. This definition perpetuates the notion that service-learning is something students do *to* communities, rather than *with* communities. In consideration of these inequitable power dynamics, socially just leadership educators should embrace equity-based critical approaches to community engagement.

CRITICAL COMMUNITY ENGAGEMENT

Mitchell's (2008) critical service-learning framework represents emerging literature on service-learning that is, "unapologetic in its aim to dismantle structures of injustice" (p. 50). Critical community engagement sharply contrasts traditional frameworks because of its consideration for social justice, emphasis on mutually beneficial partnerships, and reframing of teacher-student-community relationships toward equity. Mitchell (2008) asserted:

> A critical service-learning pedagogy moves beyond simply doing service in connection to a course's academic content to challenging students to articulate their own visions for a more just society and investigate and contemplate actions that propel society toward those visions. (p. 56)

The critical service-learning framework encompasses emergent ideologies and helps us organize community engagement for social justice. It also incorporates reflection; both as a mechanism from classroom to community, and from community back to the classroom.

Recently, scholars have scrutinized community engagement's impact (Butin, 2006; Mitchell, 2008), yet there is a gap in the literature that adequately captures students and communities as equitable stakeholders in the scope of community engagement. First, socially just designers of community engagement programs and courses are aware of the prerequisite conditions guiding community-university partnership formation. Critical community engagement partnerships depend on the authentic relationship between communities, higher education institutions, and students. Focal communities must desire connections to the university, rather than being inundated by service-seeking students. Thus, the partnership should be mutually beneficial, as defined by both the community and the higher education institution.

Communities' Knowledge, Skills, and Values

Socially just leadership educators carefully consider the alignment between community and institutional values to maximize their congruence. Higher education should not act as an imposing entity; if partnerships are not valued, pursued, and cultivated by both agents, they should not be established or maintained. Community partners in such arrangements are equipped with insight about the students with whom they will be engaging (Mitchell, 2008). Deliberation guides the development of service-learning courses to ensure they are created in response to community demands; not simply based on well-intentioned motives or academic pursuits on the part of the higher education institution. Finally, community-university partnerships advance the community agency's values and mission, rather than detracting from them in any way.

Students' Knowledge, Skills, and Values

Due to the status of community engagement as a vehicle for social justice education and social change, critical pedagogy considers students' knowledge about service-learning and the social issues being addressed. Cipolle (2004) cautioned students' ill-prepared entry into service-learning stems from a scarcity of knowledge about the individuals and communities served. Socially just leadership educators carefully design and facilitate community engagement programs to promote and advance students' preparation for engaging with communities and their membership. To combat previously held shortcomings such as the "lack [of] knowledge about the population they are serving, an understanding of their own racial and ethnic identity, and insight on institutional racism, sexism, and classism" (Cipolle, 2004, p. 20), socially just leadership educators redistribute power dynamics in community engagement partnerships, prompting students to view themselves as partners in the work.

When students lack formal exposure to identity exploration or basic understandings of self, others, and community, entry-level introductions to these topics prepare them for advanced experiences in systems of inequity evident in critical community engagement experiences (Mitchell, 2015). This is a good example of developmental sequencing in leadership education, which positions experiences "in a manner that reflects increasing complexity of content and pedagogy that compounds and builds upon itself" (Dugan et al., 2013, p. 19).

From a skills perspective, socially just leadership educators ensure students' skills match agency's needs so that time, energy, and resources are used in beneficial ways for both entities. Further, students' values should be congruent with the agency's values and the underlying values of the community engagement project.

Environment

Community engagement programs and partnerships do not exist in a vacuum; they exist at the crux of campus and community, and embody the associated dynamics. Three specific elements differentiate traditional service-learning from critical service-learning: "a social change orientation, working to redistribute power, and developing authentic relationships" (Mitchell, 2008, p. 53). Integral to socially just community-university partnerships is the emphasis on power structures and systems of inequity. Implicit within the redistribution of power is the transformation of the teacher-student-community relationship, which aligns with Paolo Freire's education philosophy. This philosophy fundamentally shifts the relationship between leadership educators and students, and posits the ideal that educators, student, and community are all colearners in the process (Freire, 1996). This transcends traditional ideals of students as recipients of knowledge. In critical pedagogy, students and community partners coconstruct their educational experiences. Rhoads (1998) affirmed this approach:

Such a vision is compatible with liberatory forms of pedagogy in which a goal of education is to challenge students to become knowledgeable of the social, political, and economic forces that have shaped their lives and the lives of others. (p. 41)

Community Partners as Leadership Educators

Critical to the establishment of socially just community-university partnerships is the relationship with community partners. Mitchell (2015) emphasized the importance of authenticity in the engagement between students, faculty, and community members "through prolonged community engagement, active learning, and self-reflection" (p. 21).

In support of these critical approaches, socially just leadership educators sustain consistent and ongoing communication with community partners who host students during community engagement experiences. Socially just community-university partnerships provide opportunities for community partners to embrace their role as leadership educators; whether or not they actively identify as such. Guthrie and Jenkins (2018) defined leadership learning as "changes in knowledge, skills, behavior, attitudes, and values resulting from educational experiences, both cocurricular and curricular in nature, associated with the activity of leadership" (p. 57). Consistent with these definitions, regardless of identification as leadership educators, community partners engage in the work of leadership learning.

Congruent with Guthrie and Jenkins' (2018) perspective that "individuals enter the task of becoming a leadership educator from different disciplinary lenses, contexts, and experiences" (p. 27), community partners also approach their roles from a vast array of ideologies, experiences, and perspectives. We contend this diverse richness enhances and advances critical community engagement as authentic relationships are developed and sustained between community and university partners.

Reflection

Reflection is necessary for learning longevity. Critical reflection focuses on power analyses and contexts (Volpe White et al., 2019). As a result, socially just leadership educators use critical reflection to empower students in analyzing the social and political contexts associated with community engagement. Complementary to the paradigm of critical reflection, asset-based community development positions communities as entities with existing resources and opposes deficit-based framing. Although community engagement often focuses on *community needs* and *social issues*, socially just leadership educators who advance asset-based community development embody the tenants of critical community engagement by considering the broader factors affecting individuals, groups, and communities.

Outcomes of Critical Community-University Partnerships

Community-university partnerships inform change at all relevant levels through strengthened community capacity, participatory democracy, and student learning, respectively.

Systemic Level: Participatory Democracy.   This theory represents a vision to change how service-learning is centered in communities, which is inherently social justice in its aims. In terms of participatory democracy (Morton & Bergbauer, 2015), this type of community engagement dismantles systems of oppression and transforms communities through active engagement from all citizens. In addition, they "surface questions of position and power within the partnership and through the ... goals of the host agency, focus attention on the structural dimensions of injustice, and direct student learning to the relationships among agency, power, and social change" (Morton & Bergbauer, 2015, p. 19).

Community Level: Strengthened Community Capacity.   Critical community engagement oriented around root causes of inequity addresses the perpetuation of unequal power structures in society. Therefore, an outcome of this type of community engagement mitigates the approach in which students "fix" communities (Cooks et al., 2004). As community capacity is strengthened, dependence on university resources and student volunteers is diminished (O'Grady, 2000).

Individual Level: Student Learning.   Students have the potential to experience tremendous benefits from this approach to critical community engagement, with the hopes that the benefits will continue throughout their lifetimes. As a result of engaging in critical community engagement, students dismantle stereotypes regarding community deficits. Further, students are educated about privilege and oppression as it actually exists and begin to understand the root causes of community needs, which requires considering "the courses of action necessary to challenge and change the structures that perpetuate those problems" (Mitchell, 2008, p. 53).

Socially just leadership educators provide mutually beneficial accountability with community partners to have invested interest in the development and maintenance of community engagement partnerships. If necessary, the reimagining of community-university partnerships can serve as a vetting instrument where community agencies decline partnerships with higher education institutions if their values and needs are not aligned with the institution's goals. In the following section, we outline some questions and considerations to guide socially just community-university partnerships.

GUIDING QUESTIONS AND STRATEGIES
FOR SOCIALLY JUST COMMUNITY-UNIVERSITY PARTNERSHIPS

- What am I doing to cultivate mutually beneficial relationships with our community partners that transcends simply communicating about service project logistics?

- Do our community partners even want or need our students? What unspoken power structures may be pressuring partners to host students for service projects?

- Are we creating more of a burden on nonprofit agency staff by asking them to give up part of their weekend and accommodate our group of unskilled, untrained students?

- How are voices of community members apparent in community engagement programs?

- How do students experience community engagement differently based on their identities, knowledge, skills, values, and positionality?

- How are community engagement programs designed to address actual community needs? Who is determining these community needs prior to establishing the community engagement experience and partnership?

- How does community engagement approach the relationship between students and communities as colearners?

- What kind of language is used in program materials and curricula regarding the community? Does the language denote an asset-based approach or deficit model?

Socially just leadership educators wrestle with the complexities of these guiding questions. We offer Grain and Lund's (2016) conceptualization of 'critical hope' in service-learning as a means to shift the mindset of community engagement and advance critical community partnerships, "aided by, the necessary tension between criticality—of privilege, charity, hegemony, representation, history, and inequality—along with a hope that is neither naïve nor idealistic, but that remains committed to ideals of justice, reflexivity, and solidarity" (p. 51). We approach critical community partnerships as relationships rooted in mutually beneficial objectives between universities and communities, consistent with pedagogy on systemic injustices, rooted in critically reflective practices, and committed to strengthened community capacity. We believe it is through this approach to partnerships that higher education will continue to work toward its embodiment of community engagement that advances equity and justice.

REFERENCES

Boyer, E. L. (1990). *Scholarship reconsidered: Priorities of the professoriate.* The Carnegie Foundation for the Advancement of Teaching. https://files.eric.ed.gov/fulltext/ED326149.pdf

Butin, D. W. (2006). The limits of service-learning in higher education. *The Review of Higher Education, 29*(4), 473–498.

Chunoo, V. S., & Osteen, L. (2016). Purpose, mission, and context: The call for educating future leaders. In K. L. Guthrie, & L. Osteen (Eds.), *New Directions for Higher Education: No. 174. Reclaiming higher education's purpose in leadership development* (pp. 9–20). Jossey-Bass.

Cipolle, S. (2004). Service-learning as counter-hegemonic practice: Evidence pro and con. *Multicultural Education, 11*(3), 12–23.

Cooks, L., Scharrer, E., & Paredes, M. C. (2004). Toward a social approach to learning in community service learning. *Michigan Journal of Community Service Learning, 10*(2), 44–56.

Corporation for National and Community Service. (2015). *College students: Trends and highlights overview.* https://www.nationalservice.gov/vcla/demographic/college-students

Dugan, J. P., Kodama, C., Correia, B., & Associates. (2013). *Multi-institutional study of leadership insight report: Leadership program delivery.* National Clearinghouse for Leadership Programs.

Freire, P. (1996). *Pedagogy of the oppressed (revised).* Continuum.

Grain, K. M., & Land, D. E. (2017). The social justice turn: Cultivating 'critical hope' in an age of despair. *Michigan Journal of Community Service Learning, 23*(1), 45–59.

Guthrie, K. L., & Jenkins, D. M. (2018). *The role of leadership educators: Transforming learning.* Information Age.

Jacoby, B. (1996). *Service-learning in higher education: Concepts and practices.* Jossey-Bass.

Kezar, A. J. (2004). Obtaining integrity? Reviewing and examining the charter between higher education and society. *The Review of Higher Education, 27*(4), 429–459.

Mitchell, T. D. (2008). Traditional vs. critical service-learning: Engaging the literature to differentiate two models. *Michigan Journal of Community Service Learning, 14*(2). https://files.eric.ed.gov/fulltext/EJ831374.pdf

Mitchell, T. D. (2015). Using a critical service-learning approach to facilitate civic identity development. *Theory Into Practice, 54*(1), 20–28.

Morton, K., & Bergbauer, S. (2015). A case for community: Starting with relationships and prioritizing community as method in service-learning. *Michigan Journal of Community Service Learning, 22*(1), 18–31.

O'Grady, C. R. (Ed.). (2000). Integrating service learning and multicultural education: An overview. In *Integrating service learning and multicultural education in colleges and universities* (pp. 1–19). Erlbaum.

Rhoads, R. A. (1998). Critical multiculturalism and service learning. In R. A. Rhoads & J. P. F. Howard (Eds.), *Academic service learning: A pedagogy of action and reflection* (pp. 39–46). Jossey-Bass.

Telles, A. B. (2019). Community engagement vs. racial equity. *Metropolitan Universities, 30*(2), 95–108.

Volpe White, J. M. (2018). Service-learning as a pedagogy for socially just leadership education. In K. L. Guthrie & V. S. Chunoo (Eds.), *Changing the narrative: Socially just leadership education* (pp. 291–304). Information Age.

Volpe White, J., & Guthrie, K. L. (2017). Good for whom? The shifting role of higher education. In C. P. Gause (Ed.), *Leadership, equity, and social justice in American higher education* (pp. 49–56). Peter Lang.

Volpe White, J. M., Guthrie, K. L., & Torres, M. (2019). *Thinking to transform: Reflection in leadership learning.* Information Age.

Yapa, L. (1996). What causes poverty? A postmodern view. *Annals of the Association of American Geographers, 86*(4), 707–728.

CHAPTER 19

CULTIVATING SOCIALLY JUST LEADERS FOR AGRICULTURE

Katherine E. McKee and Jackie Bruce

It is essential for justice and equity to be visibly enacted within in the industry responsible for feeding and clothing the growing global population. Pivotal to that visibility are with the leaders responsible for enacting it. The world is more diverse than ever before, and our challenges are increasingly complex. Impactful leaders acquire the skills needed to meet such challenges directly. Transformative leadership builds those skills by questioning the systems around our lives and work. Through this framework, and, in those questions, find ways to refashion systems toward equity.

TEACHING SOCIALLY JUST LEADERSIHP IN AN AGRICULTURE CONTEXT

The College of Agriculture Context

Agriculture, as conceptualized in *colleges of agriculture in the United States*, typically refers to conventional, Eurocentric, and nationalistic views

Shifting the Mindset: Socially Just Leadership Education
pp. 229–241
Copyright © 2021 by Information Age Publishing

and norms (Martin & Wesolowski, 2018; Murphy, 2007; Persaud et al., 2008; Rouse et al., 2013). Conventional agriculture prioritizes efficiency, scientific breakthrough, and economic vitality (Conway, 2012; Martin, 2016; Murphy, 2007). The conventional paradigm for agriculture dominates both course work and faculty expectations (Martin & Wesolowski, 2018). Further, many students in colleges of agriculture have Eurocentric and nationalist perspectives of agriculture which are typified by beliefs that the western way of life, economy, and culture are superior, casting those of European descent as superior to those of other ancestries; the dominance of Christianity among European immigrants contributed to the superiority of North American agriculture development; and that North American and European conventional agriculture is superior to other regions' (Persaud et al., 2008; Rouse et al., 2013). These views are embedded in the American psyche, and faculty perpetuate them throughout colleges of agriculture (Persaud et al., 2008; Rouse et al., 2013).

It is unsurprising, then, that colleges of agriculture are primarily composed of students who match this conventional, Eurocentric view. Two recent profiles of such colleges—Iowa and Nebraska—determined that the school population was weighted heavily toward students from farms or small towns and had family involvement in agriculture (Foreman et al., 2018; Powell, 2017). White students make up 95% of Nebraska's college of agricultural sciences and natural resources while they make up 80% of the rest of the university's student body (Powell, 2017). Agricultural employers acknowledge the need for globally minded and culturally aware employees, and the National Research Council (1996) advised colleges of agriculture to broaden their scope beyond conventional forms of agriculture. Yet, industry funding of scientific research disproportionately favors men and the teaching of conventional agriculture persists (Crowe & Goldberger, 2009; Rouse et al., 2013).

To prepare college of agriculture graduates for modern and future challenges as well as meet the expressed needs of industry, socially just leadership educators prepare students to engage in leadership that challenges worldviews rooted in Eurocentrism, nationalism, and conventional agriculture. Further, we carve out places for students who desire to collaborate across social differences, engage in the work toward justice and equity, and develop. Leadership education in colleges of agriculture has traditionally emphasized preparation to lead in and on commodity boards, Extension settings, and other agricultural organizations; however, we propose leadership education programs should prepare students to engage in transformative leadership, leading toward justice and equity outcomes in the agriculture industry and its related communities.

A New Approach

Transformative leadership questions justice and democracy, critiques inequitable practices, and addresses the individual and public good to enhance equity, social justice, access to opportunities, and quality of life (Astin & Astin, 2000; Shields, 2010). As such, transformative leaders serve the long-term interests of society by encouraging respect for difference and diversity, strengthening democracy, and promoting personal freedom and expression by reframing worldviews and identities through examination and rebuilding of systems (Astin & Astin, 2000; Caldwell et al., 2012; Christensen & Raynor, 2003; Pava, 2003; Quinn 1996).

Transformative leaders may present as learners, allies, advocates, and activists as they engage learning and action to develop such systems (Figure 19.1). Learners reflect critically to understand control, domination, and internal records of bias (Brown, 2006; Dunn, 1987; Senge, 1990). Allies support those who are oppressed or marginalized with the intention of ending the oppression (Washington & Evans, 1991). Advocates communicate urgent calls to action to others through canvassing, phone banking, letter writing, fundraising, and public speaking; often with the intention of policy or systemic change (Ganz, 2009). Activists mobilize and deploy resources in support of calls to action for policy or systemic changes (Ganz, 2009; Trueba, 1999).

Teaching Transformative Leadership

As detailed in Figure 19.1, we conceptualize transformative leadership as identity development along the student leader activist identity continuum (slaic)—learner, ally, advocate, and activist identities—through which an individual engages in the behaviors of transformative leadership (van Oord, 2013; Shields, 2010, 2016; Shields et al., 2018). As such, pedagogies and program structures support learning as identity development. Thus, a Project Based Learning (PBL) curriculum and the incorporation of Communities of Practice are appropriate (Markham, 2003; Lave & Wenger, 1991; Wenger, 1998).

To develop concepts of self that lead to engagement in the desired identities, socially just leadership educators develop capacities for authentic action (Bruner, 1996). PBL engages learners in real-world problems through driving questions, independent work, just-in-time instruction, partnerships among faculty, students, and people impacted by the problem, and presentation of solutions to related experts or impacted people

Learner	Ally	Advocate	Activist
Open to new experiences; curious; willing to hear and learn	Supports a group's rights & equality; shows up for individuals and groups experiencing marginalization; recognizes own privilege	Aims to influence others & public policy or resource decisions	Campaigns to bring about political and social change; organizes others to generate change

Increasing knowledge, skills, behavior frequency & competence, self-efficacy >

< Changes in issue, context, or community

Learner	Ally	Advocate	Activist
Listens, reads, observes, asks, believes; continues these behaviors throughout development of subsequent identities	Goes with an impacted person to an event or service; supports an individual or organization materially or emotionally; attends events, carries signs, wears the t-shirt	Engages in media campaigns; speaks or writes publicly, conducts research or polling and shares results, issues briefs; participates in phone banks/letter-writing/canvassing; donates or participates in fundraising	Lobbies; organizes fundraisers; organizes teams and events to address issues

Source: McKee et al. (2019). Reprinted with permission.

Figure 19.1.   Student leader activist identity continuum.

(Adderley et al., 1975; Guile & Griffiths, 2001; Lave & Wenger, 1991; Wenger, 1998). PBL helps students learn information and put it into practice, encourages habits that facilitate career success and civic responsibility, and leads to higher order cognitive development (Markham, 2003).

Communities of practice (CoP) contain experts, near-peers, and newcomers who work toward the same goals or practice (Lave & Wenger, 1991; Wenger, 1998). These CoP exist to perform processes and raise newcomers to higher levels of engagement and expertise (Lave & Wenger, 1991; Wenger, 1998). Newcomers to a CoP begin to consider themselves in relationship to the community, developing new identities (Lave & Wenger, 1991; Wenger, 1998).

The Oaks Leadership Scholars employs PBL and CoP to teach undergraduates transformative leadership. Each student is paired with a faculty mentor at the start of the academic year and meets at least monthly throughout the program. Faculty mentors serve as one type of expert in the CoP helping students answer the driving question, "How can you create justice and equity in agriculture?" Scholars work with their faculty mentors to develop solutions to justice and equity issues that engage them as advocates and activists. Further, second-year scholars and peer mentors, chosen from previous cohorts, serve as near-peers to new scholars. Peer mentors hold study hours, answer questions, and facilitate access to others working in justice and equity. Second-year scholars are role models in both project and cohort engagement.

Cohort sessions with guest speakers—another type of expert—help students identify specific systems of oppression, privilege, justice, and equity in agriculture; as well as skills and strategies for allyship, advocacy, and activism. While the guest speakers serve as experts in our community of practice and continue to interact with some students on their projects, the cohort sessions and required readings serve as just-in-time instruction. The instructional plan is further personalized in mentor meetings and the scholars' choices of outside participatory events.

Guest speakers also facilitate scholars' entry into other justice and equity communities wherein they find people to work with on their projects. This allows them to engage with the people impacted by the issues they are working to address and find other newcomers, near peers, and experts to learn alongside. All collaborators are invited to participate in the presentation day and provide further feedback to the scholars.

Developing Industry Partnerships for Program Sustainability

The relationship between institutions of higher education and industry is long, well documented, and often results in internships and research innovations. However, as the demand for industry-ready college graduates increases, industry steering committees in higher education settings are becoming increasingly common for curricular development and assessment purposes. This is true for the Oaks scholars as well. We convened a steering committee for purposes of curricular assessment, ensuring we were staying congruent with the needs of industry, and for development officers to secure the financial future of the program.

Traditionally, the membership of an advisory council mirrors the population being served (Edwards, 2008; Garmon et al., 1977). In the case of the Oaks scholars; however, we kept the paradigm of the CoP. Thus, the steering committee constituted steering committee a diverse group of people reflective of the 21st century agricultural industry, the college, university partners also doing justice/equity work, and the community where we are all situated. Committee members from outside the university were identified via their work with companies named in the Human Rights Campaign Index, employee resource groups, or nonprofit advocacy groups in the community. University members were identified as working with campus justice/equity organizations (NCSU GLBT Center, Women's Center), leadership initiatives (Impact Leadership Village, the Center for Leadership and Civic Engagement) or self-identified as interested faculty members from the college. The steering committee convenes twice per year, reviews the progress made on the programmatic 5-year plan, funding, and student learning outcomes. Additionally, committee members attend (and participate in) scholar cohort meetings, serve as guest speakers, and assist with scholar selection. The committee has been particularly effective with assisting scholars in articulating how their scholar experience aligns with their postgraduation plans.

While the goals of the steering committee are being met, some unexpected but important results must be reported. Members of the steering committee have hosted the scholars at their workplace, giving the students an opportunity to see justice and equity work in real time. Perhaps the most important outcome of the steering committee is that our scholars, many of whom are told implicitly and explicitly agriculture is no place for them because of one or more of their identities, see themselves in the industry professionals. Members of the steering committee have become personal mentors to students in the program; helping them navigate career preparation, finding spaces for the work they want to do within their fields of interest, and connecting to additional professionals. As a result, students see a place for themselves in an industry that needs a robust labor market to confront the challenges facing our world.

Finally, our industry partners and our community of practice overlap with internships. Several of our students have secured internships via their participation in the Oaks with local and national justice/equity nonprofits and advocacy organizations. However, as the program continues to grow, and permanent funding is secured, the final goal is to formally include internships for all scholars. The steering committee will be vital in this endeavor in a few ways. First, via intern placements in their companies, particularly those with active employee resource groups or vibrant diversity, equity, and inclusion initiatives. Second, is in funding. As several of the agencies where students would be placed often struggle to pay their staff, it is imperative the program have the financial resources for internship stipends, ensuring that the organization where the student is placed only has to provide the experience. Students must be paid for their work—as the reality of the cost of college and living require—and many would have to forsake an internship opportunity if it were unpaid. To disrupt the privilege allowing some students to take such opportunities while others cannot, the Oaks program intends all internships be paid and thus requires funding to offer these meaningful experiences.

Establishing Program Impacts

We use quantitative and qualitative approaches to evaluate the impact of the Oaks Leadership Scholars. Each scholar completes knowledge and skills surveys pre-, post-, and post-postengagement in the Oaks. This survey applies the student leader activist identity continuum (Bruce et al., 2019) to evaluate what scholars know about transformative leadership and learner, ally, advocate, and activist identities, as well as engagement in each. Students complete short answer questions defining terms and connecting them to issues, and 3-point Likert Scale behavioral items (never, once, more than once) for each identity. Results from the first two full cohorts indicate all scholars enter the program having acted as learners and as allies or advocates at least once (Bruce et al., 2019). They complete the program having engaged as advocates and activists multiple times and in many ways, such as speaking to a group about an issue of equity and justice, or organizing letter writing or public comments for policy change (Bruce et al., 2019). Additionally, each scholar creates a map of their justice and equity community before and after their scholar year. We analyze these maps for strength, specificity, and number of connections to people doing justice and equity work. Each scholar in the first two cohorts indicated one or two individuals or organizations they had engaged with prior to their scholar year. At the close of the year, each scholar indicated at least 10 individuals or organizations they interacted with multiple times. This indicates the program facilitates entry into justice- and equity- oriented CoPs.

Each scholar submits two written reflections per month encompassing what they have learned from readings, sessions, events, and their projects. The program codirectors analyzed this data through the lens of the student leader activist identity continuum for evidence the scholars were identifying as learners, allies, advocates, and/or activists. As the reflections are connected to specific moments, we were able to refine our ideas about how students engage in each identity and which events precipitate engagement. Results reinforced how students enter as learners and allies but begin to represent themselves as advocates and activists by the midpoint of their scholar year; as they move from planning to execution of their projects (McKee & Bruce, in press). Shifts in identity are not permanent; however, as students move within the continuum throughout the year often representing multiple identities within a written reflection. Events, such as our field trip to the International Civil Rights Center and

Museum and reading Representative John Lewis's *March* graphic novel, provoke students to engage as advocates and activists as they see how other students have been essential to movements. Participation in current movements and events—like the Poor People's Campaign's Moral March or the Women's Center's Gender and Equity Symposium—coincided with the scholars representing themselves as advocates. Finally, engagement in the execution of their projects—hosting panels, coordinating letter writing and commenting for policy change, and speaking to other organizations—led to representation of selves as activists. This supports the use of PBL to promote identity development.

BEST PRACTICES
FOR PROGRAM DEVELOPMENT AND IMPLEMENTATION

In creating and facilitating the Oaks program, we have learned several lessons and developed some practices that we have shared with others. We share them here for those interested in focusing leadership development programs for the purposes of justice and equity.

Listen to Your Students and Their Limitations

Our most important lesson learned is to listen to students as they articulate wants and limitations. We have found students, when given the space to do so safely and authentically, are able and willing to be forthcoming about what they want (and do not) from an educational experience. Particularly, we found five crucial areas where students have shared needs.

- Credit versus Noncredit: Our students were quite forthcoming about financial and time costs of creating the program as credit-bearing versus a noncredit bearing extracurricular. In this case, because of the stringent financial aid limitations and requirements for progress toward degree within the institution, noncredit was a favorable option for programmatic longevity.
- Funding needs: In addition to the financial aid constraints which limit the courses students take beyond those required, we learned to be cognizant of the hidden financial costs of the program. While all travel and required materials are covered, meals during travel and costs for projects were left up to students. Where possible, we include meal costs in travel costs, and where we cannot, we

endeavor to keep the costs as low as we can and are proactively transparent about the economic reality with students.

- Professional goals: While all our students pursue justice and equity initiatives as personal passions, comparatively few pursue the work as professional vocations. We balance that by engaging the Steering Committee as examples of how individuals engage in justice and equity work; from the most tangentially interested faculty members, to those who manage an industry profession with justice and equity work, to those for whom justice and equity work is the entirety of their professions. Giving students myriad examples allows them to see more of the professional pathways forward, and avenues to seek mentorship from individuals after whose professional path they would like to pattern their journey.

- Sharing experience: For students who have unique experiences, and particularly those who come back to the program for multiple years, it is important to honor those experiences by incorporating them in new ways. This can include additional responsibilities for those "senior scholars," including hosting cohort sessions about their experiences.

- Allow individualization: As justice and equity work is deeply personal, the operationalization of leadership skills related to justice and equity is as well. Therefore, Scholars are encouraged to engage in work that is as personal to them as they are comfortable. This results in Scholars engaging in deeply personal, and individual, projects.

Build Real Engagement With Partners

Our second lesson is how it takes a village to create and sustain a leadership scholars program. While this isn't news to practitioners in the field, we wanted to share a few aspects of what our village appears in this case and how we engage our college, campus, and community partners.

- Guest speaking: Many of our campus partners work in centers doing justice and equity work (GLBT Center or the Women's Center). These partners have contributed their time and expertise by serving on the Steering Committee and leading justice/equity content sessions.

- Join sessions: Our Steering committee members have also joined us for cohort sessions. While it may seem having individuals sporadically join sessions would be disruptive, in the case of our steering committee members, it works mostly seamlessly because of the relationship building our steering committee members demonstrate.

- Industry/organization tours: There is a positive impact of seeing justice and equity work live and in the field. Partnering with agricultural industry members on the steering committee engaging in justice/equity work allows students access to employee resource groups and industry tours.
- Facilitate access to students: The steering committee has also been an opportunity for industry professionals to meet the scholars. This has led to research and internship opportunities.
- Project mentoring: For our students who have projects that overlap with our industry partners, members of our steering committee serve as project mentors.

Project-Based Learning Curriculum

Project-based learning is a vital piece of the program. Students build skills necessary to address seemingly intractable issues of justice and equity in society. They build and practice those skills in a safe environment.

- Provide context for learning: Using practical problems engages all of the inquiry and critical thinking skills we need our 21st century graduates to have when they leave higher education.
- Promote individualization: Students take ownership of their learning when they can make it personal and can identify with the communities most affected.
- Connect to real world experts: Students are able to access experts in the field who are actively leading efforts of justice and equity in a variety of community contexts.
- Ignite students' passion for the work and learning: Because the work is so personal, students are able to follow their own passions.
- Provide opportunity for real impact: Students are addressing real issues in real time, and so their efforts are able to have immediate impact. This is a great opportunity to learn about how "moving the needle" any positive amount is a part of justice and equity work.

Connect Students to the History of the Struggle and the Work

The context of justice and equity work cannot be separated from the work itself. Understanding the history of the work is a part of that context.

- Readings: Students read historical and contemporary texts related to leadership justice and equity to further skill development. Texts are carefully selected to represent diverse voices.

- Field trips: We take our students to the field to examine the historical work of justice and equity and connect with individuals who are doing the work in our current context.

Facilitate Communities

The need for community among individuals engaging in justice and equity work cannot be overstated. Communities share resources, engage in one another's call to action and provide hope to each other. Scholars have said repeatedly that having a space on campus, literally and figuratively has been a key component of their development.

- Provide physical space for scholars to connect with each other: We provide The Oaks Lounge for students to use to study, read, watch documentaries and meet with each other.

- Provide emotional space for scholars to connect with each other (lunch, ice cream, going to events together): Scholars don't only meet during the cohort meetings; they are encouraged to study, eat, and work together, extending the community beyond the cohort sessions.

- Require regular updates to faculty: Faculty directors serve as mentors to scholars, keeping up with their progress meeting goals. These monthly formal meetings create another thread in the community tapestry these students weave for themselves.

- Engage partners within the university who value the work: Students have opportunities to work with university partners throughout their year. Relationships are built for these partners to become meaningful members of the students' community network.

- Engaging in transformative leadership is not easy, nor is the development of those skills. Working with students who have the drive and passion to make the world a better and more equitable place makes us hopeful. While our problems are deeply complex, the answer seems almost simple people. People, with the passion and skills to effect change, will be the answers to those complex issues. The future being imagined and built by young people is bright and vibrant. For those reasons, the hard work of transformative leadership is all the more urgent.

REFERENCES

Adderley, K., Ashwin, C., Bradbury, P., Freeman, J., Goodlad, S., Greene, J., Jenkins, D., & Uren, O. (1975). Project methods in higher education. SRHE working party on teaching methods: Techniques group. Society for Research Into Higher Education.

Astin, A. W., & Astin, H. S. (2000). *Leadership reconsidered: Engaging higher education in social change*. Higher Education Research Institute.

Brown, K. M. (2006). Leadership for social justice and equity: Evaluating a transformative framework and andragogy. *Educational Administration Quarterly, 42*(5), 700–745, https://doi.org/10.1177/0013161X06290650.

Bruce, J., McKee, K. E., Morgan-Fleming, J., & Warner, W. (2019). The Oaks Leadership Scholars program: Transformative leadership in action. *International Journal of Teaching and Learning in Higher Education, 31*(3), 536–546.

Bruner, J. (1996). *The culture of education*. Harvard University Press.

Caldwell, C., Dixon, R., Floyd, L. A., Chaudoin, J, Post, J., & Cheokas, G. (2012). Transformative leadership: Achieving unparalleled excellence. *Journal of Business Ethics, 109*(2), 175–187. https://doi.org/10.1007/s10551-011-1116-2.

Christensen, C. M., & Raynor, M. E. (2003). *The innovator's solution: Creating and sustaining successful growth*. Harvard Business School.

Conway, G. (2012). *One billion hungry: Can we feed the world?* Comstock.

Crowe, J. A., & Goldberger, J. R. (2009). University-industry relationships in colleges of agriculture and life sciences: The role of women faculty. *Rural Sociology, 74*(4), 498–524.

Dunn, J. M. (1987). Personal beliefs and public policy. In F. S. Bolin & J. M. Falk (Eds.), *Teacher renewal: Professional issues, personal choices*. Teachers College Press.

Edwards, H. C. (2008). Volunteers in leadership roles: Successfully engaging advisory councils. *The International Journal of Volunteer Administration, 25*(2), 1–16.

Foreman, B., Retallick, M., & Smalley, S. (2018). Changing demographics in college of agriculture and life sciences students. *NACTA Journal, 62*(2), 161–167.

Ganz, M. (2009). *Organizing Obama: Campaign, organization, movement*. Proceedings of the American Sociological Association annual meeting, San Francisco, CA.

Garmon, W. M., McKinney, T. T., Nesbitt, M. C., Revell, H., & West, J. P. (1977). 4-H and youth committee handbook. North Carolina Agricultural Extension Service, North Carolina State University and North Carolina A&T State University.

Guile, D., & Griffiths, T. (2001). Learning through work experience. *Journal of Education and Work, 14*(1), 113–131.

Lave, J., & Wenger, E. (1991). *Situated learning: Legitimate peripheral participation*. Cambridge University Press.

Markham, T. (2003). *Project based learning handbook: A guide to standards-focused project based learning for middle and high school teachers*. QuinnEssentials Books and Printing.

Martin, M. (2016). The polarization of agriculture: The evolving context of extension work. *Journal of Extension, 54*(2), 2.

Martin, M. J., & Wesolowski, D. (2018). Experiences of non-conventional agriculture majors in a college of agriculture. *NACTA Journal, 62*(1), 11–15.

McKee, K. E. & Bruce, J. (in press). "Any movement of the needle": The Oaks Leadership Scholars represent themselves as learners, allies, advocates, and activists. *Journal of Leadership Education.*

Murphy, D. (2007). *Plant breeding and biotechnology: Societal context and the future of agriculture.* Cambridge University Press.

National Research Council. (1996). Colleges of agriculture at the land grant universities: Public service and public policy. Committee on the Future of the Colleges of Agriculture in the Land Grant University System, Washington, D.C., National Academies Press.

Pava, M. L. (2003). *Leading with meaning: Using covenantal leadership to build a better organization.* Palgrave Macmillan.

Persaud, N., Parrish, D. J., Wang, H., & Muffo, J. A. (2008). Survey of Eurocentric views of agriculture in students at a land grant institution. *NACTA Journal, 52*(2), 32–39.

Powell, L. A. (2017). Urban cowboys: Demographics confirm that agriculture and natural resources recruiting plans cannot be one-size-fits-all. *NACTA Journal, 61*(2), 121–126.

Quinn, R. E. (1996). *Deep change: Discovering the leader within.* Jossey-Bass.

Rouse, L., Rutherford, T., & Wingenbach, G. (2013). Selected college of agriculture students' attitudes about agriculture: Eurocentric origins. *NACTA Journal, 57*(4), 31–37.

Senge, P. M. (1990). *The fifth discipline: The art & practice of the learning organization.* Doubleday Business.

Shields, C. M. (2010). Transformative leadership: Working for equity in diverse contexts. *Educational Administration Quarterly, 46*(4), 558–589.

Shields, C. M. (2016). *Transformative leadership: Primer.* Peter Lang.

Shields, C. M., Dollarhide, C. T., & Young, A. A. (2018). Transformative leadership in school counseling: An emerging paradigm for equity and excellence, *Professional School Counseling, 21*(1b), 1–11. https://doi.org/10.1177/2156759X18773581

Trueba, E. T. (1999). *Latinos unidos: From cultural diversity to the politics of solidarity.* Rowman & Littlefield.

van Oord, L. (2013). Towards transformative leadership in education. *International Journal of Leadership in education: Theory and Practice, 16*(4), 419–434. https://doi.org/10.1080/13603124.2013.776116

Washington, J., & Evans, N. J. (1991). Becoming an ally. In N. J. Evans & V. A. Wall (Eds.), *Beyond tolerance: Gays, lesbians, and bisexuals on campus* (pp. 195–204). American College Personnel Association.

Wenger, E. (1998). *Communities of practice: Learning, meaning, and identity.* Cambridge University Press.

CHAPTER 20

THE NEXT FRONTIER

Virtual Environments
for Socially Just Leadership Education

Kirstin C. Phelps

Leadership is necessary to address the dynamic and complex challenges of today's multicultural and interconnected world; particularly leadership reflective of diverse perspectives and varied contexts. Socially just leadership education prepares future generations to create positive change and support the development of a fair and more just world by including, empowering, and promoting diverse voices which previously have been ignored in leadership development literature (Guthrie & Chunoo, 2018). While integrating social justice concepts are an essential component of reframing the dominant narrative of leadership education, another shift is required—seeing leadership and leadership development as primarily a face-to-face, colocated phenomena. It is not just *how* leadership education is practiced that should be a core consideration of today's leadership practitioners, scholars, and students, but also *where*.

Digital environments are an essential element of leadership development and preparation (Ahlquist & Endersby, 2017); the types of contexts they provide is rife for leadership. I contend online contexts are crucial in leadership; particularly in promoting socially just leadership education.

Shifting the Mindset: Socially Just Leadership Education
pp. 243–256
Copyright © 2021 by Information Age Publishing
All rights of reproduction in any form reserved.

Rationale for considering online contexts in socially just leadership education will be presented, followed by an outline of how critical approaches can be applied to leadership education, and concluding with recommendations for educators.

THE NEXT FRONTIER FOR LEADERSHIP EDUCATION

Online contexts deserve consideration in leadership education, particularly socially just leadership education, for two reasons. The first is the wide-spread adoption of online learning and engagement. U.S. Bureau of Education reports show steady increases over the past decade in the number of distance learning programs and courses; as of 2015–2016 over 43% of undergraduate students participated in an online class (Digest of Education Statistics, 2018). Enrollment is expected to continue to grow as more institutions add online courses and/or degree programs. The flexibility and convenience of online courses is compelling to a wide range of students, including those who are juggling full- or part-time employment, and/or personal or family responsibilities which make attending physical classes difficult. Online learning may also increase after recent significant events, such as the COVID-19 pandemic, which forced many instructors and institutions into distance learning for social distancing purposes.

Growth of Online Leadership Education Programs

Recently within leadership education, there has been a notable increase in the number of institutions offering leadership education online. As of May 2019, over 240 institutions offered hybrid class options or entirely online degree programs according to the International Leadership Association Directory of Leadership Programs (International Leadership Association, 2020). In addition to their convenience and flexibility, online courses may be particularly beneficial for leadership learning. According to Cini (1998), the aspects of online leadership learning that make educators hesitant may also be their strengths. Cini proposed leadership learning best occurs when course *content* aligns with the *process* of delivery. Thus, a "didactic lecture (process) on the importance of teams (content) may send divergent messages to students" (Cini, 1998, p. 110) as the content of teamwork is better suited to a dynamic and participatory process of delivery. Within online settings, the roles of student and teacher become less distinct, as both parties take responsibility for learning. For example, an instructor's perceived lack of dominance encourages shared responsibility among learners as students take ownership for their learning; a perfect platform for leadership topics which encourage relational processes among groups. Therefore, online learning is a unique opportunity for the development of new pedagogical strategies to teach leadership.

Yet, there remains a dearth of research regarding online leadership education. Several scholars have explored intersections of leadership education and online learning through pedagogical strategies and on various platforms (Guthrie & Meriwether, 2018; Headrick, 2019; Jenkins, 2016), including use of technology from other disciplines (Phelps, 2012), and students' social media behaviors (Ahlquist, 2016). However, findings about online social justice education gains are nearly nonexistent. Ultimately, as online learning proliferates, socially just leadership educators will consider when, not if, to embrace the potential impact of online contexts on learning and development; not only to align content and process, but to also role model socially just leadership behaviors, and to prepare students for the same.

Preparing Students for the Realities of Organizational Life

The second reason to consider socially just leadership learning online includes the realities of daily life, which increasingly involve digital technologies and networked environments. The growth of telecommuting and the rise of the *gig economy* both reflect a restructuring of work arrangements and relationships. Analyses of 2018 American community service data highlighted the 5 million employees who work from home at least half time and the 173% increase in regular telecommuters since 2005 (Global Workplace Analytics, n.d.). Similarly, more individuals are in nontraditional work arrangements. These *gig workers* engage income-earning activities beyond traditional employer-employee relationships, including temporary or project-based work. They include professionals driving for ride-share companies after hours, stay-at-home parents who freelance as a content creators, college students live streaming video games, and educators monetizing Instagram accounts on their fitness journeys.

While the landscape of work frequencies, participation patterns, and employment statuses vary, estimates claim more than 25% of workers participate in the gig economy in some capacity (Gig Economy Data Hub, n.d.), and of those workers, about 1% use online platforms. Beyond remote work, employment environments increasingly rely upon flatter and team-based structures, which involve a variety of formal and informal influence patterns. Incorporating online learning strategies into leadership education prepares individuals to effectively and compassionately engage colocated teammates and those who work remotely. Thus, it is important for students to understand how leadership, particularly socially just leadership, translates online.

Daily Digital Interactions

The daily integration of technology-enabled environments also intersects meaningfully with the nonprofessional parts of our lives. Monthly visits to social networking sites are measured in the *millions* to *billions* (Stout, n.d.), and reports on the amount of time spent online on these sites, an average of 144 minutes per person per day, reflecting considerable personal investments (Broadband Search, n.d.). Online communities facilitate personal connection, networking and support, as well as public discourse, collective learning, and community organizing. Online communities of practice, frequently used by professional educators (Marcia & Garcia, 2016), support free-choice learning from a variety of sources (Liu & Falk, 2014). Social movements like #BlackLivesMatter and #MeToo are two examples of how emerging web technologies (i.e., Web 2.0) and social networking sites foster large-scale connective action (Lundgaard & Razmerita, 2016). Social media sites allow broad information sharing during crises, seen in the 2010 Haiti Earthquake (New Media Index, 2010), as well as grassroots organization for disaster relief, such as during the 2011 Japanese tsunami and nuclear disasters (Takazawa, 2014). Geographic communities benefit from information technologies by supporting social activity and group interaction (Kavanaughet al., 2005). Amid the COVID-19 pandemic, social networking applications like NextDoor help neighbors stay connected, share resources, and coordinate activities during social distancing (Perez, 2020).

Online community engagement occurs daily for many of us. Despite benefits associated with participation, there are substantial drawbacks to consider. Due to the user-driven nature of many sites, some act as incubators for antisocial behavior such as trolling, flaming, bullying, and harassment (Cheng et al., 2015). Many platforms insert mechanisms to thwart such practices, such as community moderation, post voting, user muting/blocking, or algorithmic obfuscation of undesirable content (Hsu et al., 2009). Although these approaches help combat antisocial sentiments in some online settings, root behaviors and attitudes remain a problem.

Part of the solution includes preparing students to make positive and sustainable change online; this is where leadership education could be more meaningfully engaged. Although research on virtual teams (Dulebohn & Hoch, 2017) and e-leadership (Avolio et al, 2000) has found important differences in leadership between online and offline settings, the leadership education remains woefully behind in preparing students for online environments. Intentionally including online contexts in leadership learning helps individuals by encouraging, testing, and role-modeling prosocial behaviors across contexts and platforms. Understanding differential expressions of leadership, and social influences in online settings, better prepares students for technology-mediated group dynamics in their organizations, associations, and communities.

Online contexts present unique challenges for social justice and leadership. Preparing students to fight inequalities is even more important when the individuals and communities at stake are marginalized, anonymous, or invisible online. Technology is one tool students should be prepared to use in respectful, inclusive, and compassionate ways. The next section discusses how critical technology perspectives support socially just leadership education.

CRITICAL PERSPECTIVES TOWARD TECHNOLOGY

Given its ubiquity in modern daily life, it is appropriate to apply a critical lens toward technology when considering socially just leadership education. Web 2.0 technologies influence and enable civic engagement and voting behaviors, activism and advocacy, social aggregation and action, and various leadership processes. Physical devices, like cellphones and tablets, as well as underlying infrastructure (e.g., fiber networks or cellphone towers) allow for digital access and connectivity. Online platforms, like learning and content management systems, create digital pathways for remote education and self-directed learning. Preparing students as global change agents means teaching how to leverage the strengths, and overcome the limitations, of technology. The crucial first step is fostering critical perspectives toward technology.

Technological innovations are often accepted uncritically within society; frequently positioned as solutions to societal challenges. In such *technocentric thinking* (Papert, 1987), technology is viewed as *the* agent of change (Bers, 2008) and problems are presented as having simple technical solutions. The oft-used term *digital divide* sums up technocentric thinking nicely. In the late 1990s, the advent of the personal computer and modem prompted a variety of reports on America's technology usage and what was necessary to harness the potential of the information age. The digital divide described the gap between Americans who needed additional resources (computers, modems, access points) to keep up with the burgeoning digital revolution.

While presented as a technical problem (i.e., more computers to support access), it was actually a, "complex intersection of social, cultural, and economic realities" (Fouche, 2013, p. 74) where citizens were ignored and given no venue for input. Rather, the approach reflected a one-way street, where technologically savvy "haves' sent computers, equipment, and other devices to the "have-nots"; assuming little can be learned from the latter (Eglash, 2002). This perspective perpetuated problematic savior tropes, while minimizing the cultural value of others' perspectives, while insidiously promoting technology as a set of, "neutral, universally applicable tools" (Eglash, 2002). Similar viewpoints and critiques can be found in other examples, like the *One Laptop per Child* initiative (Wooster, 2018).

Even when technology is used for positive social change, investigations have shown its creation, implementation, and adoption can instantiate social inequalities. Within information studies, there is a rich research history critiquing technologies and technology education. Some of the frameworks in this discipline parallel the goals of socially just leadership education, in that they "emphasize sensitivity to power structures, awareness of in- and out-group dynamics, and focus on developing capacities to help groups and communities integrate technology in ways that support social transformation" (Phelps & Wolske, 2018, para. 14). Research from this area demonstrates how a lack of criticality around technology can go wrong. Examples include:

- Innovations in face tracking software developed by Hewlettt-Packard failed to recognize darker complexions, resulting in darker skin customers not being followed by the camera like lighter skinned users. This oversight was connected to early photographic technology standardized for White faces as the more valuable subjects (Sandvig et al., et al., 2016).

- Facial recognition developed by Google incorrectly identified Black people as gorillas (Barr, 2015). Years later, updates to the app failed to solve the problem (Simonite, 2018).

- Algorithms used in various technological applications have been shown to perpetuate real-world biases. Examples include a deep learning algorithm that showed a preference for lighter skin tones in a beauty contest; the creation of a chatbot that "quickly began using racist language and promoting neo-Nazi views" (Levin, 2016, para. 5), and software programs used to predict future criminals biased against Black people (Angwin et al., 2016).

- Predictive analytics algorithms used to make important medical decisions found risk assessments are skewed toward White patients, resulting in the potential to widen health-related racial and economic inequalities (Heath, 2019).

- Even though many talent-sourcing and hiring algorithms are used to reduce subjectivity in hiring, a review of real-world applications shows many of these algorithms, "drift toward bias by default" (Bogen, 2019, para. 5). One notable example is that of an Amazon.com-created sourcing algorithm tool was found to disadvantage women applicants (Dastin, 2018).

Our reliance on machine learning, big data, and predictive analytics for decision-making is increasing. Assumptions about the positive benefits of technology are reified through the mindset of technology as a panacea to society's challenges. Technology alone is not the answer. Rather than neutral, technology should be considered as an amplifying force (Toyama, 2015); one capable of furthering both effective solutions as well as entrenching existing inequalities. In preparing students to lead with and through technology, it is increasingly important for critical technological considerations to become core components of leadership education.

RECOMMENDATIONS FOR LEADERSHIP EDUCATORS AND PRACTITIONERS

What are we as educators and practitioners to do when preparing students to lead with, and through, technology in socially just and responsible ways? Our goal is to empower students with knowledge of how to engage in leadership in virtual contexts and to develop skills to actively combat the amplifying nature of technology to promote processes that are socially just. The following section faces these questions and provides recommendations on integrating considerations of technology into courses or programs for socially just leadership education.

Develop a Critical Stance toward Technology

One of the first priorities is to develop a critical stance toward technology in ourselves and our students. Even as I suggest the incorporation of online contexts in your leadership education practices, I simultaneously empower you to question the technologies employed—and encourage your students to do the same. Emerging research is examining social power gains and losses related to scientific and technological innovation – from science and technology studies to critical technology studies to liberatory design to the contributions of critical, feminist, and gender studies scholars working across disciplines. These scholars aim to problematize the dominant narrative of *technocentrism*, to encourage human agency within technology, and to champion nondominant voices around technology. As stated by Seymour Papert, who coined the term *technocentrism*,

"The question is not 'What will the computer do to us?' The question is "What will we make of the computer?" The point is not to predict the computer future. The point is to make it" (Papert, 1987, para 4.)

At the individual level, start by educating yourself about the false narratives around 'digital natives' (Nature, 2017), and reading books by information scholars (see Eubanks, 2011, or Toyama, 2015). You may also reflect on the assumptions made about your own, and your students' skills around, access to, or experience with technology. From a leadership lens, encouraging reflection on the intersection of technology and personal identity is a valid undertaking, as well as an emerging area within leadership education, as highlighted in previous sections. Conversations about self-awareness, values, or ethics can be supplemented by virtual components—for example exploring digital citizenship, personal branding and social media sites, or evaluating individuals' online presence. Helping students understand how to engage productively online involves considering how technologies encourage the spread of misinformation. Developing skills to identify questionable sources, and evaluate the veracity of information online, (i.e., components of digital literacy; Glister, 1997), are essential skills in the 21st century for anyone; especially leaders. Therefore, developing information literacy is a worthwhile endeavor (for a list of resources, see: Cooke, 2017). Developing skills for virtual environments, role modeling positive virtual behaviors, and challenging assumptions around technology use are all important steps toward developing a critical stance toward technology.

Incorporate Virtuality Into Leadership Education

Central to preparing students for virtual and technology-infused contexts is making space for them to *practice* leadership in those contexts. Incorporate class activities that split students into different teams which require them to work across different platforms. Integrate experiences that require students to consider how they understand how leadership dynamics operate in face-to-face, hybrid, and fully virtual environments. Even if your class or program is face to face, consider going remote for one session or change the requirements of a group project to have students collaborate online. Additionally, ask students to reflect upon class activities or other experiences with remote teams or working through technology. Analyzing which behaviors do and do not cross over well online encourages students to think about virtuality and leadership.

Virtual teams literature provides insight on practices of leading remotely (Dulebohn & Hoch, 2017), which can be incorporated into experiential learning or case studies. Recent popular articles around organizational and group responses to COVID-19-related to remote work and learning can be analyzed from leadership and justice lenses. Exploring how leadership emerges online, how influence takes shape in virtual settings, and how leadership behaviors translate online are all rich topics for discussion, reflection, and experiential learning.

Do not incorporate technology in superficial or performative ways; help students explore leadership through technology. *Technology should add to students' experiences around leadership, not simply* as *the place leadership is taught.* Technology use can be justified by learning objectives *and* how well technology supports your topic. Examples of technology supporting course objectives can be found in Guthrie and McCracken's (2010) exploration of online service-learning courses, or Snyder's (2009) work on web tool-supported online learning.

Practicing Socially Just Leadership in Online Contexts

Developing socially just leadership in today's technologically infused world requires educators and students to question dominant narratives of technological solutions to complex social challenges. It also requires developing skills to engage prosocially in virtual spaces, and reflecting on personal experiences alongside questions of equity and access.

Actively Plan for Equity and Access. Social inequalities are often hidden in online settings. Assumptions about technological knowledge or skill, expectations of access to technology and reliable internet connection, and ease of anonymity contribute to inaccurate understandings of who participates in virtual settings. A key in promoting socially just leadership education is to find ways of helping students connect online actions to offline consequences and vice versa. Researchers have found robust offline communities can be supported by online resources when digital literacy is considered alongside multiple public access points, varied resources, and participatory design approaches (Kavanaugh et al., 2005). Therefore, raising consciousness about equity, access, and justice online and offline highlights structural barriers to engagement for members of disadvantaged and underrepresented groups. Tangible examples of this in practice include: encouraging students to create online and printed copies of training materials and/or digital resources for their student groups, providing paper copies of online content, scheduling in-person sign-ups for members of targeted groups, or providing information on nearby internet access points when online resources are required for participation.

Amplify Others' Voices Responsibly. Central to socially just leadership education is shifting dominant narratives to amplify other voices. How-

ever, it is not enough to empower others to speak up. We also need to prepare students to actively honor and amplify minoritized perspectives.
This means helping students understand how their own actions may subvert good intentions. A recent example of this is the #challengeaccepted
tag on Instagram, which is flooded with black-and-white selfies of women.
While one understanding of this hashtag was to direct attention to Turk-
ish femicide, critics noted these glamorous shots—posted by influencers
and celebrities—"aren't advocating for any specific feminist acts; rather,
they appear to be another manifestation of digital bandwagoning for
influencers and celebrities to partake in" (Nguyen, 2020, para. 2). On
platforms where publishing and sharing content comes at the press of a
button, extra attention should be paid to how easily justice-oriented messages can be co-opted.

With the rise in social consciousness around racial inequities after the
death of George Floyd in May 2020 and other Black, indigenous, and
people of color throughout history, the need to promote non-White experiences and voices has risen again. It is no longer adequate to celebrate
the contributions of Black and Brown people during special months or
other specifically dedicated time frames. Intentional effort behind
addressing existing inequities and breaking through structural barriers,
online and offline, is part of socially just leadership. While it is simple to
share information on social media too many individuals are operating
within digital echo chambers; similar individuals promoting similar content. Breaking out of this sameness to amplify others' voices includes: following individuals with different lived experiences through your online
network, engaging in an 'account takeover' to let someone else use your
profile (and connections) for a specified amount of time, or making a
point to ensure your online (and offline) events represent diverse and
minoritized people and their communities.

Learn to Read and Write Power Online.   Connected to amplifying
other voices is learning to question how power and influence take shape
in virtual spaces. Much of the online world is quantified and commodi-
fied; data points—number of followers, amount of citations, total time
spent on course websites—often serve as proxies for power, influence, and
engagement. However, the data upon which these metrics are created are
ripe for questioning (boyd & Crawford, 2012). The commercialization of
many online platforms, combined with the opacity of algorithms, and
complexities of anonymity make it very difficult to get a clear sense of how
much, and what kind of, influence individuals and other entities have
online. Any individual in virtual settings should consider the quality of
their interactions, alongside intended and obtained outcomes, to determine influence; remembering not everything can be accurately captured.

THE GAMBLE OF NEGLECTING ONLINE CONTEXTS

Virtual environments are the critical next frontier for socially just leadership education. Students need to be empowered and emboldened to lead authentically in offline settings, while also actively combatting social inequalities perpetuated online. When we fail to consider technology and leadership interactions, we risk reproducing the same social inequities online we seek to overcome offline. We also risk not preparing our students for lives where the growth of distance education, remote work, and daily digital engagement is ever-increasing. The ubiquity of *high tech* in our daily lives needs to be balanced by *high-touch* individuals, trained to care about people, engage compassionately with diverse communities, and support communication across boundaries; face to face and screen to screen.

REFERENCES

Ahlquist, J. (2016). The digital identity of student affairs professionals. In E. Cabellon & J. Ahlquist (Eds.), *New Directions for Student Leadership: No. 155. Engaging the digital generation* (pp. 29–46). Jossey-Bass.

Ahlquist, J., & Endersby, L. (Eds.). (2017). *Going digital in student leadership: New directions for student leadership* (Number 153). Jossey-Bass.

Angwin, J., Larson, J., Mattu, S., & Kirchner, L. (2016, May 23). Machine bias. https://www.propublica.org/article/machine-bias-risk-assessments-in-criminal-sentencing

Avolio, B. J., Kahai, S., & Dodge, G. E. (2000). E-leadership: Implications for theory, research, and practice. *The Leadership Quarterly, 11*(4), 615–668.

Barr, A. (2015, July 1). Google mistakenly tags Black people as 'gorillas,' showing limits of algorithms. *The Wall Street Journal.* https://www.wsj.com/articles/BL-DGB-42522

Bers, M. U. (2008). *Blocks to robots: Learning with technology in the early childhood classroom.* Teachers College Press.

Bogen, M. (2019, May 6). All the ways hiring algorithms can introduce bias. *Harvard Business Review.* https://hbr.org/2019/05/all-the-ways-hiring-algorithms-can-introduce-bias

boyd, d., & Crawford, K. (2012). Critical questions for big data. *Information, Communication & Society, 15*(5), 662–679. https://doi.org/10.1080/1369118X.2012.678878

Broadband Search. (n.d.) *Average time spent daily on social media (latest 2020 data).* https://www.broadbandsearch.net/blog/average-daily-time-on-social-media

Cheng, J., Danescu-Niculescu-Mizil, C., & Leskovec, J. (2015, April). Antisocial behavior in online discussion communities. *Proceedings of the Ninth International AAAI Conference on Web and Social Media.* AAAI Press.

Cini, M. A. (1998). Learning leadership online: A synergy of the medium and the message. *Journal of Leadership Studies*, 5(2), 103–115.

Cooke, N. A. (2017). *Fake News Workshop Resources* [Resource List]. Programming Librarian. https://programminglibrarian.org/sites/default/files/ischool_-fake_news_handout.pdf

Dastin, J. (2018, October 10). Amazon scraps secret AI recruiting tool that showed bias against women. *Reuters*. https://www.reuters.com/article/us-amazon-com-jobs-automation-insight/amazon-scraps-secret-ai-recruiting-tool-that-showed-bias-against-women-idUSKCN1MK08G

Digest of Education Statistics. (2018). *Number and percentage of undergraduate students enrolled in distance education or online glasses and degree programs, by selected characteristics: Selected years, 2003-04 through 2015–16.*[Table]. National Center for Education Statistics. https://nces.ed.gov/programs/digest/d18/tables/dt18_311.22.asp

Dulebohn, J. H., & Hoch, J. E. (2017). Virtual teams in organizations. *Human Resource Management Review*, 27(4), 569–574.

Eglash, R. (2002, June 21). A two-way bridge across the digital divide. *Chronicle of Higher Education, 48*(41), B12.

Eubanks, V. (2011). *Digital dead end: Fighting for social justice in the information age*. The MIT Press. https://doi.org/10.2307/j.ctt5hhgk1

Fouché, R. (2013). From Black inventors to one laptop per child: Exporting a racial politics of technology. In L. Nakamura & P. Chow-White (Eds.), *Race after the internet* (pp. 67–90). Routledge.

Gig Economy Data Hub. (n.d.) https://www.gigeconomydata.org/basics/how-many-gig-workers-are-there

Glister, P. (1997). *Digital literacy*. Wiley Computer Publications.

Global Workplace Analytics. (n.d.) *Latest work-at-home/telecommuting/mobile work/remote work statistics*. https://globalworkplaceanalytics.com/telecommuting-statistics

Guthrie, K. L., & McCracken, H. (2010). Teaching and learning social justice through online service-learning courses. *International Review of Research in Open and Distance Learning, 11*(3), 78–94

Guthrie, K. L., & Chunoo, V. S. (2018). Opening up the conversation: An introduction to socially just leadership education. In K. L. Guthrie & V. S. Chunoo (Eds.), *Changing the narrative: Socially just leadership education* (pp 1–8). Information Age.

Guthrie, K. L., & Meriwether, J. L. (2018), Leadership development in digital spaces through mentoring, coaching, and advising. In L. J. Hastings & C. Kane (Eds.), *New Directions for Student Leadership: No. 158. Role of mentoring, coaching, and advising in developing leadership* (pp. 99–110). Jossey-Bass. https://doi.org/10.1002/yd.20291

Headrick, J. E. (2019). *Leadership education and MOOCs: A content analysis approach to understanding the pedagogy and characteristics of leadership massive open online courses (MOOCs)*. Theses, Dissertations, & Student Scholarship: Agricultural Leadership, Education & Communication Department. https://digitalcommons.unl.edu/aglecdiss/112

Heath, S. (2019, October 9). *Predictive analytics algorithm displays bias, drives inequity.* Health IT Analytics. https://healthitanalytics.com/news/predictive-analytics-algorithm-displays-bias-drives-inequity

Hsu, C. F., Khabiri, E., & Caverlee, J. (2009, August). Ranking comments on the social web. *2009 International Conference on Computational Science and Engineering*, *4*, 90–97.

International Leadership Association. (2020, January 9). *Leadership education program directory.* http://www.ila-net.org/Resources/LPD/index.htm

Jenkins, D. M. (2016). Teaching leadership online: An exploratory study of instructional and assessment strategy use. *Journal of Leadership Education*, *15*(2), 129–149. https://doi.org/10.12806/V15/I2/R3

Kavanaugh, A., Carroll, J. M., Rosson, M. B., Zin, T. T., & Reese, D. D. (2005). Community networks: Where offline communities meet online. *Journal of Computer-Mediated Communication*, *10(4)*. https://doi.org/10.1111/j.1083-6101.2005.tb00266

Levin, S. (2016, September 8). A beauty contest was judged by AI and the robots didn't like dark skin. *The Guardian.* https://www.theguardian.com/technology/2016/sep/08/artificial-intelligence-beauty-contest-doesnt-like-black-people

Liu, C., & Falk, J. H. (2014) Serious fun: Viewing hobbyist activities through a learning lens. *International Journal of Science Education, Part B*, *4*(4), 343–355. https://doi.org/10.1080/21548455.2013.824130

Lundgaard, D., & Razmerita, L. (2016). *Connective versus collective action in social movements: A study of co-creation of online communities.* Abstract from Connected Life 2016, Oxford, United Kingdom.

Macià, M., & García, I. (2016). Informal online communities and networks as a source of teacher professional development: A review. *Teaching and Teacher Education*, *55*, 291–307.

Nature. (25 July 2017). *The digital native is a myth.* https://www.nature.com/news/the-digital-native-is-a-myth-1.22363

New Media Index. (2010, January 10). *Social media aid the Haiti relief effort.* Pew Research Center Journalism & Media. https://www.journalism.org/2010/01/21/social-media-aid-haiti-relief-effort/

Nguyen, T. (2020, July 30). The complicated origin of Instagram's #ChallengeAccepted. *Vox.* https://www.vox.com/the-goods/2020/7/30/21348162/instagram-challenge-accepted-turkish-womens-rights-controversy

Papert, S. (1987). *A critique of technocentrism in thinking about the school of the future.* http://www.papert.org/articles/ACritiqueofTechnocentrism.html

Perez, S. (2020, March 19). *Nextdoor adds help maps and groups to connect neighbors during the coronavirus outbreak.* TechCrunch. https://techcrunch.com/2020/03/19/nextdoor-adds-help-maps-and-groups-to-connect-neighbors-during-the-coronavirus-outbreak/

Phelps, K. (2012). Leadership online: Expanding the horizon. In K. L. Guthrie & L. Osteen (Eds.), *New directions for student services: No. 140. Developing students' leadership capacity* (pp. 65–75). Jossey-Bass.

Sandvig, C., Hamilton, K., Karahalious, K. & Langbort, C. (2016). When the algorithm itself is a racist: Diagnosing ethical harm in the basic components of software. *International Journal of Communication*, *10*(2016), 4972–4990.

Simonite, T. (2018, January 11). *When it comes to gorillas, Google photos remains blind.* Wired. https://www.wired.com/story/when-it-comes-to-gorillas-google-photos-remains-blind/

Snyder, M. M. (2009). Instructional-design theory to guide the creation of online learning communities for adults. *TechTrends: Linking Research and Practice to Improve Learning, 53*(1), 48–56.

Stout, D. (n.d.) *Social media statistics 2020: Top networks by the numbers.* Dustin Stout. https://dustinstout.com/social-media-statistics/#infographic

Takazawa, A. (2014). Action at a distance: How do ordinary people self-organize humanitarian efforts remotely and collaboratively? *iConference 2014 Proceedings.* http://hdl.handle.net/2142/47375

Toyama, K. (2015). *Geek heresy: Rescuing social change from the cult of technology.* Public Affairs.

Wooster, M. M. (2018). *The spectacular failure of One Laptop Per Child.* Philanthropy Daily. https://www.philanthropydaily.com/the-spectacular-failure-of-one-laptop-per-child/

CHAPTER 21

ADDRESSING WHITE FRAGILITY IN LEADERSHIP EDUCATION

Cameron C. Beatty, Amber Manning-Ouellette, and Erica R. Wiborg

Leadership education has a vast history, characterized by consistent evolution over the last 35 years. Leadership education, often associated with college student development, is an established field which cuts across various academic programs at postsecondary institutions in the United States (Guthrie et al., 2018). Higher education and leadership education have long been associated with cultivating engaged citizens (Manning-Ouellette, 2018). Guthrie and Callahan (2016) posited the importance of higher education's transformative role in leadership education by serving our communities' well-being. Therefore, leadership education cultivates individuals' knowledge and competencies, while solving complex systemic issues within communities (Manning-Ouellette, 2018). There are deep connections between leadership education and social responsibility (Kliewer et al., 2016). The nature of developing such broad and important skills leads to considerations regarding the social identities of those who teach leadership. What responsibilities do those who teach individualized notions of leadership and service to communities retain?

Shifting the Mindset: Socially Just Leadership Education
pp. 257–270
Copyright © 2021 by Information Age Publishing
All rights of reproduction in any form reserved.

257

This question frames our discussion on how leadership educators address systemic and social inequities.

WHO ENGAGES IN LEADERSHIP CURRICULUM

Leadership educators tend to come from student affairs traditions (Jenkins & Owens, 2016). Educators from these contexts are often indoctrinated in cocurricular design, predefined philosophies, and values which permeate the profession (Rocco & Pelletier, 2019). These professional identities are often rooted by dominant perspectives. Seventy-one percent of student affairs professional staff identify as White women; only eight percent identify as Hispanic, and three percent identify as Asian American (Bauer-Wolf, 2018). A 2016 study conducted by Jenkins and Owens on the landscape of leadership educators found 85% of their dataset identified as White. Given the lack of diverse racial representation in student affairs, and the substantial representation of these professionals as leadership educators, many leadership educators come from dominant identities, and specifically, White perspectives.

With dominant identities comes a responsibility for personal and professional critical reflection. Chunoo and colleagues (2019) suggested leadership educators

> do the work through ongoing reading and reflection about the ways in which our identities privilege our humanness in society and in ways society oppresses certain people's humanness and how at times we are all complicit in this process. (p. 93)

In other words, socially just leadership educators continually reflect on how they show up to educate and liberate themselves, and their students, when engaging in leadership frameworks. Subsequently, among White leadership educators, movement toward critical consciousness is one way to explore notions of Whiteness and privilege in the classroom, and within professional settings; particularly when teaching leadership.

Raising Critical Consciousness

Raising critical consciousness in leadership education requires students and educators to reflect on structures of power, and use the classroom as a place for knowledge exchange, which stands in contrast to the banking style of teaching discussed by Freire (1998). Freire's critical pedagogy raised questions about the relationships between theory and practice, and reflection and action, as well as considered power in social institutions. Liberatory pedagogy is a strategy for educators and students to disrupt expressions of power learning spaces through innovative teaching and learning. Educators leveraging liberatory pedagogies recognize, engage, and critically examine undemocratic practices and policies that maintain inequality and oppression (Sayles-Hannon, 2007). When educators and the students we learn alongside critically examine and identify power dynamics, ideologies, and cultures, we can engage liberatory leadership learning. Strategies for comprehensive application of liberatory pedagogy, which is beyond the scope of this chapter, require attention to curriculum development, pedagogical approaches, and learning assessment. Raising critical consciousness through reflection requires leadership educators—who are mostly White—to grapple with Whiteness and the feelings connected to it.

WHITE FRAGILITY AND WHITE GUILT

Whiteness refers to specific dimensions of racism that elevate White people over all people of color (Sensoy & DiAngelo, 2017). Basic rights, resources, and experiences assumed to be shared by all, are actually only available to White people. DiAngelo (2011) defined White fragility as an, "insulated environment of racial protection [which] builds White expectations for racial comfort while at the same time lowering the ability to tolerate racial stress" (p. 54). DiAngelo highlighted White fragility as a state where any amount of racial stress becomes so intolerable for White people, defensive reactions are triggered. These reactions include the "outward display of emotions such as anger, fear, and guilt, and behaviors such as argumentation, silence, and leaving the stress-inducing situation" (DiAngelo, 2011, p. 54).

White Guilt

White guilt is often discussed in relation to White fragility because they are both shields against racial stress for White people. Spanierman and Cabrera (2014) defined White guilt as

> remorse, self-reproach, or sense of responsibility for individual or collective wrongdoing with regard to racism. This differs from popular notions, which equate White guilt with self-serving, self-flagellation that is counterproductive in terms of addressing systemic racism. (p. 16)

When feelings of shame, guilt, or negativity arise, they recenter White feelings, and marginalize responses from people of color (POC). Sensoy and DiAngelo (2012) called for such guilt to be regarded as temporary and argued emotions should not "become an excuse to avoid action … [since] … paralysis due to guilt ultimately protects our positions and holds oppression in place" (p. 142). Using guilt to avoid acknowledging the privilege among members of dominant groups is not new; in particular, Audre Lorde addressed feelings of guilt in a 1981 speech at the National Women's Studies Association Conference: "Guilt is not a response to anger; it is a response to one's own actions or lack of action. If it leads to change then it can be useful, since it is then no longer guilt but the beginning of knowledge" (as quoted in DiAngelo, 2018, p. 148).

Influenced by Leonardo (2004), we contend understanding racism should not endorse avoidance of blame, shame, and guilt. We do not want to simply "push through" White guilt to get to action. Instead, through our praxes and leadership educator identities, we can increase our knowledge of systemic oppression and White supremacy, as well as the ways we collude with racism. This includes awareness of how collusion occurs throughout the field of leadership education, and higher education contexts where leading is taught. Leonardo (2004) warned,

> When educators advise White students to avoid feelings of guilt, we are attempting to allay their fears of personal responsibility for slavery and its legacies, housing and job discrimination, and colonialism and other generalized crimes against racial minorities. (p. 140)

When we avoid these feelings, we create an escape from the ongoing structural roots of the issue—racism and White supremacy. By adjusting and orienting around White guilt as a function of individual and collective oppression, we deconstruct Whiteness through an ongoing commitment to action.

WHITE FRAGILITY AND PEOPLE OF COLOR

Although walls of Whiteness (Mahoney, 2016) provide racial comfort for White students, the opposite occurs for students of color, and POC more broadly. Despite nearly universal appeal, hooks (1989) warned Black students in particular of the dangers hidden in higher learning. After the watershed decision of *Brown v. Board of Education*, students of color were removed from Black schools with Black instructors and were bused to White schools, with White instructors, with curricula rooted in Whiteness and White supremacy (Ladson-Billings, 2004). The precarious placement of education as highly sought after, despite its differential embedded dangers, is a direct result of historical racism carried forward. It can be reasonably predicted students of color seeking leadership education at predominantly White institutions will most likely have White instructors, and as described by Suarez (2015), "students with marginalized identities are silenced and unwelcomed by the very act of questioning why diversity, justice, and identities are relevant to leadership education" (p. 37). It is crucial to confront how White fragility operates in teaching and learning with students; to interrupt such silence as normal in leadership education.

Our feelings, behaviors, claims, assumptions, and their relation to White fragility impact how we respond to our own racial discomfort. Leadership education environments are discursive, and what we say (or do not) communicates our mindsets and affects how students perceive us. A specific pressure faced by POC, identified by DiAngelo (2018), includes "the pressure to collude with White fragility by minimizing their racial experiences to accommodate White denial and defensiveness" (p. 153). This can hinder students' sense of belonging in the classroom, leading to incomplete understandings of a topic, and disengagement in leadership education; all sourcing from students' White fragility, and educator's White fragility as well. Much like the complaint Sensoy and DiAngelo (2012) detail about how students wait for specific instructions to act:

> students often lament that they are being told about all of the problems but not given any solutions. Yet the desire to jump to the 'end' or to the answers can be a way to avoid the hard work of self-reflection and reeducation that is required of us. (p. 142)

Socially just leadership educators do the hard work of critical self-reflection and reeducation in hopes that as a collective community social change becomes a lived reality. In the next section, Erica illustrates her reflection of White fragility within the classroom as a White instructor.

Erica and Addressing White Fragility With Students

Leadership learning is a complex, multifaceted process; which includes discussions on politics, inequity, power, and influence. These interactions can elicit strong, sometimes unpredictable, reactions. In addition, leadership education often relies on personal narratives as a form of reflection; which are valuable, and can be used as a defense mechanisms devoid of social location considerations. Through our personal experiences, when social identity and social location is integrated into leadership curriculum, resistance is often perpetuated by White students. For example, in a leadership program Erica coordinated, she engaged with a small number of students, all identified as White men, who were troubled by the focus on social identities and its relation to social inequalities. The students believed by stressing the influence of social groups, we were perpetuating divisive beliefs when we should be teaching about our shared humanity. This color-blind ideology was not surprising; this can be a typical response from students based on years of socialization. Learning from this resistance, she realized the leadership program curriculum needed to center diversity, social justice, and identities; to grapple with the realities of racism and other intersecting forms of oppression.

White people, including students, are socialized to avoid conversations about race in fear of equating their own participation in racism to being a "bad person" (DiAngelo, 2018). Hardiman and Keehn (2012) found White students saw racism as solely interpersonal or particular to a setting; not as socially pervasive. In addition, since Whiteness is considered the normative and pervasive "universal" category, Whiteness has an unacknowledged position of dominance and power. Leonardo (2004) described this happening through the White-washing of history and overemphasis on individuals; forsaking structural analyses of inequities. This subversion to structural racism and White supremacy often functions to deflect personal responsibilities of power, inequality, and domination. By framing racism as individualized, and eliminating the individuals who are racists, institutional racism continues implicitly and invisibly because of the perceived elimination of racism and racist people (Ahmed, 2012).

Allowing leadership education to be an arena of racial comfort for White students damages and adversely affects students of color. This means disrupting the so-called invisibility fog, so Whites are required to confront their self-image as racialized people (Leonardo & Porter, 2010). For White students who confront their racialized self-images, and become antiracist allies, guilt and shame can still incite a fear of appearing racist (Linder, 2015). This can result in paralyses where White students remain silent in classroom conversations out of fear. However, fear can be productively deconstructed, lending to a greater depth of learning and connection. This requires awareness among White leadership educators of their own fears in addressing racism and Whiteness. Next, Amber shares how she navigates White fragility with colleagues.

Amber and Addressing White Fragility With Colleagues

Higher education institutions are uniquely suited for diversity and inclusion initiatives, for differing dialogue, and for challenging personal perspectives. As a young, White, cisgender woman—who identifies as a leadership scholar and faculty member—I often find myself confronted by colleagues who were poorly prepared to confront personal biases or assumptions affecting our work. This friction serves as an entrance into my colleagues' awareness and analysis of Whiteness, and offers a way into examining privilege. However, shouldering power complexities within our collegial relationships takes mental strength, stamina, and intention.

Points of entry into analyses of Whiteness and White fragility with anyone are complex. Regular interactions with colleagues create a web of communication, power negotiations, and emotionally charged relationships. One account of my navigation through exploring Whiteness with colleagues occurred when we were discussing prospective graduate student applications and how we evaluate their materials. A colleague suggested a rubric for rating potential interviews, which included a preselected rating system for the department. My first question was, "How does a rubric implicate an interview process?" Upon further review, I noticed a rubric section on professionalism and ratings with criteria including, "presented self in a professional manner" and "was well spoken and personable." I could not help but call out the glaring Whiteness embedded in those words. Navigating this situation with colleagues took careful consideration in how I might "call them in" to explore how problematic a rubric with ratings of "professionalism" was to our program. Given my Whiteness, I was forced to face how much harder this conversation would be if I identified as, or if they attributed to me, a different race. I also acknowledge that in my approach with colleagues, I accounted for the "protective space" where they processed the information, which would also not be the case if I held less racial privilege. While messy, confronting Whiteness with colleagues implicates our relationships, and offers opportunities to advocate for others. Lastly, Cameron shares how he navigates and addresses White fragility in the classroom as a leadership educator of color.

Cameron Addressing White Fragility as a Black Leadership Educator

Reflecting on how my identities are read by students helped me to make sense of the resistance I have experienced when intentionally centering marginalized identities in course content and discussions. Students have complained that I focus too much on race, even when the articles and authors on the syllabus represented various other marginalized identities. When discussing leadership theories and perspectives from minoritized scholars, students often focus narrowly on race in their comments, even before critical race theories were introduced. I realized students interpreted any critical theoretical perspective I offered as an allusion to racism, and an indictment of Whiteness, because they read my Black identity alongside course content. As a result, I work more intentionally to (re)center gender, sexuality, class, ability among other identities. I also struggled to help students engage intersectionally, as some fixated on resisting (or solely engaging) racial oppression, with less regard for gendered oppressions and the interlocking nature of inequity as experienced by Black women and others forced to the margins.

My teaching centers on fostering colearning environments where students and I engage in collaborative learning. I draw from critical pedagogy, challenging students to explore personal and systemic assumptions. I model this by naming my own assumptions and being vulnerable in leadership learning processes. I continuously consider my assumptions about privileged and/or marginalized identities I do not hold. How do I communicate these assumptions in the learning environment so they are used for tools of engagement? How do I address Whiteness and White fragility in our learning community? I encourage discussions on issues of power, privilege, oppression and representation, and giving personal examples on multiple levels in my own life. Our ultimate goal is to understand how leadership learning is culturally and socially constructed.

STRATEGIES TO ADDRESS WHITE FRAGILITY
IN LEADERSHIP EDUCATION

"If Whiteness allows some bodies to move with comfort, to inhabit that space as home, those bodies take up more space" (Ahmed, 2007, p. 136). Socially just leadership educators critically consider how and who they are privileging in learning, particularly when facilitating conversations across racial differences. Brunsma et al. (2012) identified universities as institutionally, demographically, and ideologically White spaces; rooted deeply in the structural legacy of American society (Brunsma et al., 2012). Leadership education was built to prioritize White student learning; however, this also insulates students from developing a critical consciousness about race and racism (Wiborg, 2020). White leadership educators are more likely to center White student learning because their identities informs their leadership spaces. Further, it can be challenging to find leadership content that challenges racism and other systems of oppression, requiring engagement with disciplines and perspectives outside the leadership canon (Wiborg, 2020). However, when we accept this as true, we adopt the responsibility to increase our racial literacy and confront how racist ideologies lead to hegemonic Whiteness as normal in leadership education. These strategies are a comprehensive list, but are offered as entry points for leadership educators doing the important work of racial justice across racial differences.

Challenging Safe Space

We have seen higher education initiatives where campuses strive to create environments, and events, where the space is safe for all students to dialogue about diversity and inclusion (Zimmerman, 2019). The discourse surrounding safe-space "provides a format for people of color and Whites to come together and discuss issues of race in a matter that is not dangerous as well as inclusive" (Leonardo, 2010, p. 147). The assumption of any space as safe for all participants is inherently flawed (Arao & Clemens, 2013). These efforts presume creating communities with the goals of undoing racism (Arao & Clemens, 2013; Leonardo & Porter, 2010). Safe space community dialogues make the assumption that the space is safe for both White participants and POC equally. Historically in the U.S., 'safety' is a misnomer because it often means White individuals feel safe or comfortable (Arao & Clemens, 2013; Leonardo, 2010). If we are truly interested in addressing Whiteness in leadership learning spaces, we must embrace the idea that for individuals with targeted identities, *there are no safe spaces*.

Socially just leadership educators seek *brave space* opportunities. Brave spaces encourage dialogue, recognize difference, *and* hold every person accountable for sharing experiences and coming to new understandings; which is understandably uncomfortable. Our recommendations of creating brave spaces come from Boostrom (1998), who argued we cannot foster critical dialogue regarding social justice by turning classrooms into solely safe spaces. "We have to be brave because along the way we are going to be 'vulnerable and exposed'; we are going to encounter images that are 'alienating and shocking.' We are going to be very unsafe." (Boostrom, 1998, p. 407). We add the need to critically address classroom guidelines frequently relied upon in leadership education (e.g., respect, trust, speak from your own experience, etc.) because they can be used to limit racial tension, minimize conflict, and revert to a state of racial equilibrium (i.e., comfort) for White individuals (Arao & Clemens, 2013). When leadership educators reframe racial justice conversations to emphasize courage over the illusion of safety, we center critical dialogue in the attainment of our learning outcomes.

Disrupting Invisibility and Meritocracy

Race scholars contend White people use defense mechanisms to hide their privilege (Cabrera et al., 2016). These mechanisms include decentering themselves as individuals with privilege, which allows White students (and educators for that matter) to project the problem of racism onto groups (e.g., White people collectively or the group who names racism as a problem; Ahmed, 2012), resulting in avoidance of individual responsibility. This deflection allows White people to retain positive self-perceptions and dominant group privileges. This leads to invisibility, "at the societal level and can thus protect both the privileges and the innocence of individual privileged actors—even when they do not individually engage in these protective actions" (Phillips & Lowery, 2018, p. 56). Socially just White leadership educators do the self-work of reckoning with their own White privilege. In doing so, they learn to acknowledge unearned benefits; continually interrogating concepts of meritocracy and mediocrity.

A meritocracy is a system where goods and/or power are awarded to individuals based on talent, effort, and achievement; rather than wealth or social class (Merriam-Webster, 2020). Popular discourse in leadership education includes the notion "anyone can be a leader," however; this sentiment ignores the realities of racism and other forms of oppression as barriers to leading (Suarez, 2015). Meritocratic myths (the perpetuation of the perception of a meritocracy where it truly does not exist) must be disrupted when addressing White fragility in leadership learning. Such myths prevent the interrogation of systemic racism and inequities in society that keeps member of some groups perpetually succeeding over those from others.

Responding to Emotion and White Guilt

Cabrera (2014) highlighted the relationship between emotions and racism, particularly within institutions of higher education. The role of emotional expression in the maintenance of Whiteness in higher education is severely understudied because racial analyses tend to implicitly adopt a cognitive framing as opposed to group and structural perspectives. As Cabrera (2014) argued, "Despite this growing literature in psychology, there are currently few analyses of how White people feel about issues of racism. Most of the literature in racial theory tends to rely on a cognitive framing of race/racism (e.g., Bonilla-Silva, 2006; Leonardo, 2005)" (p. 772). Cabrera (2014) suggested critical analyses exploring Whiteness erroneously focuses on what White people *think* about issues of racism, at the expense of how they *feel*. As previously advocated, we should not avoid feelings of blame, shame, or guilt; but increase our knowledge of our feelings about individual and collective oppression, as well as individual and collective responsibility to act.

Some scholars who study Whiteness and emotion interactions identified White guilt as self-serving (Matias, 2016), while others (see Spanierman & Cabrera, 2015) stressed how White guilt leads to increased antiracist actions. Socially just leadership educators are mindful of this when addressing White fragility in their praxes. By doing so, they enhance our understanding of conditions fostering productive and counterproductive White guilt. Allowing White students to sit in guilt and explore its roots is an important dissonance exercise. White leadership educators might model vulnerability by sharing how they navigate their own guilt. Leadership educators of Color might disclose their own intersectional experiences and any accompanying guilt. Modeling the management of White guilt for learners enhances productive possibilities by begging the question: "What do you do with your guilt and how can it move us toward positive change?

Increasing Your Racial Literacy

We realize many you may be asking—*but how?* From our varied experiences, one formative strategy for addressing White fragility is increasing racial literacy and understanding. Prioritize understanding and naming the *ordinariness of racism* across contexts (local/global, personal/professional, curricular/cocurricular, etc.) and time (past, present, and future). This priority improves your ability to challenge Whiteness in leadership education, and prepares you to respond to a range of responses when naming racism. Prioritize sources of knowing, being, and doing leadership from POC, especially those with additional marginalized intersecting identities (individuals who are queer, trans, women, etc.). Increasing your racial literacy is best accomplished through informed knowledge coupled with critical reflexivity. Consider your own responses and (dis)comfort in learning—are there any feelings of defensiveness, shame, judgment, anger, compassion, motivation, or humility? These responses naturally lead to additional actions and next steps in your learning process as an educator.

LEARNING AND UNLEARNING
HOW WE PERPETUATE WHITE FRAGILITY

We offer the following reflective questions to guide investigating how you as an educator can unlearn/relearn to navigate your own, your colleagues', and/or your students' White fragility:

1. How do I disrupt White fragility in my own life with my family, friends, and colleagues?

2. What does White fragility look like in the learning communities I cocreate with students?

3. How do I perpetuate White fragility in my own teaching, pedagogy, and learning processes?

4. How is White fragility celebrated and maintained in leadership education? How can we decenter Whiteness in leadership education?

5. How might we respond to White fragility once we stop centering Whiteness in leadership education?

REFERENCES

Ahmed, S. (2007). *Queer phenomenology: Orientations, objects, others*. Duke University Press.

Ahmed, S. (2012). *On being included: Racism and diversity in institutional life*. Duke University Press.

Arao, B., & Clemens, K. (2013). From safe spaces to brave spaces: A new way to frame dialogue around diversity and social justice. In L. Landreman (Ed.), *The art of effective facilitation: Reflections from social justice educators* (pp. 135–150). Stylus.

Bauer-Wolf, J. (2018, November). *Student affairs is a diverse profession*. Inside Higher Ed. https://www.insidehighered.com/news/2018/11/02/report-student-affairs-professionals-more-diverse-rest-college-professions

Boostrom, R. B. (1998). "Safe spaces": Reflections on an educational metaphor. *Journal of Curriculum Studies, 30(4)*, 397-408.

Brunsma, D. L., Brown, E. S., & Placier, P. (2012). Teaching race at historically White colleges and universities: Identifying and dismantling the walls of Whiteness. *Critical Sociology, 39(5)*, 717–738.

Cabrera, N. L. (2014). Exposing Whiteness in higher education: White male college students minimizing racism, claiming victimization, and recreating White supremacy. *Race Ethnicity and Education, 17(1)*, 30–55.

Cabrera, N. L., Franklin, J. D., & Watson, J. S. (2016). Whiteness in higher education: The invisible missing link in diversity and racial analyses. *ASHE Higher Education Report, 42(6)*.

Chunoo, V. S., Beatty, C. C., & Gruver, M. D. (2019). Leadership educator as social justice Educator. In K. L. Priest & D. M. Jenkins (Eds.), *New Directions for Student Leadership: No. 164. Becoming and being a leadership educator* (pp. 39–53). Jossey-Bass.

DiAngelo, R. (2011). White fragility. *International Journal of Critical Pedagogy, 3(3)*, 54–70.

DiAngelo, R. (2018). *White fragility: Why it's so hard for White people to talk about racism*. Beacon Press.

Freire, P. (1998) Teachers as cultural workers: Letters to those who dare teach. *Australian Journal of Teacher Education, 23*(1), 40–55.

Guthrie, K. L. & Callahan, K. (2016). Liberal arts: Leadership education in the 21st century. In K. L. Guthrie & L. Osteen (Eds.), *New Directions for Higher Education, No. 174. Reclaiming higher education's purpose in leadership development* (pp. 21–33). Jossey-Bass.

Guthrie, K. L., Teig, T. S., & Hu, P. (2018). *Academic leadership programs in the United States.* Leadership Learning Research Center, Florida State University.

Hardiman, R., & Keehn, M. (2012). White identity development revisited: Listening to White students. In C. L. Wijeyesinghe & B. W. Jackson, III (Eds.), *New perspectives on racial identity development: Integrating emerging frameworks* (pp. 121–137). New York University.

hooks, b. (1989). *Talking back: Thinking feminist, thinking black.* Between the Lines Press.

Jenkins, D. M., & Owen, J. E. (2016). Who teaches leadership? A comparative analysis of faculty and student affairs leadership educators and implications for leadership learning. *Journal of Leadership Education, 15*(2), 98–113.

Kliewer, B. W., Moretto, K. N., & Purcell, J. W. (2016). Emergent spaces of civic leadership education and development: Understanding the liberal arts and humanities from a perspective of civic and public work. *Journal of Leadership Education, 15*(2), 114–128.

Ladson-Billings, G. (2004). Landing on the wrong note: The price we paid for *Brown*. *Educational Researcher, 33*(7), 3–13.

Leonardo, Z. (2004). The color of supremacy: Beyond the discourse of 'White privilege.' *Educational Philosophy and Theory, 36*(2), 137–152.

Leonardo, Z., & Porter, R. K. (2010). Pedagogy of fear: Toward a fanonian theory of 'safety' in race dialogue. *Race Ethnicity and Education, 13*(2), 139–157.

Linder, C. (2015). Navigating guilt, shame, and fear of appearing racist: A conceptual model of antiracist White feminist identity development. *Journal of College Student Development, 56*(6), 535–550.

Lorde, A. (1981, June). *The uses of anger: Women responding to racism* [Keynote presentation]. National Women's Studies Association Conference, Storrs, CT, United States.

Mahoney, A. D. (2016). Culturally responsive integrative learning environments: A critical displacement approach. In K. L. Guthrie, T. Bertrand Jones, & L. Osteen (Eds.), *New Directions for Student Leadership: No. 152. Developing culturally relevant leadership learning* (pp. 47–59). Jossey-Bass.

Manning-Ouellette, A. (2018). Fostering the unification of academic leadership outcomes through democracy education. *Journal of Leadership Studies, 12*(2), 75–78.

Matias, C. E., Viesca, K.M., Garrison-Wade, D. F., Tandon, M., & Galindo, R. (2014). What is critical Whiteness doing in OUR nice field like critical race theory? Applying CRT and CWS to understand the White imaginations of White teacher candidates. *Equity & Excellence in Education, 47*(3), 289–304.

Merriam-Webster. (2020). Meritocracy. In *Merriam-Webster.com dictionary.* https://www.merriam-webster.com/dictionary/meritocracy

Phillips, L. T., & Lowery, B. S. (2018). Herd invisibility: The psychology of racial privilege. *Current Directions in Psychological Science, 27*(30), 156–162.

Rocco, M. L., & Pelletier, J. (2019). A conversation among student affairs leadership educators. In K. L. Priest & D. M. Jenkins (Eds.), *New Directions for Student Leadership: No. 164. Becoming and being a leadership educator* (pp. 39–53). Jossey-Bass.

Sayles-Hannon, S. J. (2007). Feminist and liberatory pedagogies: Journey toward synthesis. *International Journal of Diversity in Organisations, Communities & Nations, 7*(2), 33–42.

Sensoy, O., & DiAngelo, R. (2012). *Is everyone really equal? An introduction to key concepts in social justice education.* Teachers College.

Spanierman, L. B., & Cabrera, N. (2014). The emotions of White racism and anti-racism. In V. Watson, D. Howard-Wagner, & L. Spanierman (Eds.), *Unveiling whiteness in the twenty-first century: Global manifestations, transdisciplinary interventions* (pp. 9–28). Lexington Books.

Suarez, C. E. (2015). Never created with nosotros in mind: Combating colorblind leadership education with cultural competency and intersectionality of identity. In A. Lozano (Ed.), *Latina/o college student leadership: Emerging theory, promising practice* (pp. 29–43). Lexington Books.

Wiborg, E. R. (2020). *A critical discourse analysis of leadership learning* [Doctoral dissertation, Florida State University]. ProQuest Dissertations and Theses Global.

Wiborg, E. R. (2020). *A critical discourse analysis of leadership learning* (Order No. 28022412) [Doctoral dissertation, Florida State University]. ProQuest Dissertations & Theses Global. https://www.proquest.com/dissertations-theses/critical-discourse-analysis-leadership-learning/docview/2447509036/se-2?accountid=14553

Zimmerman, J. (2019, January 17). College campuses should not be safe spaces. *Chronicle of Higher Education.* https://www.chronicle.com/article/college-campuses-should-not-be-safe-spaces/

CHAPTER 22

MOVING BEYOND A CALL

Collectively Engaging in Socially Just Leadership Education

Kathy L. Guthrie and Vivechkanand S. Chunoo

Calling others into action and motivating others toward creating change is indeed important to moving forward. However, what is even more important is how we *actually* engage in socially just leadership education. Not just to talk about, but how to engage in the work with all social identities, at all levels, and contexts. The conversation is shifting from the mere need of action to the actual engagement of the work. To provide leadership learning opportunities with culturally relevance at the heart of creation, critical pedagogy intentionally used, and topics that consider the leader development of identity, capacity, and efficacy of all students. Just as the cover of this book illustrates, it takes a new perspective, looking at things differently, to shift a mindset. The symbolic nature of the reflection is literal in the sense that is takes continuous meaning making and learning to shift perspective. The subject of a tree of this perspective shift symbolizes growth and the planting of a seed to growing into something bigger. All of these symbolic features of the book cover comes together in the need for action.

Shifting the Mindset: Socially Just Leadership Education
pp. 271–278
Copyright © 2021 by Information Age Publishing
All rights of reproduction in any form reserved.

271

The imperative for action with respect to socially just leadership education is about our moral and ethical obligation as educators. The diverse voices shared in this book continues the conversation about socially just leadership education, both in considerations of social identity and various contexts. It continues to actively work towards shifting the mindset about socially just leadership education.

As we discussed in *Changing the Narrative: Socially Just Leadership Education* (Guthrie & Chunoo, 2018), moving forward through the disentanglement of people, problems, and social structures is sorely needed for socially just leadership education to be achieved. It was expressed how some current leaders are complicit in the shared leadership process and continually try to hold back the coming tide of social justice. However, the tide is here, now. We, as leadership educators, are a part of this tide of social justice. We support our students and the development of emerging leaders, who will continue to ride those waves over the walls of oppression. Those tides will not only crest the walls, but erode these barricades of oppression. The very same walls that have held us back from *all* fully engaging in the process of leadership. We must collectively reformulate socially just leadership education into the creation of all leadership learning opportunities.

ENGAGING IN SOCIALLY JUSTICE LEADERSHIP EDUCATION

Creating socially just leadership learning opportunities requires educators to not only question *what* and *how* they teach, but also *what ends* does their teaching impart to all students. Deconstructing current ways of leadership education is critical to interrupting the hitherto unchallenged forces of oppression and Whiteness that plague leadership development programs in higher education. It is time to take action, engage, and change how some have been excluded from leadership education, specifically those from historically marginalized groups. Authors in this text have given us tremendously useful tools in not only deconstructing leadership education, but recommendations of reformulating leadership learning opportunities with social justice at its heart.

Leadership Education Deconstruction

Throughout this text, authors have highlighted and brought awareness to social identities whose voices are often oppressed or forgotten. By articulating how various ways of knowing and learning have been ignored by dominate cultures for too long is a critical tool for deconstruction. Not only dominant identities, but diverse identities need to hear the stories and not only acknowledge and include these voices, but honor and learn from lived experiences and narratives. Considering contexts such as activist spaces, community-university partnerships, agricultural settings, virtual environments, and addressing White fragility, are crucial for deconstructing current engagement practices and crafting new ways of being, leading, and learning leadership in socially just environments.

Appreciating how we, as educators, are each situated in various contexts, with different strengths to influence and obstacles to overcome, we can no longer ignore structural oppression and professional barriers. If we do not advocate for ourselves, our profession, and our context, then we cannot promote new ways of leadership education for our students. We need to remember our students are watching and learning. Our leadership practices become their leadership learning.

Many more authors provided ways to frame leadership learning situated in social justice and therefore aligning these areas rather than just teaching at the intersection. Reconsidering students' lived experiences are at the heart of these recommendations. Considering how students' histories inform their leadership learning as well as that of others. These recommendations are useful guidance in creating equitable contexts for socially just leadership education to thrive. Although we acknowledge context is critical in how these recommendations may be useful in various learning opportunities, we encourage all educators to think and innovatively act to integrate more of these recommendations then currently seem possible.

Leadership and Social Justice Reformation Recommendations

Susan R. Jones and Adrian L. Bitton's remarks in Chapter 14, on applying intersectionality to leadership learning, helps leadership educators complicate and acknowledge the conceptualization of leader with intersections of identities in mind. As Jones and Bitton stated powerfully in their chapter, "intersectionality requires leadership educators to examine their practices through lenses of marginalization, inequalities, and higher education power structures; including those contexts where leadership education is emphasized" (Jones & Bitton, 2021, p. 163)

At the heart of this text, listening to the lived experiences, scholarship, and practice of those who sit at different intersections of identities. provide educators strategies to reducing engagement barriers. Closely examining how leadership is defined, how invitations to development programs are made, and decolonizing the curriculum were all common recommendations. Those with military identities, student employees, international students, and student athletes all recommend expanding on who may identity as leaders in varying contexts. Disrupting the dominant narrative of who is a leader and when they are able to lead is a powerful tool in honoring the complexities and conceptualization of leader.

In this text, we specifically include chapters on social identities and leadership development. However, we also recognize our omission of others. Although not all voices were included here, all educators need to consider how all individuals from various social identities are invited into the conversation and can significantly alter the conversation in leadership education. Every time we make space for a new and different leadership learner, and their identities, to be an active part of our praxis, we shift the mindset of leadership education toward social justice in our local context. This shift can create a widespread sea-change when we all commit to being part of this tide.

In Chapter 15, Jasmine D. Collins and Shane L. Whittington encouraged us to think about the *presumed centrality* of moral and ethical development to socially just leadership education. They offered an ethical leadership values braid, which showed how morals, values, behaviors, responsibility and accountability are intertwined. This braid provides educators a reflective framework to infuse into their pedagogical approaches to explore what it means to lead ethically, given a specific value orientation.

Lastly, we recognize how navigating White fragility can not only be challenging, but exhausting for not only White allies, but especially people of color who live in the reality of oppression and White supremacy daily. Helpfully, Cameron C. Beatty, Amber Manning-Ouellette, and Erica R. Wiborg have provided recommendations for navigating fragility with students and colleagues from different perspectives and identities. Recommendations for working through and with resistance are provided in order to create socially just leadership education and projects more leaders and leadership based in justice.

COLLECTIVELY MOVING FORWARD

Although we have attempted to open conversations about socially just leadership education in various spaces, we still have a long way to go regarding integration of social justice and leadership education. Beyond teaching at their intersection, full alignment of providing socially just leadership learning opportunities continues to be filled with obstacles. To provide further actionable direction to advance this integrated socially just approach to leadership education we propose, we humbly offer the following questions to support leadership educators' thinking and engagement in this work. These questions are organized into categories of: critical challenges, to further develop opportunities for change towards socially just leadership education; critical hope, to continue deconstructing various barriers potentially encountered; and critical innovation, proposed to spark creative, as well as encourage personal and professional action to make meaningful, positive, and sustainable changes in leadership education toward social justice.

Critical Challenges

The numerous hurdles to engaging in socially just leadership education are deeply rooted in systems of oppression and are, at times, hard to readily identify. These barriers are so deeply embedded in structures, practices, and culture, that simple recognition of this oppression can be challenging. To sharpen the focus of leadership educators in socially just program development, we offer the following:

- How can we learn and apply the Indigenous Knowledge Systems in order to provide nuanced and authentic leadership learning opportunities (Oxendine & Taub, Chapter 3)?
- How do gender constructs invite and repel transgender students from leadership development programs and initiatives (Lange & Todd, Chapter 6)?
- As educators, how can ensure leadership learning is situated with feminist underpinnings to maximize socially just learning from a gender lens (Owen, Devies, & Reynolds, Chapter 8)?
- How can we redefine leadership learning opportunities for international students in the U.S. context by using a global lens (Cecil & Hu, Chapter 12)?
- As educators, how do we facilitate learning for college student athletes beyond their "field of play" and competition (King & Badger, Chapter 13)?
- In meaningful discourse of ethics in leadership education, how do we challenge and support the presumed centrality of ethics in all leadership learning opportunities (Collins & Whittington, Chapter 15)?

We hope the questions provided here can support educators in developing socially just leadership development programs. Although honest answers may lead us to uncomfortable conversations with colleagues in our institutions, and perhaps in our own personal reflection, it is essential to critically challenge the current ways leadership learning opportunities are being provided. These potentially uncomfortable conversations lead to shifting thoughts and therefore actions necessary for positive change towards socially just leadership education. These changes also require critical hope to continue deconstruction of current ways and critical innovation to formulate new ways.

Critical Hope

Resistance is common to any change initiative (Quinn, 1996). This resistance to change can be seen in active and passive ways. We acknowledge and honor those who have been passionately working towards socially just leadership education and join their efforts on this journey. We hope by highlighting diverse voices that we can collectively continue this important work. Critical hope (Bozalek et al., 2013) is required to continue this journey towards transformative ways of providing leadership learning opportunities. With this in mind, we offer the following questions to consider when attempting to address resistance you may encounter when moving forward on this collective journey:

- How can we center love and healing, especially in the context of masculinity, for socially just leadership learning (Travers & Craig, Chapter 7)?
- What opportunities are offered to reframe underlying ablest assumptions that dominate leadership education (Scruggs & Watkins, Chapter 9)?
- In better understanding the history of leader development in the context of military, how can we use these lessons to enhance socially just leadership education for all (Gray, Marshall, & Dixon, Chapter 10)?
- How do we take current contexts of on-campus employment to develop leadership learning to enhance career readiness of current students (Runk & Piers, Chapter 11)?
- What opportunities do we currently have to connect leadership learning to student resistance in the frame of student activism (Shenberger & Guthrie, Chapter 16)?
- How do we, as educators, maximize leadership learning opportunities beyond campus to include community engagement for further and future commitment to communities (LeBlanc & Guthrie, Chapter 18)?

- How can we address White fragility in making leadership education socially just (Beatty, Manning-Ouellette, & Wiborg, Chapter 21)?

As we collectively move forward in this work, critical hope is essential for us to make meaning from the challenges and successes in implementing socially just leadership learning opportunities. Acknowledging there will be setbacks and we will not always get it completely right, having hope that we will continue this journey together will produce meaningful changes in programs and initiatives that are long overdue. Being creative and innovative in curriculum, program development, pedagogy, and assessment will continue our engagement in this work and perhaps provide continual motivation to continue the journey.

Critical Innovation

Last, we honor that reformulating leadership development programs and initiatives is a large task and takes a considerable about of time and energy. However, by focusing on creativity to do this work, we can harness unknown resources, including energy and motivation within ourselves and partners. To think creatively, we offer these questions for reflection:

- As educators, how can we rethink what "counts" as leadership for Asian American students who lead from in-between (Luutran & Chung, Chapter 4)?
- How are we attending to important factors in the cultivation of Native, Asian American, lesbian, gay, bisexual, and transgender leaders (Oxendine & Taub, Chapter 3; Luutran & Chung, Chapter 4; Pierre & Okstad, Chapter 5; Lange & Todd, Chapter 6)?
- By interlocking the dynamics of social identity and social location, how can we enact critical tenets in socially just leadership education (Jones & Bitton, Chapter 14)?
- How can we expand and reframe essential elements of the culturally relevant leadership learning model to make it operational for my specific context (Chunoo & French, Chapter 17)?
- Using project-based learning, how do we expand opportunities for leadership learning in agricultural contexts (McKee & Bruce, Chapter 19)?
- How do we continue to be innovative in virtual online contexts to maximize learning for various learners (Phelps, Chapter 20)?

Considering the current complexities in higher education, we have all been asked to do more with less. In fact, creativity has been required of us as educators to meet our goals and objectives in supporting not only our students' development, but our students as their whole selves. As we continue to encourage educators to use critical perspectives when developing creative ways to integrate leadership and social justice, we want to also find new ways to do this work with more educators' voices being included and highlighted. Only through collectively doing this work and infusing innovative practices will we be able to truly be able to reformulate leadership education with social justice at the heart of all we do.

Socially just leadership programs can no longer be the exception, they need to be the norm. Framing leadership education in culturally relevant ways (Guthrie et al., 2016) and from critical perspectives (Dugan, 2017) should be the standard in higher education and support the core mission of higher education institutions. The time to collectively engage in this work is now. We are past a call to action or even beginning the conversation. Action is long overdue for justice, fairness, and equity. Together we can shift the mindset of the dominant way of teaching leadership and make socially just leadership education the model we all are using. We now not only invite you to stand with us, but to collectively engage in this work with us.

REFERENCES

Bozalek, V., Leibowitz, B., Carolissen, R., & Boler, M. (Eds.). (2013). *Discerning critical hope in educational practices*. Routledge.

Dugan, J. P. (2017). *Leadership theory: Cultivating critical perspectives*. Jossey-Bass.

Guthrie, K. L., Bertrand Jones, T., & Osteen, L. (Eds.). (2016). *New Directions for Student Leadership: No. 152. Developing culturally relevant leadership learning*. Jossey-Bass.

Guthrie, K. L., & Chunoo, V. S. (2018). *Changing the narrative: Socially just leadership education*. Information Age.

Quinn, R. E. (1996). *Deep change: Discovering the leader within*. Jossey-Bass.

ABOUT THE EDITORS

Kathy L. Guthrie (she/her) is an associate professor of higher education at Florida State University. In addition to teaching in the Higher Education Program, Dr. Guthrie also serves as the director of the Leadership Learning Research Center and coordinates the Undergraduate Certificate in Leadership Studies, which are both partnerships between the College of Education and the Division of Student Affairs. Kathy's research focuses on leadership learning, socially just leadership education, online teaching and learning, and professional development for student affairs professionals specifically in leadership education. Kathy has developed and taught both undergraduate and graduate courses in leadership and higher education. Kathy has authored/coauthored over 45 refereed journal articles and book chapters, and coedited four monographs in the New Directions series. She coauthored *The Role of Leadership Educators: Transforming Leadership* and *Thinking to Transform: Reflection in Leadership Learning* and coedited *Changing the Narrative: Socially Just Leadership Education*. She has received awards including FSU Transformation Through Teaching Award, Graduate Faculty Mentor Award, ACPA Contribution of Knowledge award, and honored as an ACPA Diamond Honoree and NASPA Pillar of the Profession. Guthrie has served on several editorial boards and is currently the associate editor of the *New Directions in Student Leadership* series.

Vivechkanand S. Chunoo (he/him) is an assistant professor of agricultural leadership, education, and communications at the University of Illinois at Urbana-Champaign. He teaches courses in leadership communications and collaborative leadership. His research centers on the cultural aspects of teaching and learning leadership, the social justice outcomes of leadership learning, and online leader development. Dr. Chunoo also serves as one of the graduate degree coordinators in his academic area. His scholarship on becoming and being a socially just leadership educator has most recently been featured in the *New Directions for*

Student Leadership series. V. is also a contributor to the 2020–2025 National Leadership Education Research Agenda, calling for a renewed focus on critical and socially just approaches to leadership learning. He presents his research regularly at annual meetings of the International Leadership Association and served as one of the closing keynote speakers for the 2020 meeting of Leadership Educator Institute. Dr. Chunoo works closely with LeaderShape, LLC as their senior research fellow. In 2021, V. will be a scholar-in-residence for the virtual National Leadership Symposium. He lives in Urbana, Illinois with his partner, Marilé Quintana and their two dogs, Charley and Milo.

ABOUT THE CONTRIBUTORS

Catherine A. Badger (she/her) is the director of academic affairs and senior associate director of student athlete academic services at Florida State University. Catherine has over 10 years of experience advising student athletes, along with serving as the primary liaison to student affairs partners within the university. A former Division I soccer player, Catherine earned a bachelor's degree in secondary English and chemistry education from Western Michigan University. She also earned two master's degrees from Florida State University in Higher Education and Athletic Administration.

Cameron C. Beatty (he/him) is an assistant professor in the Educational Leadership and Policy Studies Department at Florida State University. Dr. Beatty teaches courses in the undergraduate leadership studies certificate as well as conducts research with the Leadership Learning Research Center. Dr. Beatty's research foci includes exploring the intersections of gender and race in leadership education, leadership development of Black and Latinx student on historically White college campuses, and racial battle fatigue for undergraduate students.

Adrian L. Bitton (she/her) is a doctoral student in the Higher Education and Student Affairs program at The Ohio State University. She earned her MA at the University of Maryland and BA at the University of Richmond. She held several leadership educator positions prior to pursuing her PhD. Her research interests include women in leadership, leadership efficacy, leadership educators, and socially just leadership education.

Jackie Bruce (she/her) is a leadership educator and faculty member in the Department of Agricultural and Human Sciences at North Carolina State University, where she teaches courses in leadership development, advises undergraduate and graduate students and tries to find good parking every day. Dr. Bruce serves as a coordinator of the Oaks Leadership

Scholars Program; an Equal Opportunity Institute Graduate scholar, and a GLBT Center advocate. She enjoys great discussions on how educational environments can become more inclusive for our increasingly diverse student population. Jackie is the current editor of the *Journal of Leadership Education* and is honored to work with a vibrant community of leadership scholars and practitioners. When not in Ricks 213, Jackie is wife to Danny, mom to Ainslee Mae, and kibble provider to Maggie, the family's Bernese mountain dog.

Ben Cecil (he/him) serves as the assistant director of International Student Life at the University of Georgia in Athens (UGA). In this role, he works directly with transition and support services for international students as well as oversees engagement opportunities and intercultural competency development programs. Ben is a doctoral student in UGA's Institute of Higher Education and is actively involved in a number of professional associations related to international education. He received his master's degree in higher education from Florida State University and a bachelor's degree in international affairs from the University of Georgia.

Jessica Chung (she/her) serves as the curriculum and instruction coordinator for the undergraduate leadership minor at the University of Minnesota Twin Cities. She has spent years studying and practicing leadership education and development pedagogies to better serve all students through course curriculum and instructor training. Her hope is for every student to see how their own unique gifts are, in fact, leadership. She is endlessly fascinated by the intersection between leadership and art.

Vivechkanand S. Chunoo (he/him) is an assistant professor and graduate program coordinator in the Agricultural Leadership, Education and Communications program at the University of Illinois at Urbana-Champaign. Dr. Chunoo's research interests involve improving the leadership learning experiences of first-generation college students, undergraduates of historically underrepresented racial and ethnic backgrounds, and collegians from underserved socioeconomic communities. V. teaches undergraduate courses in leadership communications and collaborative leadership. He is also coeditor of *Changing the Narrative: Socially Just Leadership Education.*

Jasmine D. Collins (she/her) received her PhD in educational organization and leadership with a concentration in higher education from the University of Illinois at Urbana-Champaign, and remains there as assistant professor in the Agricultural Leadership, Education, and Communications program. Through her teaching, research and service, Dr. Collins is shifting leadership education toward critical conversations of race, power, ethics, and equity and empowering emerging adults to lead as agents of social justice and transformative change within their communities, industries, and broader spheres of influence.

John Pierre Craig (they/he) is a Black, queer, community organizer with Black Youth Project 100 and student services specialist. They hold an MEd in higher education administration from North Carolina State University. They are a first-year PhD student in social justice education at the Ontario Institute for Education, University of Toronto.

Brittany Devies (she/her) is a second-year doctoral student at Florida State University studying higher education. Brittany currently serves as a graduate assistant for the Leadership Learning Research Center and a lead instructor for the Undergraduate Certificate in Leadership Studies, including teaching a gender and leadership course. Her research interests include the intersections of gender and leader identity development.

David F. Dixon is the assistant director of leadership development at the Center for Leadership and Ethics at the Virginia Military Institute (VMI). He serves as the principal member of the center's staff responsible for the leader development programs provided at VMI. David has also helped to create the core competency modules for incoming cadets. He advises the cadet superintendent advisory board for developing leadership skills from an organizational and strategic perspective. David earned a bachelor's degree from VMI where he was also a Division I athlete on both the baseball and football teams. He has earned two master degrees from West Virginia University in secondary education and educational leadership. David is currently charged with the design and execution of three professional development training programs for incoming staff, midlevel faculty and staff members, and rising committee/department chairs at VMI.

Gregory E. French (he/him) is a doctoral student at the University of Illinois at Urbana-Champaign in education policy, organization, and leadership with a concentration in higher education administration. He also earned a master of arts in organizational leadership from Gonzaga University and a bachelor of arts in business administration from Washington & Jefferson College. Gregory has research interests in student leadership development and leadership motivation, and has previously worked full-time within admissions, student affairs, and human resources.

David Gray, U.S. Army (Retired), is director of the Center for Leadership and Ethics at the Virginia Military Institute. Dr. Col. Gray serves an academic course director and manages the center's curricular and cocurricular leadership, character, and ethical development programs. He earned a doctorate degree in military history from The Ohio State University and a master's degree in strategic studies from the U.S. Army War College. He has served as a faculty member and academic leader at West Point, University of Maryland, The Ohio State University, Saudi Arabia's War Course for senior officers, and as a federal executive fellow at Brookings Institution. A proud alumnus of the U.S. Army education system, he commanded progressively larger units from an infantry platoon through a multifunctional brigade combat team during deployments to Haiti, the Balkans, Afghanistan, and Iraq. Colonel Gray's research and publications focus on leader/leadership development, modern military history, and national security policy/strategy.

Kathy L. Guthrie (she/her) is associate professor in the higher education program at Florida State University. Dr. Guthrie serves as director of the Leadership Learning Research Center and coordinator of the Undergraduate Certificate in Leadership Studies. She currently serves as associate editor for the *New Directions in Student Leadership* series.

Pei Hu (she/her) is an international doctoral student in the Higher Education program at Florida State University. Her research interests focus on academic leadership programs and international student leadership identity development. Currently, she serves as a graduate assistant for the Leadership Learning Research Center, responsible for conducting leadership research projects and teaching in the Undergraduate Certificate in Leadership Studies. Pei received her bachelor's degree in Chinese literature and linguistics from Jianghan University in China and obtained her master's degree in higher education at Florida State University.

Susan R. Jones (she/her) is professor of higher education and student affairs at The Ohio State University. Dr. Jones earned her MA at the University of Vermont and her PhD at the University of Maryland. She held several position in student affairs, including dean of students, prior to becoming a faculty member. Her research focuses on college student development, social identities, intersectionality, and qualitative methodologies.

Kathryn C. King is the associate athletics director of academic services and assistant dean of undergraduate studies at Florida State University. Dr. King has 20 years of higher education experience, with more than 15 years in working directly with Division I student-athletes. Kathryn completed her undergraduate work at Wittenberg University where she was a member of the field hockey program. She earned her graduate degrees from Michigan State University in the Higher, Adult, and Lifelong Education program.

Alex C. Lange (they/them) protects a restless, impatient, and enduring hopefulness for a more equitable and compassionate world. They are currently a doctoral candidate in the Higher Education and Student Affairs Program at the University of Iowa. Their scholarship focuses on queer and trans college students' development and experiences as well as the ways patterns of dominance (e.g., White supremacy, heterosexism) show up on college campuses.

Julie B. LeBlanc (she/her) is a doctoral student in the higher education program at Florida State University. She works in the Leadership Learning Research Center as an instructor for the Undergraduate Certificate in Leadership Studies program. Julie has over seven years of experience designing community engagement and leadership education programs. Her research interests focus on leadership education and community engagement's role in elevating community capacity. Julie believes in the power of mutually beneficial community-university partnerships to transform communities.

Valerie Luutran (she/her) received her master's degree from Florida State University where she began critically exploring her identity as the daughter of Vietnamese immigrants, conducted research on leadership development in Asian American students, and advised the Asian American Student Union. She is currently a coordinator for Orientation, Transition and Parent Programs at the University at Buffalo where she is able to advocate for radically inclusive practices and learn from dedicated, inclusive, diverse teams of orientation leaders.

Amber Manning-Ouellette (she/her) is an assistant professor in higher education and student affairs at Oklahoma State University. Her scholarly work and research foci include socially just leadership education and pedagogy, college student learning and identity development, and first-year student transition. Previously, Dr. Manning-Ouellette worked in student affairs administration for over 8 years in various roles while completing her doctorate of philosophy in educational administration and higher education at Southern Illinois University Carbondale.

Daniel R. Marshall (he/him) is the assistant director of assessment at the Virginia Military Institute. Dr. Marshall earned his doctor of education from Florida State University where he focused on policy and leadership studies in higher education. Prior to his doctorate, he earned a bachelor's degree in kinesiology from the College of William and Mary, a master's degree in sport and entertainment management from the University of South Carolina and worked in campus recreation at the University of North Carolina at Chapel Hill and Tallahassee Community College. His research interests focus on the development of leadership in the curricular and cocurricular environment as well as how different experiences contribute to an individual's development of leadership capacity, efficacy, and identity.

Katherine E. McKee (she/her) is an assistant professor in the Department of Agricultural and Human Sciences at North Carolina State University. Dr. McKee codirects The Oaks Leadership Scholars; a transformative leadership development program, teaches undergraduate leadership courses, graduate courses across the agricultural and extension education domain, and carries out extension programming in leadership development.

Jonathan J. Okstad (he/him) is a doctoral student of higher education at Loyola University Chicago and higher education consultant. Previously, he served in various higher education roles within academic affairs, advancement, alumni relations, and student activities. He has over 10 years of higher education and international humanitarian non-profit work experience.

Julie E. Owen (she/her) is an associate professor of leadership studies at the School of Integrative Studies, George Mason University. Dr. Owen is the author of *We are the Leaders We've Been Waiting For: Women and Leadership Development in College*.

Symphony Oxendine (she/her/hers), Cherokee/Choctaw, is an assistant professor in higher education at the University of North Carolina Wilmington. Dr. Oxendine worked as a student affairs practitioner for over 6 years before pursuing her doctorate. As an Indigenous quantitative scholar, her research centers the social and institutional issues that affect the educational performance and institutional support related to Indigenous people in higher education, appreciative inquiry in higher education, campus engagement and leadership, historically Native American fraternities and sororities, and pathways into the student affairs profession.

Kirstin C. Phelps (she/her) studies leadership in digital and sociotechnical systems; namely, exploring group processes around organizing and information sharing, as well as the information behaviors of individuals serving in leadership roles. Her work is informed by an interdisciplinary background in communication, advertising and education as well as over a decade of professional experience serving as a leadership educator within higher education. Dr. Phelps received her PhD in information sciences from the University of Illinois at Urbana-Champaign.

Darren E. Pierre (he/him/his) is a clinical assistant professor of higher education at Loyola University Chicago. Dr. Pierre's teaching and research focuses on college student development, the student affairs profession, and leadership within higher education.

Rebecca Pettingell Piers (she/her) is a program coordinator at Florida State University's International Programs Office, where she works with faculty to create and implement quality study abroad experiences. Previously, Becca worked at WFSU, where she supervised a student staff each summer. Becca received a master of science degree in higher education from Florida State University in 2017.

Michael Promisel is assistant professor of politics at Coastal Carolina University where he teaches political philosophy and American politics. Dr. Promisel specializes in classical political thought and writes on topics concerning leadership, virtue, and religion and politics.

Danyelle J. Reynolds (she/her) is the assistant director for student learning and leadership at the University of Michigan's Ginsberg Center for Community Service and Learning. In her work and research, she is committed to applying justice-oriented frameworks to leadership development and community engagement.

Amie Runk (she/her) has been supervising student employees for nearly a decade. Amie began serving as a program coordinator at the Florida State University (FSU) Askew Student Life Center (ASLC) in 2011. Since 2017, she has been program manager for the FSU Student Life Cinema and ASLC Gaming. She received her master of science degree in higher education from FSU in 2018.

Spencer Scruggs (he/him), MS, currently serves as the assistant director of the Office of Accessibility Services at Florida State University, promoting equitable educational and campus living experiences for students with disabilities. He holds extensive experience in working with students with disabilities through the interactive accommodations process, listening to their narratives of their educational experiences and how they succeed with their disability, not despite it. Through this work, Spencer has developed scholarly interests in the experiences of students with disabilities, especially those around leadership and identity development, and accessibility in higher education in general. Having presented at previous annual conferences and through his work with students with disabilities, Spencer prides himself on being an agent of change in higher education focused on equity, inclusion, wellness, and most importantly student success.

Michaela A. Shenberger (she/her) is a first-generation student currently working on her doctoral degree in the higher education program at Florida State University. Her research passions revolve around student activism, leadership development, and institutional response to both. Outside her doctoral student duties, Michaela works at the Hardee Center for Leadership and Ethics in Higher Education and teaches undergraduate courses in the Leadership Learning Research Center. While her master's degree is also from Florida State University, her undergraduate alma mater, Appalachian State University, will always hold the top spot in her heart.

Deborah J. Taub (she/her) is professor and chair, Department of Student Affairs Administration, at Binghamton University. She has served as a faculty member in graduate preparation programs for 25 years (Purdue University, the University of North Carolina-Greensboro, Binghamton University). Dr. Taub is a prolific author and frequent conference presenter on many topics including college student mental health, entry into the student affairs profession, student development theory, and Native college student involvement. Her real claim to fame, however, is that she was once a contestant on Jeopardy!

Kieran P. Todd (they/them) is currently a research project manager at the Center for Sexuality and Health Disparities at the University of Michigan. Their research arenas include sexual and reproductive health for trans folks, constructions of masculinity in nonmen and how that influences their health behavior and outcomes, and nonbinary health needs.

Christopher S. Travers (he/him/his) is an educator, writer, and speaker. His work explores the intersection of faith, love, and masculinity among Black men in education. He has published in several journals including the *Journal of Negro Education*, *Spectrum: A Journal on Black Men*, and the *Journal of Diversity in Higher Education*. Dr. Travers earned his PhD in higher education and student affairs from The Ohio State University and currently serves as the director of young adults at the New Salem Baptist Church in Columbus, Ohio.

Sally R. Watkins (she/her) is a specialized teaching faculty in Leadership Studies at Florida State University. With over 20 years of professional work in higher education, Dr. Watkins has taught a variety of leadership courses and facilitated numerous co-curricular leadership learning opportunities for college students. Dr. Watkins fosters interactive classroom communities where students can focus on leadership learning, personal growth, and applying their learning beyond the academic space. Her doctoral work and research interests include the history of leadership education at the collegiate level and leadership learning and pedagogy. She completed her bachelor of arts in communications at the University of Alabama, a master of education in art education at the University of North Georgia, a master of education in post and secondary education at Arizona State University, and a Doctor of Philosophy in higher education at Florida State University.

Shane Whittington (he/him) is the social justice coordinator at the Center for Leadership and Social Change at Florida State University (FSU). With his bachelor's degree in social work and master's degree in higher education from Indiana University-Bloomington, Shane went on to work in state politics, international business management, and nonprofit workforce development. Shane currently manages several major diversity and inclusion-oriented programs at FSU, in addition to teaching courses on social justice theories and practices. Shane's leadership is grounded in critical connections through depth in relationships and welcoming transformative thoughts overtime, exploring curiosities, living on purpose, navigating with humanity, and loving abundantly.

Erica R. Wiborg (she/her) is a critical, qualitative scholar passionate about deconstructing systemic racism, the sociohistorical influences of race and racism, and hegemonic Whiteness in higher education. Dr. Wiborg's overall research focus is within curricular and cocurricular student engagement. She studies college access and inequity in leadership learning and teaching; critical race theory and Whiteness in leadership; critical leadership pedagogy; and college student leadership development. Previously, Erica served as a research assistant in the Leadership Learning Research Center and worked full-time as a program coordinator in the Center for Leadership and Social Change at Florida State University, where she coordinated college student development programs focused on the outcomes of leadership, social justice, identity, diversity, and community engagement.

Made in the USA
Las Vegas, NV
15 July 2022